THE BOYS AND ME

THE BOYS AND ME

My Life in the Country Music Supergroup Sawyer Brown

A Memoir

MARK MILLER

with Robert Noland

Forefront
BOOKS

Published by Forefront Books.
Distributed by Simon & Schuster.

Library of Congress Control Number: 2023918166

Print ISBN: 978-1-63763-201-7
E-book ISBN: 978-1-63763-202-4

Cover Design by Bruce Gore, Gore Studio, Inc.
Interior Design by Mary Susan Oleson, Blu Design Concepts

TO MY MOM, who is truly my hero
and whose example of hard work
and faith taught me that,
with God, anything is possible.

AND TO MY BROTHER, FRANK,
who has been my biggest fan
and without whom none of this
would have ever happened.

Contents

FOREWORD by Kurt Warner 9

INTRODUCTION: All These Years 13

1. That's the Way It's Done 'Round Here 17

2. I Got a Plan 35

3. Six Days on the Road 51
    Hobie 71

4. Gypsies on Parade 75
    Jim 95

5. When Twist Comes to Shout 99
    Smokin' Hot Wife 123

6. Big Picture 127
    Bobby 151

7. Blue Denim Soul 153
    The Joes 171

8. Soul Searchin' 175
    Duncan 197

9. Going Back to Indiana 199
    Ain't That Always the Way 213

10. Tryin' to Find a Way to Make It Last 217
    Transistor Rodeo 241

11. Glory to the King 243
    The Walk 259

12. Travelin' Band 279

SAWYER BROWN DISCOGRAPHY 303

ACKNOWLEDGMENTS 325

Foreword

IN MY PRO FOOTBALL Hall of Fame speech, I stated, "Moments matter, both the moments to be impacted and the moments to impact!"

Life, for all of us, is made up of millions of moments that determine the destination of our journey—journeys defined by the moments others seize to impact us and the ones we seize to impact others. In *The Boys and Me*, Mark Miller does an incredible job of showing both sides of that coin and how those moments directed Sawyer Brown's incredible career.

The Boys and Me lays out in fascinating form the critical crossroad moments of Mark's life and the people who helped him navigate the road to and through stardom. The moments he ran, the moments he walked, the moments he listened, the moments he talked, the moments he stood firm in his convictions, and the moments he let others take the lead—each moment important, each moment shaping the arc of their career, each moment defining the man and the band that would impact the music world.

Using a sports metaphor, it's easy to point to one single moment in a game or one single player as the reason a team won or lost, but those of us who have been involved in a team sport, for which life is one, realize that it takes so much more than that to be successful. Each moment shapes the next, each decision has consequences, both good and bad, and every player plays a pivotal role in the final score. It's the beauty of being a part of something bigger than yourself.

This theme, of life being the ultimate team sport, is depicted beautifully throughout the book. Mark weaves together fascinating stories of the multitude of players (friends, music partners, band members, pro athletes, iconic performers, and of course, family members) and forums (from small bars to station wagons to tour buses, from festivals to stadiums to international invitations, and even James Brown's birthday party) that helped him reach the pinnacle of his sport: music. (I know many may not call it a sport, but with the way Mark approached it, after reading this book you might change your mind!)

Yet, while navigating each of these moments on the way to the top, Mark never strayed from who he is. He knew that what truly made him unique was the person God created him to be and his conviction to be that person whether everyone agreed with him or not. In a world that is constantly trying to change us, to make us into what it thinks we should be, I often find that it's those who are willing to be themselves, that embrace their differences and see them as strengths, not weaknesses, that make the most indelible impression.

Sawyer Brown and Mark Miller never fit neatly into a box and it almost cost them everything, but ultimately it would be standing outside that box that would lead them to places only few have gone.

The Boys and Me takes you on a tour of one group's pursuit of their dream through the highs and lows, from the unthinkable to the unbelievable, and everywhere in between. It shows us that there are many ways to achieve success in this world and it encourages us to do it our way.

Mark has spent his life embracing the idea that "moments matter." Moments with family, friends, and teammates . . . moments in the studio, on stage and with fans . . . moments of fear, doubt, and indecision . . . moments of breakthrough and success . . . once-in-a-lifetime moments and fleeting moments in a one-time interaction. You never know which moments will be the ones that define who you are or that help define the life of others, so you must take advantage of every single one. In the pages that follow, you will be reminded of this important truth through the life of Mark Miller and Sawyer Brown, and you will hear the story of a group of men who did their best not to "miss the moments" God has presented to them and how that has made all the difference.

—*KURT WARNER*
Pro Football Hall of Fame Quarterback

All These Years

THERE'S AN OLD SAYING that goes "Man plans and God laughs."

For me, the point is not that the Almighty makes fun of us, but rather, life rarely turns out the way we think it will. That is especially true if the choice is made to follow Him. Because if He's running the show, He gets to call the shots. That's the way it works.

Take my story, for example.

Picture a small, blond surfer-looking kid from Ohio. An introvert who wants nothing to do with the spotlight, except for the dream to one day play in the NBA. Then, down the road after a successful career, to become a basketball coach.

That was me, for my first twenty years.

Not a singer. Certainly no dancing. *Zero* desire to be an entertainer. While I loved music, that was limited to listening to the radio and records. No thoughts of *ever* being on a stage. The only hardwood I wanted to stand on was a court, with me, nine other guys, a ball, and a hoop—totally focused only on winning the game, blurring out the people in the stands.

That was *my* plan. But what actually happened was, well, a bit different.

I ended up the lead singer and front man for a country-rock band called Sawyer Brown. For four decades and counting.

How do you explain that? Well, I just have to say, if God is laughing, then I'm laughing right along with Him. Because the band's legacy makes no sense any other way.

But I'm not here to make sense of it, just to tell you the story. So jump in. This is going to be a fun ride with the boys and me ... and you.

CHAPTER ONE

That's the Way It's Done 'Round Here

That's the way we live and
that's the way we love 'round here
Strong hearts and folded hands

—FROM THE SONG "'Round Here"

I WAS RAISED by a single mom.

My dad was overseas in the Korean War when he contracted rheumatic fever. While the Air Force was able to fly him back home, he was in and out of the hospital and never recovered. At just twenty-four years old, my dad passed away with my mom by his side.

So, at the age of twenty-one, still a kid herself in some ways, my mom, Irene, had two little boys to raise alone. I was fifteen months old, and my brother, Frank, was four months old. (I was born in 1958 and Frank in 1959.)

Mom, Frank, and I grew up together. For that reason, we were always more than a family. Closer than close, we were a team. If you've ever heard of "the power of three," well, together, we were a force to be reckoned with. (I believe this is the likely reason why, throughout my life, it was just in my nature to be part of a strong team, never solo.)

My grandparents—Mom's parents—were a constant presence in our lives. They were amazing influences and offered loving support. There were even seasons where we lived with them or they lived with us. My grandfather was a character. Bigger than life. Regardless, my mom would never relinquish any of her roles as our only parent. She worked hard to be the very best mother and do all she could to fill the roles of mom and dad. The leader and the nurturer. The disciplinarian and the healer. The provider and the protector.

Because my dad had been in the service, Mom was able to go to college on the GI Bill. (After high school, Frank and I also benefited from that program.) She enrolled at Eastern Kentucky University. We lived in Dayton, Ohio, two and a half hours away. Mom got a room in the dorm and would leave us with our grandparents during the week while she was at school. Then on Fridays when classes were done, she would drive home for the weekend. However, there were weeks when she took us with her, smuggling Frank and me into the dorm. Her suitemates would help Mom out by watching us.

She worked as many hours as possible in and around school to pay the bills, until she eventually reached her goal of getting a math degree and her teacher's certificate. One of my earliest memories at around five years old is being at my mom's college graduation, with all of us celebrating her accomplishment and hard work. From there, she began teaching at Jefferson Township Elementary where Frank and I attended. When we started kindergarten, Mom taught first grade there. When we got to junior high, we moved to Trotwood and she went to teach algebra at Jefferson Township Junior High. Mom's career as a math teacher continued until she retired.

My mom was a multitasker, fearless, and an overachiever with an eternally optimistic spirit. She was the first person in her family to graduate from college. Her work ethic and energy were unmatched. In our farming community, because of the spring planting, there weren't any men available who could coach our Little League team. So Mom coached one team and my aunt Nadine coached the other. Mom also coached the senior league boys' team and took them to the state playoffs. (Side note: She didn't know a thing about baseball, but she was one heckuva recruiter.)

Mom was a diehard born-again Christian on a relentless mission to tell anyone and everyone about Jesus. For example, right after Shayne Hill, our guitarist, joined the band in 2004, I wasn't in the room when Mom introduced herself to him for the first time. After he told me, "Hey, Mark, I met your mom," I asked him, "So, how long was it before she asked if you were a Christian?" He grinned and answered, "Oh, like the second sentence after she said, 'So nice to meet you.'"

When Frank or I would tell her we were going on a date, she always asked, "So, is she a Christian?" If we ever answered with an "I don't know" or "I'm not sure," it was game on for Mom. She never left the privilege of sharing the gospel to someone else. She was always compelled to let anyone in on the good news.

I know there are people who witness or ask those kinds of personal questions and their motive is out of judgment or some sort of holier-than-thou attitude. But that was never my mom. In fact, of the countless people she asked about their faith, I never saw anyone take her wrong or be offended. Her gracious and generous spirit was so evident that you knew she really cared. She just wanted people to know what she had found—that Jesus loves us and a relationship with Him is available, no matter who you are or what you may have done. She was a woman of great love and compassion who took her faith very seriously every day of her life.

On many occasions, I have shared that if you shot my mom and then, at some point, somehow, came to her to ask for forgiveness, she would tell you, "Come here, honey, and give me a hug. Of course I forgive you." Mom's grace and ability to move past any offense was absolutely amazing. To her, that was just part of her relationship with Jesus.

When I was growing up, we were members of a Pentecostal church. Especially back then, women in that denomination couldn't wear makeup or pants, and their hair was uncut and always up in a bun. But my mom was a maverick. She wore makeup. And pants. And her hair was cut and fixed the way she wanted. Because she believed the Bible and knew Scripture, Mom didn't see where rules like those from the church made sense. But we never missed a Sunday. She would tell us, "Boys, you listen to what the Word says." She believed that part of being a Christian was learning to feed yourself spiritually.

Her attitude and approach to life always gave Frank and me permission to have a spirit of independence. Not rebellion, but the ability and opportunity to think for ourselves.

Everyone who knew my dad always said nothing but great things about him. He was a man's man and also a passionate follower of Jesus—evidently very charismatic, not just in the expression of his faith, but his personality as well. (That's probably where the DNA came from for me to front a band.) Often, extended family would tell me, "You look like your dad and you act just like him too." Even though I never knew my father, when people made those comparisons, their affirmation always made me feel very proud and connected to him.

Boys to Men

One of Mom's most important goals for my brother and me was that we would grow up to be strong men. For that reason, she was tough on us and her standards were high, from our behavior and character to our grades and goals. Because we were only eleven months apart, Frank and I were always in the same grade. My brother has always been smart. Like really smart. While I never made a C in all my years at school, I was not the straight-A student he was. I always knew Mom would not tolerate anything below a B from me, so I had to work extra hard. Her constant challenge to us was that we were going to step up in life. No matter how tough the fight we faced, our job was to bring it on. Mom was always our role model because she talked truth and walked truth.

Once Frank and I were both in elementary school, my grandfather pulled us aside and said, "Okay, boys, I need to teach you how to fight. You have to know how to defend yourselves at school. You're both little guys, so there's no shame in helping the other one out, even if you have to jump in together." My brother and I had never fought each other, much less anyone else, so we figured we better listen up and learn.

Right in the middle of him demonstrating the technique for how to throw a good punch, Mom walked in. Ruh roh! Let's just say she had a little talk with our grandfather, and he abruptly ended his impromptu self-defense class. (For the record, we did get enough of the lesson in to know how to handle an elementary school bully.) My grandfather was a tough-as-nails farmer. All through our growing up, like so many men in that era, he smoked. On the Sundays when Mom had to work, he would drive my grandmother, Frank, and me to church. He'd park, and we'd get out of the car and go inside while he waited outside. An hour or so later, the three of us would walk to the car. He would snuff out his cigarette on the ground with the other men, and we would drive home. When Frank and I got older and he realized we didn't like being around smoke, he actually quit for us. He taught me what it meant to be a dad.

I know my grandfather had his own unique relationship with God. Maybe that's where my mom got her approach to faith, because he didn't follow the expectations of people, but he did follow the Lord.

Mom also wouldn't allow Frank and me to argue and bicker with each other. We would get along. We would work it out. We would work together. So we never fought in any way—like, to this day. I don't recall us ever having an intense disagreement. From our earliest memories to the present, we have always been closer than close. Couple that level of love and grace with Mom's constant encouragement—"Boys, you're smart, so there are no limits. You can do whatever you want to do. We live in a country where you can accomplish anything that you set your mind to do." We believed her, because we watched Mom prove it every day.

There are a lot of family photos from our childhood of Frank and me dressed alike, to the point that most everyone thought we were twins. For a single mom with sons not even a year apart, going to a store and buying two of everything was just easier and made sense. But around the sixth grade, Frank and I went to Mom and told her, "Hey, we're getting teased at school for wearing identical clothes. We're about to go into junior high, so if you want us to be men, then we need to stop the dress-alike thing." Thankfully, she agreed.

My mom was very proud. Not prideful, but proud. There's a big difference. Mom was obviously great at math, but she was also a master of finance. What she was able to provide for my brother and me over the years was amazing, all while being obviously challenged by our circumstances. The old saying "She could get a dollar out of a dime" was certainly true for Mom. A bit tongue-in-cheek, she often told us, "You know, you boys were raised like the Kennedys." (If you're under the age of forty, just google the name.) The older I got, the more understanding I gained of the enormity of what Mom dealt with day in and day out to raise Frank and me the way she did.

While Mom was tough on me and my brother, she never spanked or paddled us. Her punishment was always a good tongue-lashing or a talking-to. I mean, my mom could absolutely throw down on bad behavior, mixed with a little guilt trip and a whole bunch of oh-no-you-won't-not-on-my-watch! I still laugh about the time when we were older, right in the middle of one of her long-winded sessions, Frank finally broke and pleaded, "Mom! Please! Would you just whip us and get it over with?!"

Growing up in the 1960s, with busing and integration, we saw racial diversity slowly increase in the area where we lived. This social shift gave us a new group of friends, exposed us to a higher level of sports competition, and broadened our perspective of music. Our farming community was a bunch of good people just trying to get by. To me, we were all the same—families trying to make it through the next season and pay the bills. So this diversity was an exciting change.

Those same influences introduced me to music. My first favorite group was The Jackson Five. I loved the beat, the harmonies, and Michael. I also loved the fact that he was a kid like me, out front and center with his brothers. But then my cool, older cousin Judy introduced me to her music. Once she played me "Sloop John B," I became a huge Beach Boys fan. In 1969, the first single I saved up to buy was "Get Back" by the Beatles, with the B side, "Don't Let Me Down." (Looking back, my earliest influences were bands with solid musicians and writers, not solo artists.)

Speaking of music and solo acts, let me rewind a bit here: When I was just a little guy, Mom would have me sing in church. And I hated it. I got so nervous being up there all alone in front of everyone. My personality is most definitely introverted, so the spotlight was never natural for me.

When I was in the second grade, there was a citywide talent show. Mom had me sing an Elvis song from one of his popular movies with my cousin Jerry playing guitar. Once again, I hated the experience, but I gave it my all and won. Although Mom was so proud, I finally broke down afterward and confessed to her, "I just don't wanna do this. I don't wanna get up and sing in front of people anymore." She responded, "Well, okay, Mark, but you have to at least take piano lessons." Mom always had a gift for seeing the big picture. She obviously saw something in me that she felt needed to be nurtured.

So with the piano now being a rude interruption in my life, the teacher would come over to the house once a week and we would sit together at Mom's old upright. I made sure that no one knew I was taking lessons. Even though I was supposed to be learning to read piano music, I would just memorize the song. I figured out how to fake it. Instead of actually reading the notes, I followed the words on the sheet music. While I played along, I made sure to turn the page at the right time in the song. I took piano lessons up until about the sixth grade and then I quit. I guess Mom felt like I had enough training, because she allowed me to stop.

By that time, I had a decent knowledge of chords. Later in college, I started teaching myself how to play guitar. Today, I'm actually a better guitar player than piano player. Regardless, I'm grateful to my mom for making me take lessons after I begged her to stop making me sing.

Nothing but Net

With each passing year, I became more consumed with sports. Throughout elementary school, I could dribble a basketball better than anybody at my school. While I was always a good shooter, by high school, I was playing with some really solid players who challenged me to keep getting better. I loved anything athletic, but basketball was my thing.

Also, as I got older, my introverted personality and fear of being in front of people got worse, to the point where I wouldn't even read out loud in class. I don't know if I was traumatized or freaked out more than I realized as a kid from having to be onstage, but I never wanted to be the focus in any situation. While I would get nervous when I played basketball in front of people, there was something different about competing on the court with a team.

Out there on the hardwood, everything else seemed to fade away and I could focus on the game.

With Mom working so much, and my grandparents being of the generation that thought sports was only for fun, none of my family ever watched me play, except my brother. Frank was a great baseball and soccer player. So I would go to all his games I could and he would come to mine. Aside from being a math teacher, Mom worked other jobs on nights and weekends, so she was never able to see me play throughout junior high, high school, and college. That was a different day, when a parent asking off to go watch their kids play wouldn't fly. Plus, if you didn't work, you didn't get paid, so that made it impossible for her.

For many years, after the band was well-established, I was the captain of a team for an annual charity basketball game at Belmont University in Nashville. One of the first years, when I was in my mid-twenties, we were playing against Vince Gill and his team. Mom had come to watch. Afterward, looking pleasantly surprised, she commented, "Wow, Mark, you're a really good basketball player." I just grinned and said, "Well, thanks, Mom."

All through school, the more I played, the better I got, and basketball became the passion of my life. Even though I was often told, "You're too small to play," I never let that stop me. That criticism just motivated me to work harder and get better. In high school, we had a really good team with some great players. And I couldn't wait to play college ball.

Fresh Start in the Sunshine State

When Frank and I were in the eighth grade, Mom took us to

Florida for spring break. After only a day or so, she decided she loved it there. Calling a few schools in the area, she inquired about teaching positions. One invited her to come in right away for an interview and she was hired to start the next school year. We finished out those last two months of school in Ohio, then packed up and moved to Apopka, Florida, a town northwest of Orlando.

Mom's decision wasn't on a whim, but from a desire for a fresh start that had been brewing for quite a while. She wanted and needed a new beginning. Frank and I were on board with it all. We thought by moving to Florida, we had found the promised land. The weather was always warm and sunny, the lake or the beach was a short drive away, and in October of 1971, Disney World opened. (Mom was never afraid of change and bold moves. Later, she would officially change her name from Irene to Jackie, inspired by Jacqueline Kennedy Onassis, one of her heroes.)

The only difficult part of our move was leaving family behind. Besides my grandparents, my mom had three sisters. There were twenty-one cousins in total, with one aunt having twelve kids. We all lived near one another and went to the same church. All of us were, and still are, really close. In fact, when I would hear people say they had a best friend that wasn't family, I always thought that was so strange. About a year after we moved, my grandparents made the decision to leave their home and move down to join us in Florida.

Within my first week in Apopka, I was all in. Right away, I was proud to be a Floridian. Because of that at-home feeling, I settled in and quickly made close friends. Throughout high school, my classmates and I were one big family.

Life in Florida also grew my passion for music. The vibe

there was much more laid-back than in Ohio, and that came through in the music my friends and I listened to. In the 1960s and 1970s, so many artists were using their platforms to preach on social issues. I believe one of the main reasons I loved groups like The Beach Boys and The Jackson Five was because I just wanted music to be fun. To feel good. To make you forget about the troubles of the world, not remind you of them. (That mindset definitely stuck with me.)

Being on the beach and around water so much, always hanging out with my friends, the songs on the top forty were the soundtrack to my life. Once I got my license and began to drive, I had the radio on all the time. These factors definitely increased my appetite for music, forming and influencing what it was about for me.

As soon as Frank and I were old enough to work, we jumped in to help Mom pay the bills. If we made a dollar, we would walk in the door and lay it on the kitchen table. In our home, there was no mine, only ours. Nothing was singular with an I, always plural as in "we." The three of us were truly "all for one and one for all." Whether it was ten bucks from mowing a yard or a paycheck from a steady job, Mom would make the deposit in our account the next day. I never recall her ever telling us to pool our money. Yet, Frank and I didn't think twice about it. We just knew we had to take care of each other.

So with that work ethic, the day I turned sixteen, I knew what I needed to do.

Disney World had exploded in popularity and was where every young person in central Florida wanted to work. Knowing I could make decent money there to help our family, I made the forty-five-minute drive through the back roads of orange groves to apply. They paid more than most starting jobs, plus you got to work at "the most magical place on earth." As a small-town kid, that was living the dream.

After being hired, I attended an orientation where they showed us all the different facets of the parks. I started out working in an ice cream shop at the end of Main Street for a few months. Then they announced there were openings in entertainment and I figured that might be my ticket out of food service.

At the audition, I began to watch the people in line ahead of me. You had to do a simple dance routine after they showed you the steps. Now, I had never danced or done anything like that since the trauma of singing solos as a kid. But with the thought of endless ice cream scooping and screaming kids as motivation, I decided I had to go for it. I thought to myself, *Okay, looks simple enough. I can do this.* So when my turn came, I went up and did the routine.

Boom! I got the call that I was hired into Disney entertainment.

After another orientation, I started in the character department. One of the big events at that time was the water ski show. Being an athlete and realizing I could get paid to be out on the water, I knew that's what I wanted to do. But there were two immediate problems: first, there wasn't an opening in the show, and second, I didn't know how to water ski.

For a couple of weeks, I was assigned to various character costumes, until one day, David Hill, the supervisor who hired me, said, "Hey, Mark. Someone got hurt in the ski show. We need you to go out and be a spotter in the boat." (That was someone who stood in the back and helped with the ropes, etc.)

I couldn't believe it. This was my big break. I changed as

quickly as I could and headed over to the lake. (I need to pause the story here and tell you that David went to bat and covered for me several times when I could have easily been fired. I was so appreciative of his generosity, that years later after he had left Disney, I hired David on as our merch manager. And then eventually, he became our road manager for many years.)

I've Got No Strings to Hold Me Down

At the time, I was still sixteen, and the two character skiers were twenty and twenty-one years old. Great guys and great skiers. We quickly became friends. On weekends, I was out there with them in the boat for every show. One day, David came up to me and said, "Hey, Mark, we found out the guy who got hurt is not coming back. We have to replace him in the show. By chance, do you ski?" I hesitated for a moment and then answered, "Yes. . . . Yes, I do." I was thinking to myself, *I didn't dance either and I nailed that. How hard can water-skiing be? Looks easy enough.*

Obviously glad for my answer, David then added, "Great! But it's not just skiing. You gotta trick ski." In a heartbeat, my confidence exploded. With a big grin and my mom's inspiration of "This is America, son. You can do anything you set your mind to," I answered, "David, that is my specialty." Yep, I lied so good I think I even believed me! (Now, let's put this in context: I was a teenage boy naturally loaded up on testosterone. Very athletic and equally as cocky. If something involved any type of sport, I genuinely believed I could do it.)

Hearing my answer, David gave a grin that outdid mine. His relief and surprise showed, as he gushed, "Oh my gosh! Why didn't you say something sooner? This is great!" From there, he proceeded to tell me what I had to not just learn but master, from the tricks to driving the boat to all the safety protocols. He told me I had a month of weekends to work with the guys and learn the routine. After that, he would come out and watch me in an audition to make sure I was ready to perform.

The next day, my new skiing partners said, "Hey, Mark, congratulations! This is going to be great. We had no idea you could do this. Let's get started on the routine." I took a deep breath and confessed, "Hey guys, I gotta tell you something ... I don't know how to ski."

After an awkward moment of silence, they both busted out laughing. "Oh, that's a good one, Mark. You don't know how to ski. Yeah, right. You're probably a hot dog. Come on, man." I insisted, "No, guys, I'm totally serious. I'm telling you. I've never even been on skis."

The laughing stopped.

One asked, "So, how in the world did you get the job?" I answered, "I told David I could." The laughing started back up again. "Are you kidding us? You told him you could trick ski when you can't even ski?!" By now, I knew these two guys well, so I said, "I've been watching you both for a while. It can't be that hard." Respecting my over-the-top confidence, they asked, "Okay, Mark, so what's your plan?" I offered, "Well, you guys are gonna help me. You're gonna teach me. David's given me a month. We've got four weekends, so let's do this!"

They looked at each other, shrugged, and laughed. "Alright, if you got that kind of nerve, we're in. Let's go!"

So, after each show where I was spotting them from the boat, we would drive down to a private area of the lake, out of view from guests. During lunch breaks, show breaks, and any other free time we had, we'd head out there to practice. Just as I had promised the guys, I started to pick it up quickly. Before long, I was skiing and able to start on the tricks. I had to learn everything from taking off from the beach and the dock to jumps.

One of the biggest issues was safety, as we had to navigate around the other boats. If you've ever been to Disney, then you know that characters can appear anywhere. We had to ski by the Contemporary Hotel, the Polynesian Hotel, and Fort Wilderness Campground, around ferry boats and any watercraft. The biggest challenge was, while in a character costume, you could not fall. Disney heroes are supposed to be incredible at everything (except Goofy, of course), so seeing one crash and burn quickly ends the fantasy. The illusion had to be protected at all costs. So, the pressure was on as we were closing in on my big audition day.

Now, let's review.

Learn to ski? *Check.*

Learn to trick ski? *Check.*

The last and final step—trick ski *in character.*

For that, my assignment was delivered.

You ready? Okay.

Pinocchio. Me, Mark Miller, would be Pinocchio.

Kind of makes sense, right? What with me lying about being able to ski and all? Ironic, huh? Maybe you were thinking something a bit cooler? Captain Hook? Tigger, maybe? Nope. I was a wooden puppet with the funky outfit and adjustable lie-detector nose.

For my first practice run, I put on the trademark costume and then slipped on the head, which had a motorcycle helmet encased inside it. I will never forget the first time I fell while practicing. The "face" had two small eye holes with screens over them. That's the only way I could see and there was zero peripheral vision. As soon as I hit the water, it covered the screens and I was totally blind. The water rushed up into the helmet, creating the sensation that I was drowning. I panicked. Started kicking and flailing, even though I'm a strong swimmer.

Through the helmet, I could hear the muffled sounds of hysterical laughter. The guys started yelling, "You have on a life jacket! Stop fighting, Pinocchio! Float! Just float!"

Finally, after several more tries, I got the hang of skiing in costume, found my balance, and got most of the routine down. (Yes, I said *most*.)

On the big day, at 5:00 in the morning in front of the Polynesian Hotel, David walked out on the dock. I was good to go, except for one thing. We hadn't had time for me to learn to ski backwards and that was supposed to be the final stunt in my audition.

We took off from the beach and I started going through all my required moves. Everything was going great. But in the back of my mind, I knew the backwards thing was coming. Finally, the routine was over and we were coming back around for my final pass in front of David. I told myself, *Okay, you just gotta do this. Don't think. Just make your move.* For some reason, I have always been able to focus and concentrate well under pressure. I get this strange tunnel vision, forget everything around me, and just live in the moment.

When the guys gave me the signal, I closed my eyes and spun around. Boom! In a flash, I was backwards on the skis, holding the ropes behind my back for the first time. On the boat, the guys were hooting and hollering. Not wanting to risk a fall after everything had gone so well, I just stayed backwards until David was out of sight. As I let go of the ropes and went down into the water, on the walkie-talkie, I heard him say, "Hey, the kid's fantastic! Love it! Mark's got the job."

Crazy story? Yes. But entirely true. Yet, even as a teenager, I think this was the moment when I began to overcome my fear of performing and start to build my chops as an entertainer. This would serve me well where life was about to take me, sooner than later.

CHAPTER TWO

I Got a Plan

I wake up with this peaceful feeling
In my heart, my soul and my mind
What was once a weight on my shoulders
Is now the hand of something divine

—FROM THE SONG "I Got a Plan"

FOR THE NEXT FIVE YEARS, my job was trick-skiing for "the Mouse." I worked part-time during the school year and full-time in the summer. Frank and I even bought an older, cheap ski boat for me to practice and also for us to just have some fun. Since this was what I was going to be doing for a living, I wanted to keep getting better.

Eventually, I started putting in overtime with some of the live stage productions. I would sign up, learn the dance routine, and then perform with the cast in the show. I also began to take part in the Main Street Electrical Parade. While my only motive was to make extra money, being a part of the entertainment was always fun. Another place that connected me to artists was when I became a runner for acts that performed at Disney, such as KC and the Sunshine Band, Chuck Berry, and The Spinners. (More on KC later.)

Disney offered me a safe place to stretch myself and grow in these new skills, things I never imagined doing before. Once again, this experience provided more evidence of whatever Mom obviously saw in me at an early age. I also think I was beginning to translate playing ball in front of a crowd into these other areas, from people watching me play to performing—just a different version of the same concept.

But in all those years of performing, I never *sang* at Disney. Here's one of the major reasons: after puberty hit, my voice started to drop and just kept going. My pitch got deeper and deeper, which made me even stronger in my determination to *not* sing.

Mom had always been a huge country music fan. Anytime we were in the car, the country radio station was on. Even though I was not a fan yet, I was still exposed to all the Nashville legends at an early age. Along with the music I discovered from friends and family, my tastes continued to expand as I got older to include rock bands like Creedence Clearwater Revival and pop musicians and songwriters, such as Billy Joel. Throughout my teens, music was slowly catching up with basketball as a passion of mine.

During my senior year in high school, I began to look at nearby universities. My first college visit was at the University of Central Florida (UCF). At that time, their basketball program was really strong in Division II on the national level. The head coach was Torchy Clark, who was a legend. I had the opportunity to meet with him during my campus visit.

After the introductions, Coach Clark said, "I saw you play in the districts. I didn't realize you were this small." He looked over at his assistant coach and asked, "Hey, did *you* know he was this little?" The response was, "No, Coach, I didn't." Coach looked me over a minute and then tested me with, "You only scored six points in that district game." I nodded. "Yessir."

After letting me sweat a bit more, he half-smiled, and added, "Those two Harris boys you played with … it's hard to get a shot in with them." (The "Harris boys" were twins, each standing at about six feet seven. They were *really* good.) Again, I nodded and agreed, "Yessir, it was."

After deciding he had enough fun with me, Coach started laughing, then said, "Well, Miller, you don't have to be tall to play here. You've got what we need. You got speed. That's what *we* need . . . speed." Coach paused, thinking, then continued, "But I don't know what we have in scholarship money for you," I was ready for that subject and offered, "I don't need a scholarship, Coach. I'm going to school on the GI Bill. My dad was in the service." He smiled. "Well, then, it's a done deal, son. You can play for us."

That was such a huge moment for me. I walked out of that gym, thinking, *Wow! I'm going to get to play college basketball!* I had planned on visiting a couple of other schools, but after that brief meeting with Coach Clark, I was sold. Totally onboard at UCF, I was very excited about the opportunity.

Full-Court Press

In the fall of 1977, I started college at UCF, less than an hour from our house. Although Coach Clark was tough, I learned so much from him about leadership and motivation, and I carry that with me to this day. I quickly saw two things about him: one, he was a real character, and two, he was an incredibly godly man. Those qualities would make him a solid role model for me in my time at

UCF.

During my freshman year, we were ranked number one in our division and number four in the nation with three All-Americans on our team that season. For all those reasons, I didn't play much that first year. But our practices were intense, going full-court press the majority of the time. Before long, I was beginning to feel burned out from playing so hard every day with very little game time.

One afternoon, I was walking toward the gym when Coach Clark called out, "Miller! What are you doing right now?" I answered, "Nothing, Coach, just waiting to start practice." He motioned toward his car and said, "C'mon, ride with me. I need to go to the dry cleaners." On the way, we just small-talked until he asked, "So, who's the toughest guy to guard on the team?" Without hesitating, I answered, "Bo. Bo is hard to guard." (Bo happened to be Coach's son who was an All-American and led the nation in scoring. I gave him that answer only because it was the truth.)

Coach then asked me, "Do you know *why* Bo is an All-American?" A bit confused by the question, I answered, "Well, he's the best shooter I've ever seen." He came right back with, "No, Miller. He's an All-American because of *you*." I was completely shocked by his statement. Then Coach continued, "Bo has to go up against you every day in practice. There's not a person in the nation that guards him the way you do. You eat his lunch *every ... single ... time.* So much so that when he goes out to play in a game, it's like taking the day off for him."

Hearing Coach's explanation, I recalled the times that Bo had come to me before practice and asked, "Hey, man, can you please back off today?" I'd politely look him in the eye and answer,

"Sorry, Bo, I can't. I have to play a hundred percent."

Regardless of Coach Clark's motive, his words stoked a fire in me. Whether my guarding Bo was significant or not, he sure made me believe it was. By the end of that short car ride, my focus was no longer playing in a game, but about getting our team ready to play *every* practice. This was an amazing example of how Coach Clark led young men to become their absolute best. His encouragement taught me to "take one for the team"—how to discover and understand my purpose anywhere God placed me.

Moments like that were spread throughout my formative years, delivered at just the right time, to lay the groundwork for me to become the leader for Sawyer Brown. And as far as I'm concerned, being in a band *is* a team sport.

If you walked into my home today, you wouldn't find gold records on the wall or industry awards on the mantel. What you *would* find hanging in my office is my most prized possession— my college basketball jersey. A few years back, my kids had it framed for me for Christmas. That first major life goal, a huge dream that became a reality for me, was accomplished in getting to play ball at UCF for Coach Clark.

Three Chords and the Truth

In my free time in and around school and my job at Disney, I had started to take the chords I learned from piano lessons and figure them out on guitar. I would sit around and play, trying to nail down popular songs I heard on the radio.

One night during my junior year at UCF, I had my guitar out and my friend Scott Peterson said, "Hey, I've written a poem.

Why don't you try to put it to music?" I stopped strumming and laughed. "No, I wouldn't have a clue how to do that." But he pressed me, "Come on, man. You play guitar. Why can't you just figure out how to put my words to your chords?" As Scott was leaving, he said, "I'm going to leave a copy of my poem with you … in case you decide to give it a try."

A few minutes later, his challenge had gotten the best of me. I looked over the page and started experimenting. I had to move a few words around to make them rhyme, but in about ten minutes, I had a melody framed around Scott's poem. I grabbed my portable cassette player, hit record, played, and sang my first song all the way through. The main reason I recorded the song was just so I wouldn't forget what I had done.

A few days later, when I saw Scott, he asked, "Hey, Mark, did you do anything with my poem?" I told him what had happened after he left. Well, of course, he wanted to hear the song right then. I told him no, that I wasn't ready to play it for him. Eventually, he wore me down and I let him hear the cassette. Bottom line— Scott freaked out. He *loved* the song.

Not long after that, I went to a party at Scott's place. Suddenly, the loud music playing on his stereo stopped. With no warning, the next thing I heard was me singing. Now *I* was freaking out. And not in a good way. Quickly, people started asking Scott who the singer was. He answered, "Mark Miller!" Standing in the background, I could see some of them looking at each other, smiling, and saying, "Oh wow, cool." But before anyone could locate me, well before the song was over, I slipped out the door—got the heck outta Dodge.

But that moment of seeing my friends' responses was now stuck in my head and made me even more curious, as I started to ask myself, *What if I could write my own lyrics?*

The next free night I had, I sat down with my guitar, a pencil, and a legal pad. Within an hour or so, I had written an entire song on my own—melody *and* lyrics. When I finished, I played it through from top to bottom, then thought, *Well, that was pretty easy. I think I'll write another one.* So I did. By the end of the evening, I had two complete songs. The best way to describe them was a blend of country and pop ballads.

During my time at Disney, I made a lot of friends. One was Ron Feldman, a band leader in the entertainment department. One day, while we were eating together in the cafeteria, I casually asked him, "Can I play you a couple of songs I wrote sometime?"

Now, to paint the picture for you, Ron was really confident. Rightly so, because he was super-talented. He also gave voice lessons on the side, so he made a good living being a musician. Ron stopped eating and looked at me like I was an alien. He started laughing, then loudly called out, "Mark Miller? ... The jock? ... Has written a couple songs? I would *love* to hear them!"

No matter what he was thinking, I was serious. I was ready for someone to be brutally honest with me, not just give me the friend answer: "Yeah, Mark, that's awesome." I knew Ron would love nothing more than to deliver the unvarnished truth to me of how horrible I was. So I pulled out my cassette, popped it into a player in the room, and sat back to watch as he listened.

When both songs finished, Ron sat there in silence, staring into space. Then he slowly looked over at me and asked, "You wrote those?"

"Yeah."

Ron pressed, "You *swear* to me that you wrote those songs?"

"Yeah."

He continued, "Well, okay, but *who* is that singing?"

"Me."

"*Really?*" he said, his voice loaded with sarcasm.

"Yeah."

Ron was obviously having trouble processing all this. "Well, I don't believe you. I just don't believe you." He started laughing again. "*If* that's true, then let me hear some of your earlier songs."

I answered, "Well, I can't, because that's all I got."

Another pause, then he asked, "So these are the *first* two songs you've written?"

"Yeah."

"Okay, *when* did you write them?"

"Last week."

Deciding he was going to call my bluff, Ron challenged me, "Alright, this week, why don't you write a couple *more* songs and bring them in? You did it last week, so do it again this week. I'll listen to them next weekend."

Over the following week, in and around classes, studying, and workouts, I wrote two more songs. The next weekend at Disney, I walked up to Ron and said, "Here's a cassette of the songs I wrote this week, just like you asked."

He popped the cassette in. As the songs played, he went from casually listening to visibly upset. When they ended, Ron blurted out, "You swear to me that you wrote these songs?! And that's you singing?!"

I answered, "Yessir. I promise it is."

Ron gave a deep sigh and got a serious look on his face. "Well, Mark, I'm just gonna tell you. *This* is a gift. *You* have a gift. I've been doing music for twenty years and I can't do what you've done in the last two weeks." He looked me in the eye and said, "I don't know what you're willing to do about it, but you *do* have a gift."

His response threw me. I had wanted the truth from Ron, but this was not what I was expecting at all. He had just validated my songwriting *and* my singing. And this was someone who would have absolutely enjoyed roasting "the jock." In fact, he was fully expecting to do just that, but I had unknowingly turned the tables on him.

So, with Ron's words as motivation, before long, I had written ten songs.

One night, I was sitting at the local Pizza Hut where a good friend of mine, Gregg Hubbard, worked. You know him as Hobie, although his nickname didn't become his aka until Sawyer Brown was in full swing. Although we had known each other for years, we had become friends during my senior year, his junior year. I had to get another elective in to graduate and decided to take chorus. Hobie was the piano player for the class.

To this day, Hobie and I both laugh when we recall how in chorus, the teacher always thought I was singing off-key. One day before class started, she told him, "Hey, Gregg, could you get Mark to sit over by you, so you can help him stay on pitch?"

The reason it was so hard for me to sing choral songs was because my voice was so much lower than everyone else's. I would either sound like a foghorn or just couldn't hit the notes at all. They were too high for me. After all, we were singing choir pieces, not pop or country songs. I spent a good bit of her class humming along, just to look like I was singing. Plus, I never sang very loud, *anywhere*.

I hadn't seen Hobie in a couple of years at that point, and I was ready to get my songs sounding a little better. So while he was working at Pizza Hut, I walked over to him and asked, "Hey, Gregg, would you consider playing piano for me to record some songs I've written?"

Looking a bit surprised at my question, Hobie agreed to play keys on my songs. Full disclosure—he told me later that the only reason he said yes was his curiosity to hear what I had written. Like most everyone else, he was thinking, *So the jock has written some songs, huh? I gotta hear this.*

Another Disney buddy of mine, Fred Langer, had an eight-track recording setup at his place. He agreed to record the songs for me and also offered to play drums. In his small studio, I laid down an acoustic guitar track. Hobie played piano while Fred was on the drum kit. After we recorded my vocals, I ended up with a decent demo tape of all ten songs I had written.

By this point, my brother, Frank, was 1,000 percent on board with my music. He started pushing me like a freight train, encouraging me, "Mark, you gotta go to Nashville! You have to give this music thing a shot!"

You Have to Be Here

In 1980, during spring break of my junior year at UCF, I took the week off from Disney. When I told Hobie what I was planning, he let me know he wanted to come with me. Borrowing my buddy Jack's van, the two of us, along with another friend, Alan Cramer, who would act as my "manager," hit the road. For the entire week in Nashville, with very little money, we would live out of the van.

When we got into town, we went straight to Music Row. This was back in the heyday when every major record label and publishing company was lined up and down those famous streets, from Broadway to Belmont. As the three of us began walking into office after office down that iconic stretch in Music City, I was totally surprised at the places we managed to get into. (Something that hasn't been possible at all for many years.) When we went into RCA Records, I politely told the lady at the front desk, "I have a cassette of some songs I've written." She took my tape, told us to take a seat, and disappeared. A few minutes later, she came back out and sat down at her desk while we waited.

In about a half hour, this guy walked out. He smiled and said, "I just wanted to come out here and see who walked in with this tape. Man, it's pretty cool." I couldn't believe it. Then he stuck out his hand, and said, "I'm Tony Brown. Why don't you guys come on back?"

Being new at who's who in music, especially songs produced in Nashville, I had no idea who Tony Brown was. At that point, he had played keys for Elvis's final two years of touring and then joined Emmylou Harris's band, all well before he became a legend at producing hit records. I found out later that Tony "just so happened" to be screening tapes that day for RCA's A&R (artists and repertoire) department.

We went back into an office, and Tony hit play to finish listening to my songs. When the tape ended, he said, "Mark, I'd like to hear a real band around you, because this is pretty cool." (Real band meaning Nashville studio players.)

Every single place we walked in that week took me seriously—RCA, Warner Brothers, all the big dogs. Everywhere we went, they listened to my songs. Someone would come out and meet us, staring at this young, blond, tan, long-haired surfer-looking kid in shorts and flip-flops who was walking into the command center of country music. What that proves, though, whether back then or today, is that the music business is built on one thing: songs. If you name your five favorite artists right now, you will also quickly associate them with *what*? Great songs. Artists come and artists go, but Nashville has always been built on songwriting, on storytelling.

Whether labels or publishers, everyone seemed to like my songs, but the unexpected draw was my voice. They were all surprised at this big sound coming out of this little guy. One exec said, "It's like Merle Haggard meets The Beach Boys." (With that, the Sawyer Brown theme was definitely starting to emerge. All with Hobie right there beside me.)

By the end of the week, after hearing all the feedback from so many industry professionals, I had clearly seen that there was something to this music, songwriting, and now singing deal for me. What I never expected was definitely happening. But I wasn't quite sure what to make of it yet.

Legendary country artist and songwriter John Anderson had gone to the same high school as me. By that time, he was already in Nashville, so I actually knew someone from my hometown who was making the music thing work. That was encouraging to me.

The one consistent piece of advice every person gave me during that week was this: "Mark, you can't do this from Florida. You gotta move to Nashville. To make it, you need to be *here*. And from what we hear in these songs, it's worth you coming to town."

As I went back home to school, basketball, and Disney, that week had created a new discipline to add to my life—songwriting. Once again, here was another place where I believe God was leading me, to get me where He wanted me to go in *His* plan.

A plot twist that occurred around this time was a friend at Disney had played my demo tape for KC (of the Sunshine Band) when he performed at the park. Then, when I was working as a runner for his show, KC saw me, told me that he liked my songs, and invited me to come to his studio in Miami to talk. While there, we discussed the potential of him producing a record for me. He believed in my talent and was very supportive, which was a major confidence boost for me. But with the Nashville connection starting to happen, KC and I never ended up creating music together, although we have remained friends all these years.

Late that summer, just before I was about to begin my senior year and only two semesters away from getting my credentials to coach and teach, a conversation at a family dinner changed everything. To set the stage, Mom's ultimate goal for me and my brother was for us to graduate from college. Since she was the first in our family to get a degree, she wanted the second generation to keep going and start a new legacy.

Mom, Frank, my grandparents, and I were all sitting around the table after a meal. Seemingly out of nowhere, Mom looked at me and said, "Mark, why don't you go up to Nashville and give music a shot for a year? If you don't make it, you can come back, finish your senior year, get your degree, and move on with your original plan. You can red-shirt this year in basketball. Take a year off and go give it a try."

I was absolutely speechless. Those were *the last* words I ever thought would come out of Mom's mouth. I was in shock, trying to process what she said in front of God and everybody.

Now, to be clear in that moment, my honest feelings were not, *Alright, I'm going to go to Nashville and become a star.* No. To me, Mom had just given me permission to go on an adventure!

And my mama didn't raise no fool. She didn't have to tell *me* twice.

Because I was already signed up and enrolled for the semester, first thing the next morning, I went to the admin office at UCF and let them know I wouldn't be attending in the fall. Next, I went straight to the gym to talk to Coach Clark. Seeing he was in his office with his assistant coach, I knocked on the door. He invited me in, and I sat down and started telling my story. "Coach, I wanted to come tell you that I'm dropping out of school for a year and going to Nashville." He stared at me for a minute, then asked, "Okay, what are you gonna do?" I answered, "Well, I've written some songs and I'm going to give the music business a shot."

He turned to our assistant coach and asked, "Ray, did you know about this?" When Ray shook his head, Coach continued, "Well, if he's going to Nashville, then he's gotta be good." He looked back at me and said, "Miller, you're good, aren't you?" I answered, "I ... I don't know."

Coach looked back at his assistant and said, "I'm telling you right now, Ray, if he's going to Nashville, he's good. I know this kid." Turning to me again, he said, "Well, here's the deal, Miller. You're gonna be famous one day. You're gonna be rich. There's going to be a day when you'll think that you should donate money to the school. But you're not. You're going to give it to me, because I believe in you." At that, all three of us started laughing.

I was so relieved my coach not only understood my decision, but told me he believed in *me*, no matter what I did. (True to his word, Coach Clark and I stayed in touch over the years, and he was a huge supporter of the band until he died in 2009.)

Everyone important in my life was validating this idea of me going to Nashville to give music a try. But trust me, I was clueless with a capital C. Yet, I think that's also how you beat the odds. You just don't know any better. Because if you did, you *wouldn't* go. If you don't know enough to *be* scared, then you don't *get* scared.

On a Gas Card and a Prayer

In September of 1980, when I should have been starting my senior year in college, instead, I had $600 saved up and was ready to go to Nashville. Hobie had decided if I went, he wanted to go with me and make a go at this adventure too. So we set our launch day, loaded up the car, and hit the road late one night, headed north.

I have to be honest—leaving my family was traumatic for me, because I had no idea if I would be coming back. Driving away from my mom and my brother was one of the most heart-wrenching things I have ever done. I was the first one in our tight-knit team to venture out.

But little did I know things were about to get even tougher and more emotional.

Hobie and I made our first stop in Gainesville to get something to eat. With everything I owned and all my money in a small bag, I wasn't about to leave it in the car. I decided to carry it in with me into the restaurant. After we ate, Hobie walked outside and I went into the restroom, making the huge mistake of leaving my bag in the booth.

When I came out, it was gone—everything I had and every dime I'd saved—stolen.

Heartbroken and kicking myself, I went to a pay phone and called collect to our house. Through tears, I told Mom what had happened, ending with, "I just feel like it's a sign from God that I'm not supposed to do this—that I'm just supposed to turn around and come back home."

Calmly but firmly, Mom said, "Yeah, you *could* look at it that way. Or it could also be Satan trying to keep you from doing something great. You decide, Mark."

Pausing a moment to let that thought sink in, as she was always so good at doing, Mom then continued, "Mark, do you still have your grandmother's Texaco gas card in the glove compartment of the car for emergencies?" I answered, "Yeah, I think so." She said, "Good. Then go to Nashville. You can buy gas and some food on that. Once you're there, I'll wire you a hundred dollars until you can figure something out."

Deciding Mom's wisdom was once again dead-on, Hobie and I got back on the road.

And back to the plan.

CHAPTER THREE

Six Days on the Road

And I'm a-gonna make it home tonight
—**FROM THE SONG** "Six Days on the Road"

HOBIE AND I drove all night, pulling into Nashville bright and early. Never being one to waste time trying to get traction, I had made calls to some of the folks we met during our spring break trip and scheduled a few meetings. Hobie's mom's best friend from college lived in Nashville and knew Linda Hargrove, a song-writer with a major publishing deal who had a lot of cuts at the time. The friend graciously made a call to Linda to set up our first meeting that morning. A fellow Florida native, Linda wrote songs for everyone from Asleep at the Wheel to Olivia Newton-John, as well as being an artist and producer.

Still a bit bleary-eyed from the all-night road trip, Hobie and I sat with Linda while she listened to the cassette of my songs. Like the others from our first trip to Nashville, she said she liked my writing but was intrigued by my voice. Linda was very encouraging and quickly said that she would like to work with me.

This first meeting started to take the edge off my frustrations over the stolen bag. And now, with little money, I had no choice but to hustle to be able to stay in Nashville.

As I had planned the move to Music City, I contacted John Anderson, since he was from Apopka and his own career was taking off. He had agreed to set up a meeting for me with Norro Wilson. Norro wrote songs for artists such as Charlie Rich, George Jones, Tammy Wynette, Reba McEntire, Kenny Chesney, and Shania Twain. John met Hobie and me at Norro's place to make the introduction.

After listening to a few songs, Norro said, "What in the world is in the water down there in Florida?! You *and* John both look like kids but have these *big* voices." Laughing, he continued, "Mark, I'd like to work with you, but if Linda wants you, that's great. Go with her. I'm here, regardless."

So, as crazy as this sounds, by noon on my first day in Nashville, I decided to sign a production deal with Linda Hargrove. Four hours in town and I was handed what so many people spend years trying to land. I never worked with Norro after that, but we remained friends until he passed away years later. His offer and encouragement that morning, along with Linda's, let me know I had a real shot at songwriting. Mom was proved right *again* and, as always, I'm so glad I listened to her.

While I met with Linda that morning, she said, "Hey, there's a guy I've been writing with who's doing a set at the Exit/In tonight. His name is Dean Dillon. You ought to go hear his songs." (Exit/In is a small venue in Nashville with an incredible history of performers, from Etta James to the Red Hot Chili Peppers, from Chuck Berry to Johnny Cash.) Ready to take in as much of the Nashville music community as fast as we could, Hobie and I went to the iconic venue that night. Dean walked out onstage with his guitar and trademark look—long hair flowing out from under his cowboy hat. His first song was "Unwound" that he co-wrote with

Frank Dycus and that went on to become George Strait's first big hit at country radio.

After Dean strummed his last chord, I was already thinking, *That's it! I'm going home. What he's got? I ain't got that. Wow. He is unbelievable.* While, of course, I wasn't really going to leave, Linda telling me to go hear Dean was smart. On my first night in town, the standard was set for me in songwriting. Just like learning to trick-ski in a month or guard Bo in basketball practice, I have *always* been up for a challenge.

The next day, I went by to see Linda and told her, "Hey, I'd really like to cut Dean's song 'Unwound.'" She responded, "Yeah, that's a great song, but there's one he and I wrote that I really want you to demo." Before long, I was in the vocal booth on the mic. That was 1980. In 1981, the song was cut by David Allen Coe, the outlaw country artist. But then in 2015, Chris Stapleton recorded it for his *Traveller* album.

The song title? "Tennessee Whiskey."

Crazy that my first vocal demo to sing was that incredible song. Another example of the rich history of stories that have been written in Music City, as well as how a great song *is* a great song in *any* generation and will stand the test of time.

While working with Linda created no real traction for me, the biggest blessing was that she gave me a professionally produced demo of three solid songs that I was able to use to land work in town.

Takin' Care of Business

Needing to bring in a steady income to pay my bills, I started looking for a job that had flexibility for whenever I got an opportunity to co-write or sing on demos. At that time, racquetball was rising in popularity as a recreational sport. Because he was in Nashville a lot and loved to play, Elvis had opened a racquetball club downtown. (Yep, the King of Rock and Roll. No kidding.) When he realized there wasn't a good place for people to play, he built his own facility. He could play anytime he wanted, while also investing in a business. I thought the club could be a great option for me to work a sports job *and* make connections. (Plus, then I could also sort of say I worked for Elvis, right?)

When I walked in to inquire about a job, Dot Dixon, the manager, looked me over and then asked, "So, do you play?" I answered, "Oh, yeah." *Here we go again.* I had never played racquetball in my life. But if a sport involved a ball and competition, I was confident I could learn fast. Next, she asked, "Great. Can you *teach* people how to play?" I quickly thought to myself, *Once I learn, I know I can teach. After all, I'm going to be a coach one day.* So I answered, "Sure!" With that, Dot hired me.

Getting started, the biggest challenge wasn't learning the game but getting all the rules down. But the job worked out perfectly for me. The first reason was that I was able to meet a lot of artists, songwriters, singers, and musicians who came in to play. One was a backup singer named Becky Foster. After Becky and I got to know each other, I played her my demo. From there, she introduced me to a jingle producer. Once again, I heard, "Your voice is really unique. You've got a cool sound."

I began getting calls to sing on a lot of local commercials and was also able to do some voice-overs. My most memorable job was for a car dealership that was giving away a pig with every test drive. (Totally serious. You can't make this stuff up.) I also got to sing on a few national-brand jingles. That kind of studio work is like an assembly line. You walk in and crank 'em out, because the room is full of musicians with the clock ticking and money being spent.

Another huge reason the racquetball club was a great job for me was that Dot allowed me to work around my music—jingles, songwriting, and demo sessions. She was and is an amazing woman who became like a second mom to me. (She's now in her eighties, and we still stay in touch.)

While Hobie was hustling to get work playing keys, his steady job was being a waiter in the little diner inside a Walgreens, just a few miles south of downtown Nashville. (Yes, a Walgreens. I guess eating in a pharmacy didn't fly and they eventually canned that concept.)

An artist named Don King was a regular at the racquet- ball club and we started getting to know each other. He had just signed a deal with a major country label, was beginning to book some live shows, and was putting a band together. Don offered me a small publishing deal as a songwriter and also asked me to start going out on the road with him as a crew member. When I realized he needed a piano player, I helped Hobie land the gig. Now we would both be going out on the road to work with Don. Plus I now had a place to take the songs I was writing.

And here comes another one of those you-couldn't-write-a- better-script-if-you-tried divine appointments. When Hobie and I went to Don's first rehearsal, we met the rest of his band: Bobby Randall, who played guitar and sang backup vocals, and Jim Scholten, who played bass. Bobby and Jim had known each other since grade school, growing up in Midland, Michigan, together. For a while, Don brought in different drummers for the weekend

THE BOYS AND ME

trips. But eventually, he told us he had a guy named Joe Smyth coming to play. Once everyone heard "Joe-Joe" that weekend, the drum chair was covered.

Don King's touring band was the genesis for the original Sawyer Brown.

C'mon, Just One Song

Now everyone was in their spot, except me. I was a roadie who was questioning if I could take a career in music past songwriting. Could I overcome being an introvert and the shyness to do more? As I got to know the guys better, I started asking them to play on the demos I recorded for Don. I soon realized with a solid self-contained band, we had everything covered. Besides guitar and vocals, Bobby could also play fiddle, pedal steel, and just about anything else needed. So once I would finish writing a new song, I'd line them up for a studio session to cut a demo and I would sing the lead vocal. Through the publishing company, I was able to pay each of the guys twenty-five dollars per song. Even when a new song I'd written didn't get approved for a demo, I would sneak them into the studio late at night and record anyway.

Like all musicians in Nashville, the guys worked any chance they could. While playing for Don on the weekends, they landed the Monday night slot doing cover songs at a small local club. Bobby was handling all the lead vocals. The only difference in the lineup for this band was that Hobie wasn't involved because he wasn't able to get Monday nights off from Walgreens.

One night, the guys asked me to go with them, just to hang out. Sitting there listening and looking around, I found it was a very typical bar crowd. People were there to drink; music was just background noise.

Right away, I noticed this venue was different than Exit/ In where Hobie and I had gone to hear Dean Dillon. There are venues where people go to hear someone and they can drink. Then there are the places where people go to drink while a live band is playing. Best I can recall, that was my first time in a club like this where folks were getting drunk and most of them were ignoring the band.

After a couple of sets, the guys asked me to come up and sing during one of their fifteen-minute breaks. I was fast and firm on my answer—no! I was not interested in singing live.

But at each break, they kept asking. As the night went on, I began to think, *Nobody's really listening. Give it a shot. If I could get up and dance at Disney, why can't I try singing here?* One problem, though. I didn't really know a lot of popular songs. And, trust me, singing along with the radio or doing karaoke is *very* different than getting up on a mic and selling a song to a crowd when they expect you to be a pro. I had already seen that Bobby was great at learning and remembering the lyrics to a huge catalog of songs.

Finally, they convinced me to get up and sing "just one song." I have always been a huge Eagles fan, so I told them I could do "Lyin' Eyes," which, of course, they knew.

So I walked up onstage behind the mic as the band started that classic intro with the great guitar line. Right after I sang, "City girls just seem to find out early, how to open doors with just a smile," the whole place stopped. The crowd went silent. Everybody turned and looked at the stage. I quickly went from *How bad could it be?* to freaking out. And then it hit me: I had picked the *longest* hit song in modern history, coming in at around six and a half minutes. With people watching, it felt like an eternity. Another verse, another chorus, another verse, more choruses. When the song finally ended, I couldn't get off that stage fast enough. But the crowd was applauding. Something had connected.

But then an interesting break came one weekend when we were all out on the road with Don. He was booked to open for a show where Reba McEntire was the headliner. We were all sitting at catering, eating dinner with the other band members and crew, when Reba walked in, grabbed a plate, and sat down right next to me. In her familiar style, with that contagious Oklahoma drawl, she turned to me and asked, "So, what do you do?" I answered, "Well, I'm a roadie for Don, but I'm in Nashville because I'm a songwriter." My answer seemed to get her attention. "You write songs?" I responded, "Yes, ma'am." Reba continued, "Well then, why don't you write *me* a couple songs? Send some to me. I'll give you the address."

So when we got back home, I went through every song I had written with Reba's style in mind. I chose two that I thought, *She'll love these. These are so right for her.* Then I decided to throw in one more, just for good measure, that was completely different than the other two. As is so often the case when you pitch songs, the "sure thing" is not picked, but instead, it's the one you never thought they'd choose. "Over, Under, and Around" became song number five on Reba's *Unlimited* album, released in June of 1982. My first major artist cut.

Not long after that, Don told us he was losing his record deal and wouldn't be able to keep us on anymore. That meant I would lose my publishing agreement with him. Through my connection to well-known songwriter Bill Shore and the attention I had gotten from the Reba cut, I was able to quickly land a new deal as a staff songwriter with country legend Charlie Pride's publishing business. I worked with Blake Mevis, who was running the company for Charlie. Both Bill and David Wills, who wrote "Leona," were there, along with Byron Gallimore, who would go on to work with Tim McGraw.

I started going in to their offices every day to write. I once heard Bill Shore say, "I knew Mark would make it, because he was the first one there in the morning and the last to leave." My starting salary was around a hundred bucks a week. That was huge for me back then. Of course, in songwriting, any money paid out is just an advance on your future royalties. The goal of a publisher signing a writer is to have an exclusive arrangement where you eventually get enough cuts to recoup advances and you both make money. If a writer doesn't produce in a reasonable amount of time, the song publisher will most often cut their losses.

Around that same time, word got around town that a new club would be opening soon and the owner was going to hire a house band. Every musician wanted in on that deal. A regular gig with steady money and no traveling was gold. When Bobby, Jim, Joe-Joe, and Hobie found out, they came to me and said, "Hey, Mark, we want to audition for this new club called Knight's Corral, but we want you to be our lead singer."

I was still really unsure about taking my talent that seriously, but I saw how much they all wanted this to work, so I finally agreed. *Buckle up, here we go.*

As we started rehearsals, I wanted to feel as comfortable as possible, so I decided to play guitar too. Because I didn't know many songs by heart yet, I printed out the lyrics and chords for every song and put them on a music stand in front of me. (I think I subconsciously built a barricade between me and the crowd.)

We worked up a set list of popular country songs that were on the radio at the time, from The Bellamy Brothers to George Jones, Waylon and Willie to Merle Haggard. I was working really hard to keep up with the guys who were already established at doing live shows. By now, Hobie had really found his sweet spot and was gelling with the guys.

One of the biggest issues any band faces is coming up with a name. That process is rarely easy. While it can sound strange to someone outside the music industry, every member agreeing on a name can create major stress, even breaking up bands before they get started. At the time, Alabama was blowing up on the charts, so in our brainstorming, we began to look at Southern city names that had that kind of feel to them. One that stood out and even looked and sounded like Alabama was Savannah—a city known for its Southern charm, horse-drawn carriages, and antebellum homes. The name and the vibe worked well for us.

So, the band's first name was Savanna. We decided to leave the "h" off to be different from the city spelling.

On the day of the club audition, there were so many bands signed up that the process took hours. But, to our surprise, the call finally came from the club owner that we had gotten the gig. We were hired as the house band at Knight's Corral. Now Joe-Joe, Jim, Bobby, Hobie, and I had steady work together as a band in Nashville.

On that first night out of the gate, there I was in the middle of the stage with my guitar and my music stand. While singing, I followed the lyrics and the chords on paper, just like I had done back at home as a kid with my piano teacher. Standing totally still, I was trying to get through one song at a time. No movement. Not selling the song for the crowd. I just wanted to survive the night in this new role as lead singer.

While the owner was trying to get the word out about his club, news was traveling fast around town about this new band named Savanna. But evidently he was burning money faster than it was coming in. Even though the crowds were growing, by the end of the first month from opening his doors, the owner told us he was going to have to close down. Almost as quick as we started, we were done. We opened the club up and we shut the club down!

The good news was, I had gotten much more comfortable and was gaining confidence onstage. With the night-after-night, set-after-set repetition, I was memorizing lyrics and getting rid of the music stand. I even started putting the guitar down on some songs and holding the mic. Still a long way from where I would end up, I was at least settling in on my journey of becoming a performer, not just a singer.

Finding Our Fans

Two local talent agents who worked at Buddy Lee Attractions, Rick Ship and Ken Levitan, had been coming to the club to listen to us. (Both went on to have great success in the music industry.) They reached out after hearing we had lost our steady gig and said, "Hey, we think we can book you guys in the club circuit. We can do it on the side without signing you. But we really believe we can keep you busy with weeklong gigs, playing Tuesday through Saturday nights at one venue."

All five of us were now ready to keep going as a band. Enjoying the energy and synergy of what we were creating together along with this new opportunity from Rick and Ken, we felt like we had nothing to lose and everything to gain.

Right away, the agents called us early one week to tell us that the lounge at the Holiday Inn in Corinth, Mississippi, had just fired their band. The manager needed a replacement for the week, starting that night. They asked if we could leave right away. Sitting on go, we got all our gear together and made the four-hour drive south of Nashville.

Right after we pulled up in the parking lot in front of the hotel and started to unload, the club owner busted out of the door. To paint the picture here, we all had long hair and looked more like Bon Jovi than The Oak Ridge Boys. He planted his feet, crossed his arms, and with the personality of a marine drill sergeant, yelled, "Just get back in your van, boys! You can go home! They told me you were a country band, and you *surrrrrrre* don't look like no country band! So you can get on outta here!" Thinking he'd been lied to by a slick Nashville agent and was back at square one with no band for the night, the guy was furious.

Knowing we all needed the work and trying to think fast, I blurted out, "Wait! We got a fiddle!" His eyebrows went up and, with a smirk, he asked, "*You* got a fiddle?!" I turned and looked at Bobby. He ran back, rummaged through the gear to pull his fiddle case out, popped the latches, and, in record time, had his bow on the strings.

The club manager decided to call our bluff. "Alright ... prove it. Play me somethin' country." Bobby called out, "I can do 'Orange Blossom Special'!" Knowing that was the standard for fiddle playin', the guy answered, "Alright then, let's hear it!"

So, out in the parking lot of the Holiday Inn in Corinth, Mississippi, standing on the boiling blacktop on a blazing-hot

August day, all of us wet with sweat, Bobby broke out the very best "Orange Blossom Special" he had ever played. A performance that would have made Charlie Daniels declare Bobby had beaten the devil down in Mississippi. I bet you could have heard that fiddle breakdown for miles around.

As Bobby's last note died away, the guy was obviously surprised and lightened up a bit. "Okay. I'll let you play tonight. But if I don't like you, you're gone! Understand?" We all agreed with our best, "Yessir!" as we started to unload our gear.

That night, we did five forty-five-minute sets. Start at the top of the hour, do a solid round of country covers, then take a fifteen-minute break, before doing it all over again the next hour with different songs. The crowd looked happy and bought a lot of drinks, so at the end of the night, the owner walked up with a much better attitude than before. "Alright, I like you guys. You're good for the week. I'll get you keys to your rooms and set you up to eat in the restaurant."

By the weekend, word had gotten around Corinth that a rockin' country band from Nashville was tearin' it up down at the Holiday Inn lounge. On Saturday night, the place was packed. For that, the club manager *loved* us. After that week, he had us back on a regular basis and became a friend of ours.

In all our time playing clubs, I have never tasted alcohol of any kind. Through high school and college, I was never a party guy. I stayed busy with schoolwork, sports, and my job. Plus, I had a mom who wouldn't put up with any kind of foolishness. Her standard, coupled with my faith, were constant motivators for me to try to stay out of trouble. So when the band started playing in clubs, I had never been around drunk people before. I didn't understand when a guy got mouthy and aggressive that it was the

63

beer or whiskey talking. If someone said something I didn't like, I was ready to fight. I can remember Bobby pulling me aside and saying, "Mark, dude, the guy's drunk. Just let it go. Not worth it."

While Bobby was right, I didn't care what the guy's excuse was. If someone popped off at me, I was thinking, *Okay, get ready to get knocked out.* Because I had never been around liquor or experienced being drunk personally, that took a while for me to understand. This was also back before smoking was not allowed indoors, and like I said earlier, I have always hated cigarette smoke. So to avoid the whole scene, I started going outside on our breaks.

Singing night after night, I was able to find my groove, loosen up, and feel the music. I also learned to focus on the people who were actually listening, enjoying our music, and appreciating us. I had to learn to be a Christian man anywhere, in *any* environment, and be grateful for the people who were engaged with us. After all, those early days were about us starting to build relationships with our fans—the people we have come to love and appreciate over the years. From back then to today, those are the good folks who have always received our full attention and who we love to see and entertain.

But, being totally honest, there were some very sad moments for me in those days playing clubs. I remember thinking to myself, *What has to be going on in someone's life that he or she is getting drunk in here on a Tuesday night? Why aren't you home? Why are you in here drinking?* Like I had learned from my mom, those feelings weren't about judgment from me. Not at all. Just compassion for some of the people I saw who were out to drown their troubles night after night. People go to clubs for a lot of different reasons, but the ones who are hurt and lonely, looking to medicate themselves from some invisible source of pain, my heart went out to those people.

In our first year out on the road, from Cincinnati to Daytona Beach, we started to pack in the crowds, usually at capacity by our last night in a town. Our reputation on the circuit was growing because of the energy in our live shows. Club owners were calling to get us back as soon as the calendar would allow. Because of our track record and demand, our agents were also getting us more money each time we returned. All this was built on the reputation that we played country while looking like a rock act. Our sound and image were working from the heartland to the beach towns, from blue collar to white collar to no collar, from folks on the farm to workers in the factories to people in the corner office. We were building a united fan base of diverse people everywhere we went.

Because I had started my journey in music as a songwriter, I knew what we would eventually have to develop and introduce was our own original music. That was our next natural step to grow as a band. So, when I wrote a song and we put it together, we'd work it into our set. We quickly noticed the crowd didn't respond any different when we played our own material instead of the covers. There was no letdown on our own songs, which is the biggest telltale sign when a cover band plays one of their own. Crowds can quickly tell the difference in quality. What we were writing was holding its own with the top ten hits in our sets. That was a huge test, as well as a great experiment for where we were headed. Before long at our shows, we could see that our songs were becoming just as popular as the covers when we began to get just as many requests to hear our own songs.

I'm Not a Cowboy

Back home in Nashville, I began to struggle in my publishing deal because I was being paid to write straight, traditional country songs. What I was hearing in my head, and what was working for us live out on the road in front of real people, was very different from the expectations of what I was *supposed* to write.

So, while my latest song was killing it in our live shows, I knew I had no chance of getting it approved to demo. I decided to take matters into my own hands. Around 1:00 in the morning, I snuck the guys into the studio to record a new song. Right in the middle of a good take, the door flew open. It was Blake, my boss with the publishing company.

Evidently, he was headed home late from some event and his route took him by the studio. He saw all the cars at an odd hour, and I'm sure he recognized mine. Knowing that something unapproved was likely going down, he was *not* happy with me.

We all stopped and looked at Blake, as he stood there staring at me. After gathering his composure in front of the guys, he said, "Mark, come see me tomorrow and bring this song. I wanna hear it." With that, he turned and walked out with the guys now looking at me—like one of those moments with your buddies when the teacher walks back in the room, catches you all doing something, but everyone knows who the real ringleader is.

The next day, as ordered, I went into Blake's office, ready for a verbal beatdown. He told me to play the song he'd heard us recording. Now, when Blake would listen to a song, he'd turn his chair around with his back to you and the room. While he was probably just wanting to avoid showing any expression until he heard the cut, those moments were always totally intimidating for me. As the songwriter, I was torturing myself with thoughts like, *Am I any good? He's hating this. This is probably terrible.*

After only a verse and a chorus, Blake whipped his chair back around with his head down, motioning for me to stop the tape. With a scowl, he glared at me. "Mark! Son! I don't even know what this is! What can I possibly do with this song? *Who* would cut this?"

Respectfully, I answered, "Well, I would."

He took a deep breath, and then said, "But *you* don't have a record deal! You aren't getting paid for you. You're getting paid to write country for other artists. ... Look at you! You got long surfer hair. You wear flip-flops. You look like you walked out of some exotic dumpster! If you ever want a deal, then get a cowboy hat. Buy some boots. You need to look the part."

I shook my head and responded, "Blake, I'm not a cowboy. That's just *not* who I am."

After all the dressing down, he sighed really heavy, and ended with, "Mark, I don't know what to do with this song here in Nashville."

The song? "Step That Step," which in 1985 would become our first number one hit.

Let me stop for a moment and fast-forward you to that year, right after we won the CMA Horizon Award. Backstage after the awards, Blake walked up to me, wrapped me in a huge bear hug, and literally picked me up off the ground. I will never, ever forget his words: "Mark! You showed us all! You did it! I'm so proud of you."

The reason I could take moments like that in Blake's office is because I knew how much he cared about me as a person. We had a close enough relationship that I could handle his blunt honesty. The fact is, Blake had produced Keith Whitley and George Strait. He knew straight-up country better than *anybody*. That was his thing. He and I knew that just wasn't me. But moments like backstage at the CMA Awards, those are the ones I will always remember and cherish.

Now, back to the story …

During that same time in the early eighties, Alabama had exploded on the scene as the first self-contained band ever played on country radio. Before them, you had solo artists that had named their bands, like Merle Haggard and the Strangers or Buck Owens and the Buckaroos. The players could be easily interchanged, because the music was all about the name at the front. But now, here was Randy, Jeff, and Teddy—no cowboy hats, wearing jeans and football jerseys, with their drummer, Mark Herndon looking like a rock star in long blond hair and sunglasses, behind a giant drum kit. While this was new to the genre, the industry still wasn't ready for a full shift. Yet, in my mind, if Alabama was the Eagles of country, then we were going to be The Rolling Stones.

As a band, we were most definitely going down a different path. Gaining notoriety each month on the road, we were becoming less and less popular in Nashville. Like rebels who weren't trying to be rebellious, we were just being us with our own image and our own sound. We had spent a lot of our own money putting on showcase after showcase for country record labels in town. But the result was always the same. Every time, we heard, "It's too much. You're just too much for us. We don't get it."

We had hit a massive brick wall called the country music business. While we were out winning every night with the people who forked out hard-earned money to hear a good band, the major labels, managers, and booking agencies refused to connect the dots.

That is, except for this one guy—Lynn Schultz, an A&R rep for Capitol.

Capitol's Nashville office had Kenny Rogers, but every decision still went through the iconic circular tower in downtown LA. For that reason, Lynn didn't really have the ability to sign an act. But after hearing about the band, he decided he wanted to see us in our element, in front of a packed house. So he flew in to watch our show at a club in Cincinnati.

Afterward, Lynn took us out to eat and said, "Boys, just don't stop what you're doing. I can't sign you. But I'm telling you right now, *do not* quit! Something will come together soon, and this will work for you."

Lynn was a devoted music lover and, once he saw us, he got us. He experienced firsthand why we were working and winning. What we didn't know at the time was that he felt like the Capitol LA record execs would be interested in us. We had proved to be too much for Nashville, but maybe we were just right for LA.

If only there was some way for us to be heard there …

Hobie

I FIRST MET GREGG "HOBIE" HUBBARD after my family moved to Apopka the summer before he started the eighth grade and I was going into the ninth. His mom was the high school English teacher and his dad was a professor at a local college. Everybody knew that "the Hubbard boys" were really smart. His brother, Glenn, was a grade ahead of me. After graduating from college with two degrees in three years, Glenn went on to get his doctorate in economics from Harvard. From 2004 to 2019, he served as the dean of the Graduate School of Business at Columbia University. Today, he still teaches finance and economics there. That's the kind of stock Hobie comes from.

When we graduated from high school, Hobie procrastinated getting into college, maybe out of some rebellion, coming from that intellectual DNA. He was always kind of a rebel with long hair and was more rock and roll than academia. But he ended up going to a community college while I was at the University of Central Florida. By the time he joined me at UCF, he was a sophomore and I was a junior. That was when we started hanging out together on a regular basis. Because I was only in college to play basketball, there were many days when Hobie and I would leave for school but never actually make it to class. During that time, we also started playing music together.

Besides being the band's keys player since day one, he has

always handled the background vocal arrangements and also sings the lion's share of those. I have never been able to sing harmonies, but I've also never had to worry about it because Hobie is incredible at hearing the parts. His expertise has been amazing and his contribution matchless.

I think a huge struggle for Hobie in our early years was that he was very talented in so many areas. So music just came along at the perfect time for him, fitting his life as well as filling the creative void. The two of us got on board with music very naturally, even though he has always been a far better musician. While I could come in with a song, Hobie would be able to formulate it and make it sound like the record. After that first trip to Nashville, our music and our friendship grew even more. We created a definite bond that has stood the test of time. Neither of us had any idea where it would take us, but we just knew it was going to be together.

With Hobie's family being so smart and all three being in education, I know the expectations for him were high. But his dad was really cool about our decision to make a go at music. He was a bit of a maverick himself with a cool sense of adventure. I'm not sure, but his dad might have thought, *Do it now. Don't wait until you're older and wonder what might have been.* At the point Hobie left home with me, he certainly had a whole lot more to lose than I did. He could have done something in academics, like his family.

That is exactly the reason why, in later years, I heavily encouraged Hobie to go back to school and finish his degree. So, he went to Belmont to graduate and then went on to get his master's. He eventually became an adjunct English professor at Belmont, scheduling around our tour calendar. With most of our shows being on weekends, that has worked out well for him. Hobie also assists in the writing center, working with students to improve their writing. Getting both his degrees while we were touring was not easy. But I'm really glad he has been able to continue his family's tradition, all while staying with Sawyer Brown.

Here's my bottom line on Hobie Hubbard—he's the heartbeat of the band.

He lives the band. With Hobie, I always know that nothing is going to slip through the cracks concerning us. He's the most sensitive of any of the band members to the way the music industry, fans, and critics view us. He takes it very personally. Even when I would let something somebody said slide, Hobie ain't forgettin' nothin'! He has an amazing ability to consider how we might be perceived, along with if and how we should respond.

Hobie is fiercely protective of the band's vision. Over the years, he has constantly reminded me to trust my gut, because we have been right far more than we were wrong. Hobie wanted us to stay true to who we are rather than bend to what anyone else told us to do.

In our personal lives, Hobie is an incredible uncle to my kids and my two grandsons. He is full-on hands-on. My kids will invite him to things before they invite me. We're family. True brothers. He believes in me and I believe in him.

One of my best memories of Hobie is driving with him from Tennessee to Texas late one night. We were somewhere in the middle of Arkansas. I was at the wheel and Hobie was riding shotgun to make sure I stayed awake—even though I don't sleep much. That night, I was working on "Step That Step," so he was writing down lyrics as I was working them out. Hobie's inside joke became, "You may have written 'Step That Step,' but I wrote it down!"

Even when I was writing songs that were way too far outside the box for country radio, Hobie championed them all. When I would play a demo but then question it, often he would tell me, "But, Mark, that's just who we are." He's always been on board with the direction of the band, whatever that looked like at the time.

Our fans have always known the irreplaceable role Hobie has had in the band and in my life over the years. One of the amazing things about him that has made this partnership work so well is that, from day one, he has always responded to my leadership. But with that, I have always needed and valued his incredible contribution. We have the same kind of chemistry and connection as Jagger and Richards. David Lee Roth and Eddie Van Halen. Bono and The Edge. Robert Plant and Jimmy Page. There's a unique dynamic that exists in modern music between a lead singer and his right-hand musician in the band. That synergy definitely exists between the two of us.

With Hobie, I have always had a teammate who had my back for anything. I have been so blessed for over four decades to have such an incredibly talented guy walk alongside me, to blaze the trail with me. Like I said, he's the heartbeat of the band.

CHAPTER FOUR

Gypsies on Parade

Our name is in lights on the billboard sign
In every town we play
But if you may, all it really need say are gypsies
gypsies on parade

—**From the song** "Gypsies on Parade"

THROUGHOUT MY NASHVILLE ADVENTURE, Plan B was always in the back of my mind—go back home to Apopka, finish my last two semesters at UCF, get my teacher's certificate, and become a coach. As the high achiever my mom raised, I always had an ultimate goal of coaching in the NBA someday. No matter how immersed in music I became, basketball remained a major passion for me. But every single time I would think the end was in sight in Music City, something would happen to give me just enough motivation to stay.

Lynn Schultz with Capitol Records encouraging us to not quit was one of those moments. From being introduced to the jingle producer, to meeting the guys after agreeing to roadie for Don, to Reba asking for songs—every time I was tempted to give up and go home, circumstances like that would keep me going.

But now, as a band, we were staring at a bleak future after every label in Nashville had told us no. And I'm not just talking about a little pushback; some industry people were downright abusive to us.

The Domino Effect

One day, we received a letter from an attorney who represented a band that was also named Savanna. He stated how they had signed a record deal, creating a legal claim to the name, and was notifying us to cease and desist our use immediately.

Without money for an attorney, we saw no choice but to comply. Together, we came up with a list of about twenty possibilities for a new band name. In Bellevue, a beautiful area in southwestern Nashville where the historic Natchez Trace Parkway begins, there is a Sawyer Brown Road. After a little debate and some healthy discussion, we unanimously agreed on Sawyer Brown as our new name. (Today, everybody thinks the road was named for us, but trust me, the road was there first.)

On one of our first dates out as Sawyer Brown, we were playing in Jackson, Mississippi, and there was a guy there wearing a Panama hat. I told him how much I loved his hat and asked if he would let me try it on. Not only did he say yes, but he insisted I take it. Obviously, I obliged him. I decided the Panama could become a trademark look for me for several reasons. First, I was already starting to lose my hair and decided I wanted to cover up my head. Second, that was the closest thing to a cowboy hat I was ever going to wear. Third, the hat reminded me of Florida. And finally, with the vibe of our new name, thematically, it fit great, in more ways than one.

By mid-1983, we had hit the ceiling on how much we could get as a club band, making $3,000 a week on average and splitting that between the five of us. While that was good money back then for working musicians, we, along with our agents, knew we had maxed out those rooms. That is, until one day, when Rick called. "Hey, guys, there's a club out in LA that is really interested in you. They'll pay $4,500 a week." Our answer was, "We're in! When do we leave?"

Expecting our response, Rick explained, "Hold up, there's a bit of a catch. They want to see you first. As an audition, they want a videotape of you performing. To approve you." In the early eighties, that was a pricey ask, so we answered immediately, "Rick, you know we can't afford that. We're out." Knowing we wanted to expand our reach and make more money, he said, "Let me see if I can come up with something. I'll get back to you soon."

A couple of days later, Rick called back. "There's an outfit coming to Nashville that's going to be filming some artists. I've gotten you guys in with them. They'll shoot you doing a few songs and then they've agreed to give you a copy of the performance. We'll send that tape to the club in LA." Thinking this was a bit hard to believe, I asked, "For *free*? Who are these people?" Rick answered, "Not sure. Doesn't matter. Just go on the day and time they say, do the songs, and you'll get the tape. I'll call with the details soon."

On the appointed day, when we walked into the room, immediately we noticed a big sign that read "Star Search Auditions." Of course, we had *no* idea what that meant. A guy named Steve Stark came up and introduced himself. He quickly began giving us instructions. "Okay, we'll shoot you guys playing three songs, then send the tape to New York and they'll review it. We'll see what happens and let you know." (Now, remember, all we cared about was a video to send to the club in LA so we could go out there and play for the $4,500 a week.) So I asked, "Now, we're going to be able to get a copy of the tape, right?" Steve answered, "Yeah, yeah, sure, but we have to send it to New York first. They'll look at it. And *then* we can get it to you."

More curious now, I inquired, "So, what is this for and why does the tape have to go to New York?" Steve answered, "It's *Star Search*, a nationwide talent show on TV. We've already shot the first four episodes and we have the next twenty-two booked up. We're here looking for acts to be on the final four episodes." Being Mr. Persistent, I responded, "Great, but we're still going to be able to get the tape, right?"

After we got set and they were ready to record, we performed "Smokin' in the Rockies," "Leona," and "Step That Step." When we were done and packed up, I figured I better check one last time. I found Steve and asked, "Okay, so *when* can you get us the tape?" He answered, "Next Monday. They'll send it back to you on Monday." When I got home, I called Rick. "Hey, we did three songs for the *Star Search* thing. They're going to get us the tape on Monday for us to send to LA." That was the end of the matter as far as we were concerned.

We were scheduled to leave Monday night to drive to our next weeklong stint at a club. Typically, we started playing on Tuesday nights and ended on Saturday nights. But Monday morning, my phone rang. It was Rick. "Hey, Mark, the people from *Star Search* called. They're going to be calling you. They want to talk."

Surprised and really confused, I asked, "*What?* ... What's up? ... I hope nothing happened to the tape." Rick continued, "I really don't know what it's about, Mark. The guy said they couldn't tell me because you aren't officially signed with us or Buddy Lee Attractions. They just want to speak to you. So don't go anywhere. Wait by the phone." (Remember, this was 1983. Landline corded phones. No cellphones. No internet. No email.)

As promised, within a few minutes, Steve Stark, the guy we had met at the shoot, called. "Hey, man, listen. You guys made the show. But here's the situation. You've been bumped in front of *everybody*. We don't want to wait. We want you on the very next episode." *What?!* None of us had even considered getting on the show as a possibility. In shock, I asked, "Okay, so what does *that* look like?"

Steve answered, "You guys have to fly here to LA tomorrow morning." I swallowed hard and responded, "Man, Steve, I gotta be honest with you. We can't afford *that*." Steve laughed and said, "Oh no, no, no, Mark. *We're* gonna fly you out here. We'll take care of the flights." My mind was reeling with more questions. "Well, we've never been to LA. I don't know where we'd stay." Steve interrupted, "No, we got that covered too. Mark, we've got *everything* covered. In fact, we're going to pay you to be here. I just need you guys to get on a plane to LA tomorrow. All you have to do is say the word and everything else will be handled."

Still thinking this could not possibly be happening, I unknowingly gave the biggest yes for Sawyer Brown I would ever give. Steve was obviously pumped. "Great! I'll get back to you right away with all the details. You guys get ready to leave."

With this sudden change of plans, I had a lot to take care of fast. Because Monday was a day off before hitting the road again, everyone was out running errands all over Nashville. That meant I had to start making calls and driving around to try and locate

Hobie, Bobby, Jim, and Joe. If I could find one of the guys quickly, he could help me with the others.

Within a few hours, I had them all rounded up, shared the crazy story of how we evidently impressed the *Star Search* people, and told them they wanted us in Hollywood *the next day*. Plus we had to tell our agents to call and cancel our week at the club that was supposed to start the following night.

Suddenly, ironically, Lynn Schultz's encouragement had turned into a strange prophecy. After hearing no so many times in Nashville, we not only got a yes in LA, but a get here *now*!

Go West, Young Man

The next morning, all five of us were at BNA boarding a plane to California. I swear to you, that entire trip, from staring out the plane window to driving down the streets in Hollywood, the theme to *The Beverly Hillbillies* was playing in my head. I literally thought, *This must have been the way Jed Clampett felt*. The entire experience was like a strange and surreal dream.

When we walked out of the jetway at LAX, back before airport security was any issue, there was a limo driver standing there with a professional sign that read "SAWYER BROWN." We drove down the freeway, and before long we turned onto Sunset Strip, experiencing sights we had only witnessed on TV and in movies.

Then, just when we thought this couldn't get any better, the limo pulled up to the front door of the iconic Hyatt Hotel. We had heard a lot about this place. Little Richard had taken up permanent residency there. Keith Richards of The Rolling Stones made room 1105 famous by throwing a TV set out the window into the pool. John Bonham of Led Zeppelin rode a motorcycle into the hotel and down hallways during the band's stay in 1975.

Besides those legends, The Doors and The Who also created rock history there, causing the hotel to be dubbed "Riot Hyatt." Knowing those stories, we were all *fuh-rea-king* out, big time. But we also knew we had to behave ourselves, because at that point, we couldn't afford to get billed for a broken lamp.

After getting checked in, we all went out on the hotel balcony overlooking Sunset Boulevard, watching everything from Bentleys to Porsches drive by, wondering what famous people were in those cars. Being country boys, we were in awe of Hollywood.

Before long, a show rep came to take us to our first meeting with the producers. There, we were told, "Tomorrow we're going to do a blocking rehearsal, and then on Thursday we'll tape the show." We had no idea what "blocking" meant. But I quickly got sick to my stomach when they explained the process. They told us that all the instruments would be pre-recorded in a studio and then at the taping we would fake our playing. *But* I was going to have to sing live on air.

That took the pressure off the guys in playing on TV, but millions of people were going to hear me sing. In the clubs I could hide within the band. But now, I was going to be fully exposed in front of the largest audience I could ever imagine. The kind of nightmare that would make me wake up in a cold sweat.

The blocking rehearsal was held in a large dance studio with mirrors surrounding the walls. All the other acts for the episode were there with us. When our turn came, they played the pre-recorded tape, while we faked the instruments and I sang live with Hobie and Bobby doing the harmonies. With everyone staring at us, I felt like some kind of trained monkey. After we performed

"Smokin' in the Rockies," the director came over and said, "Hey, I need you to do the song again." I started to panic, thinking, *We've come all this way and he doesn't like the song. Everybody else has done their act in one take. They must love them, but they hate us.* Likely the lingering effects of rejection from all those showcases in Nashville.

I went back over to the director and quietly said, "Hey, man, if you don't like that song, we got a lot of others we can try. I mean, we came all this way, sir, and we'd really like to be on your show. So, we can play you our other songs until you find one you like." He just smiled and said, "No, no, no. I want you to do that song again *exactly* the way you just did. There's some people I want to bring in to see you perform."

Within a few minutes, the door opened. Three men and a lady in expensive clothing filed in and stood by the director. As they gave us the cue to do the song again with the tape, I felt like I was performing inside a fishbowl. After we finished, all four people spoke quietly to the director, then turned and walked out. We were all looking at each other, thinking, *What was that about?* We had no idea that what just happened might have been a good thing.

At the studio the next day for the TV taping, they showed us to several dressing rooms that all had the band name on the door. But being accustomed to tiny rooms backstage in small clubs, we picked one and moved all our stuff in together. Soon, I was in a bathroom stall feeling like I was going to throw up, praying hard, *God, I don't think I can do this. You're gonna have to do this, because I know I can't. Please, help me.*

Then, with a knock on the dressing room door, our time came. "Guys! We're ready for you!" With one final check in the mirror, we grabbed our instruments, went out in front of the studio audience, took our marks, and got set. The next thing we heard was the legendary voice of Johnny Carson's sidekick, Ed McMahon, introducing us, "First, let's meet the challengers. Featuring lead singer Mark Miller, they're a group from Nashville called ... Sawyer Brown!"

The audience applauded and the pre-recorded music to "Smokin' in the Rockies" began playing through the system. We went to work, just like we always have. Selling the song, smiling, moving, eye contact with the crowd, looking like we were having the biggest time of our lives. I was so nervous that, throughout the entire song, nothing sounded right with my live, raw vocal performance. In my head, I was *awful*.

But at the end of the show, when they brought us out with the previous week's vocal group winner, Ed announced that the celebrity judges had given them three stars and us three and a quarter stars. (Four stars was the highest score.) We had edged out the competition. Being asked to be on the show at all was the first surprise, but now here came the next one we didn't see coming—we won.

When we were back in our dressing room, Steve Stark came bounding in. He was so pumped. The credit of "discovering us" in Nashville was going to him, even though our agents had actually worked out the taping for us to get the video. He was happy because this was a good look for him with the producers. "Congratulations, guys! You're moving onto next week's show!"

He began talking about the schedule going forward, and we immediately got really nervous. Steve saw our faces and asked, "Hey, what's wrong?" I answered, "Well, to be honest, we just thought we were coming out here for *this* show. We only brought enough clothes for a few days." Steve thought for a minute, then said, "Okay, wait here. I'll be back as quick as I can."

Soon, he walked back in with five envelopes in his hand. "We got you booked on a red-eye tonight to Nashville. Then day after tomorrow, first thing, you'll fly back here. And guys, this time ... bring *a lot* of clothes."

Steve also told us more about what would happen if we continued on the show. For each week we won in our category, we would receive $5,000. Then, after the AFTRA (American Federation of Television and Radio Artists) pay to appear on TV, we would get $1,600 each. That was crazy money for us at the time—about three times what we were making in a club playing all night for five nights. Except no drunks, no breathing second-hand smoke, and the audience was 100 percent engaged.

Game On!

Back in Nashville, we knew we would have to provide the show with pre-recorded tapes of our music, so the next day we found an available studio and quickly cut several songs. For the rest of our time on the show, every few weeks, we would fly back to Nashville to record more songs for them. We never cut a single song in LA.

After packing up a couple of suitcases each and flying back to LA, we hit the ground running, going through the blocking rehearsals, which we now understood. The next day, we did the taping for the second show. Week after week, we just kept winning. *Every* show. Regardless of the style of our challengers, we stayed true to our sound and carried on.

A lot of the bands they brought in to compete against us were much more seasoned and experienced artists than we were at the time. We quickly discovered they were a very different beast from the Nashville crowd we knew. No such thing as Southern hospitality from these guys. Some were mean. Rude. Arrogant. Condescending. Abrasive. And, of course, that meant they would make fun of us.

My favorite story from that time involved Brad Garrett, the legendary comedian who later spent nine years on the hit comedy show *Everybody Loves Raymond* with Ray Romano. Brad got his start on *Star Search* in the stand-up comedian category. He kept winning, too, so we got to know him really well. One of the LA bands that came in walked right over to us and popped off, "Hey! Where'd you boys leave your tractors?" They all laughed, hoping for a response.

Just as I was opening my mouth to tell them where we were *about* to put our tractors, Brad stepped in between us. As you probably know, he is a *huge* guy with a massively deep voice. He looked down at them and, in his trademark style, stated, "I want to tell you something about my country boys here. They have a permanent parking spot outside the studio for their trac- tors. They're gonna still be here tonight when the show's over and you punks will be going home." Enough said. And just as Brad predicted, that night, those guys were gone and we were moving on to the next week.

Aside from our dealing with a few snarky bands, LA was really good to us *and* for us. Our music, our style, and our image were all being validated by America. Playing in clubs, night after night, we saw how people responded to us. *Star Search* just broadened that reach to the entire country, to people who would have never seen us in a club. From kids to grandparents, we were making new fans of all ages. As more and more people started watching the show, our platform grew bigger by the week.

Because *Star Search's* format presented a winner with a new challenger each week, that became a huge motivator for me. On the basketball court, or with any sport I played, I always had the attitude of *I'm going to win, but if you should beat me, I'll make you never want to have to play me again.* The show wasn't just about playing music, it was a competition. Every week when we met our challenger, I thought, *Okay, now you've entered my arena. My team against your team. I'm going to give the audience 110 percent, everything we've got. It's game on!*

That mindset also called for a clear strategy to win. Somewhere around the third week, I figured out a formula. I knew what we needed to do. For each episode, we were given a specific amount of time, down to the second. Each week when we picked the next song, our motto was, "Don't bore us. Get to the chorus." Also, we stuck with up-tempo, fun songs, never changing things up with a ballad. We stuck to our game plan. Fortunately, we had enough original songs for our entire run and never had to write anything new while in LA.

The morning after our fifth week and win on the show, I woke up to the phone ringing in my hotel room. It was 7:00 a.m. in LA, 9:00 back in Nashville. I answered to hear Lynn Schultz's voice. "Mark! Dude! Everybody here is talking about you guys. All of us at Capitol want to talk to you as soon as possible." That was the first call from a label, but then the floodgates opened. Next was Warner Brothers. I'm not sure why week five on *Star Search* was the magic number, but we started getting major buzz throughout the music business after that show.

Because we were kept so busy every day, we didn't get out and about much, but one afternoon, we decided to go clothes shopping in Beverly Hills. (Swimmin' pools, movie stars. Cue the banjo music.) All five of us were in the mall when suddenly a group of girls recognized us. To our surprise, things got crazy fast. As people started pointing and saying who we were, more girls started running toward us. Within minutes, we were mobbed. Mall security ended up having to escort us out to our car.

I mean, it looked like one of the scenes from *A Hard Day's Night* where the girls chase The Beatles down the street. We thought it was so funny and couldn't believe the response. But that was the first time we had ventured that far out of our TV bubble. Producers can tell you all day long that the show is going out to millions of people, but when you're in a situation like that, it's still hard to wrap your brain around the concept of sudden fame. With no internet or social media back then, we had no idea how many people across the country knew who we were until that moment in the mall.

As the months went by, going out in LA became harder to manage. Champagne, fruit, and gift baskets were being delivered to the hotel from artist managers and booking agents all over the country who were trying to sign us. But even with the circus going on all around us, I was determined to not get distracted from the game. We had to stay focused on the prize until the very end. The winner in each category of the finals received $100,000. Twenty grand each would have been a nice bonus on top of what we had been getting each week.

Raising the Stakes

As the offers were pouring in from every area of the music business, this was the first time any tension started to show up inside the band. Bobby was looking at our window of fame and felt like we needed to strike fast and nail down a deal. But I wanted to hold off, to wait it out. When Bobby would bring up signing with someone, I would say, "Look, we're gonna win this. I don't want to do *anything* until then." He would respond with, "But what if we *don't* win? The momentum is high *now*."

There were no fights or arguments between us, just conflict for the first time ever. I was well aware that this very thing had happened to a lot of bands and caused their downfall. It makes sense, because success can change a lot *for* people and bring out a lot *in* people.

Once a week, the *Star Search* team started taking me, and sometimes Bobby, out to a nice lunch to talk. They would throw out ideas of how to continue the relationship when the show was over. While hearing them out, I always responded with, "That sounds great. We'll see." I wasn't going to sign anything at that point.

At that time, the California laws would not let people in the entertainment industry cross over to another business category. The laws specified that *Star Search* could only be a TV show. So the show's producers weren't legally allowed to offer us any kind of music deal. To give a current contrast today when those laws no longer exist, the TV shows *American Idol* and *The Voice* have contestants sign their lives away to even be on the show. That concept didn't exist back then. That's why the prize wasn't a record deal or Las Vegas contract, but cash. *Star Search* couldn't officially make any kind of offer until after the show was over. So they just kept pitching ideas, trying to get us to commit to some sort of relationship with them afterward, whether that be taking a percentage or total control. Whatever we decided to do after *Star Search*, they wanted to be on board the train.

Looking back, I was young, oblivious, and, honestly, very naive. I never suspected anybody was up to anything that I should be cautious about. So I wasn't putting the producers off because of distrust as much as just wanting to be sure we were doing the absolute best thing for the band. I've always trusted to a fault. I am just fine to stay blissfully ignorant. That is, until something happens where I see the real truth and have to take action. (With forty years in this business, I eventually came to the point where I don't trust everyone, but I focus more on finding people I *can* trust.)

With each passing week, more and more music execs started showing up at the tapings. I was never quite sure how they got in, or who knew who, but it was clear they were there to see us. One of those was Dick Whitehouse with Curb Records. From the moment I met Dick, I liked him. He stood out from the pack.

The really funny and very ironic aspect of this onslaught was that all the LA and New York offices of these record labels were calling their counterparts in Nashville with questions like, "Why did you not sign this band when they were there?" and "How did you not know about them?" I would have loved to have heard those answers from some of the people that had turned their noses up at us at our showcases. But, regardless of their excuses, they were being told to figure out a way to get a shot at us now. One major label literally said, "Just tell us what you want." (Had you told us just a few months before that there would be a day all those labels would be at our door with their hats in their hands, we would have said you were crazy!)

But one thing was now certain—the tables had taken a full-on one-eighty turn in our favor.

We were out in Hollywood on *Star Search* for nearly six

months. We began our fairy-tale journey in October of 1983 and won the finals in February of 1984. We played our own songs, our way, in our style, with our image, staying true to who Sawyer Brown has always been. (The same band we are today.)

Right after the win, the producers booked a show at Carnegie Hall in New York. The day tickets went on sale, they sold out in minutes. The event was also going to be televised. The bill included us, comedian Brad Garrett, and singer Sam Harris. I had never been to New York, so when I found out we were going and that we were staying at The Plaza Hotel, I phoned my mom. That was such a fun call for me.

"Hey, Mom," I said. "I'm gonna fly you to New York. You're going to stay with me in my room at The Plaza Hotel and then go with me to the show at Carnegie Hall." I knew one thing—my mom *had* to be a part of this with me. She *had* to sleep in that hotel room. She *had* to experience this. While I *got* to be there, Mom *deserved* to be there. That night at the hotel, I slept on the floor and gave her the bed. Only first class for her. With all the sacrifices she had made for so many years for Frank and me, any chance to bless her back felt so good.

On the day of the show, they sent limos to pick us up from the hotel. Of course, Mom was with me. When the car pulled up to the stage door access, there were people everywhere, mostly young ladies. The venue had a few security guards there to keep things civil, but when the door opened and I stepped out, the walls of women collapsed around me. Suddenly, I was covered up to the point that they knocked me down. They were all over me. Security had to push through, pull me out, and escort me in the door. That scary moment for me was sheer fun for Mom. She was still sitting in the limo with the door open, laughing hysterically and watching me get mobbed. As far as Mom was concerned, she already had a front-row seat to the entertainment and was absolutely loving it.

That night after we were introduced on stage and hit our first note, we couldn't hear a single thing. The screams were so deafening that I couldn't hear myself sing. It's crazy how loud a few thousand girls can be. Every Beatles and Elvis scene I had ever watched as a kid was playing in my head. When a crowd responds like that, there's absolutely nothing you can do except press on and sell the song. No matter how we feel in the moment, we always want to look like we're having a better time than anyone there. And that's exactly what we did that night.

After that show, while we were still in New York, the *Star Search* creators and producers had set up a meeting with me and Bobby at the William Morris Agency. We walked into their huge corporate conference room where about twenty people were sitting around a giant table, including some TV writers and the president of A&M Records. They wasted no time jumping into their presentation: "Gentlemen, we want to do a spinoff right away. Give you guys your own TV show, along with a record deal for the songs you'll play on the show, and you'll tour in the off-season. It's a 360 deal. Everything will work together to promote the band and our show."

Next came the concept—mostly comedy with a little drama mixed in, all built around our life as a band with us "playing ourselves." (Proof that reality TV isn't actually new.) I just listened and kept my head down to show no immediate response.

Recalling moments in our career like this one is where I have to be really honest about how my faith affects my life, career, and any major decision. I have always known when the

Holy Spirit is giving me peace or telling me something isn't right. Early on, I learned to trust Him more than myself. As the pitch went on, I started getting a sick feeling in my stomach. When the guy was done and I could tell they wanted me to say something, I just looked up and asked, "So, you mean we're gonna be the country Monkees?" (For the younger crowd—*The Monkees* was a hugely popular TV comedy show from 1966 to 1968 that was built around a band of four guys the show's producers had put together.)

After my accurate clarification, there was total silence. Like drop-dead quiet. Finally, one of them answered, "Well, Mark, I guess for lack of a better description, *yes*, but you guys are a *real* band. You'll write all your songs and ..." Because of my obvious pushback, next came the hard pitch as to the level of fame and fortune that could come our way if we said yes.

The meeting ended with us promising to consider their offer. But I knew there was no way Sawyer Brown was going to follow up all the momentum from being on TV for almost six months with a comedy show.

We had agreed to fly back to LA from New York and do more follow-up press for *Star Search*. Back in Hollywood, the pressure from the show's producers to agree to their plan reached a new level. This caused the tension between Bobby's vision for the band and mine to simmer just under the surface. The short version was he wanted us to take the deal and I wasn't interested.

After all our interviews were finished and we were back at the hotel getting ready to fly home to Nashville, we had a band meeting to talk about the show's offer. Bobby presented his case to sign and stay in LA, then I simply said, "Guys, we're not actors. We're musicians. We're a band. I came to Nashville to do music.

I wanna be like Alabama or Kenny Rogers. I just want to make music. Write songs, cut records, and play shows. That starts by going back to Nashville and deciding which record label we should sign with."

That meeting was such a pivotal make-or-break moment for us. To choose to stay on our own path or walk according to someone else's? Stick with the plan or roll the dice?

The next day, Joe, Jim, Hobie, and I flew back to Nashville. The show's producers wanted to keep talking, of course, so Bobby decided to stay in LA to keep the dialogue going. Even though we were a tight-knit band, each member was always free to make his own choice, for his own future.

For me, with every door now wide open in Nashville, I knew the game was ours to win.

Jim

SMALL TO HOBIE and me, Jim and Bobby had known each other since the second grade in Midland, Michigan. Jim's dad was a chemist for Dow and his mom was a teacher, so, like Hobie, he was from some solid intellectual stock.

When we all met, Jim and Bobby were the two best musicians, the oldest, and more seasoned than the rest of us. For any band, Jim was a rare find because he was highly capable at playing both live and in the studio.

When we first started playing together as a band and were working hard to gel and get better, Jim was already at a much higher skill level than the rest of us. During those first couple of years, I assumed Jim would get offered a better gig and move onward and upward. He was a GQ-type, good-looking, strong guy who played incredible and was just so cool. He's the guy every band wants—the total package.

Jim is the quintessential bass player, quiet and stoic. It's funny how there are definite stereotypes for each instrument in a band. Think about the legendary bassists and their onstage personas, like John Paul Jones of Led Zeppelin, John McVie of Fleetwood Mac, Timothy Schmit of the Eagles, and then the iconic studio players who have recorded with everyone, such as Leland Sklar and Pino Palladino. There's a distinct pattern and, for the majority of bassists, it applies.

While Jim was very quiet for quite a while, as success came, he grew very vocal about how he felt about the band. It was really cool how he went from the guy we all suspected would move on to the one who was our biggest encourager. To hear Jim talk about us, you would think he thought we were The Rolling Stones. He would come off stage, go around to everyone, and dish out the compliments. Many nights, he has looked at me and said, "Miller, you're the best front man in the business!" He would tell us all, "We are the best band on the planet!" Jim has always believed that about us, individually and as a group. That kind of attitude motivates and inspires anyone on any team to win in a competition. You have to believe you are the best at what you do. Jim took on that role in the band. Because we all respected him so much, his encouragement was a huge confidence booster for the rest of us.

Jim played on every record, even back in the day when there was a crazy stigma about live musicians playing on records. But Jim was that good. He could hold his own in the studio and on stage. I said before that Hobie is the heartbeat of the band, but Jim has always been the *soul* of the band because of who he is and his belief in us all.

Jim has also been the most easygoing among us. It didn't matter what we did, he was up for it. It didn't matter if we had to ride a bus for twenty-four hours and then make three plane changes. No matter how difficult the circumstances, Jim kept his cool. His attitude has always been, "Let's go!" Nothing rattles him, because he believes we can pull off whatever we need to do. It has always amazed me that as intense as some of the travel would get at times, when the rest of us might be stressed out, you could look over at Jim, and he would be kicked back with his feet up. Just total chill. His bass player attitude was: Whatever happens, we'll make it happen.

While Jim is really easygoing, if he ever did snap, it was all over. Game on. He has a really long fuse, but if something lights it, you better watch out. A huge explosion is coming. Once, we had just played a massive outdoor festival in Baltimore as the headliner. We were in the bus pulling out of the parking lot of the venue. When we got to the gate—one of those places with the little booth and the arm that goes up and down—there was an attendant standing guard. He came out and waited for our driver to open the bus door. He then said, "It's gonna be twenty-five bucks for parking here." Our driver said, "Hey, this is the headline band, Sawyer Brown." Putting on his best Barney Fife impression, tucking his thumbs into his belt, and throwing his head back, the guy smirked, and said, "I don't care who you are. Nobody's gettin' outta here without paying the twenty-five dollars."

While the rest of us were sitting in the bus lounge laughing hysterically, the longer the guy insisted we pay before he would let us out, the more Jim's blood boiled. Suddenly, he jumped up, went out the bus door, grabbed the red-and-white crossing arm on the gate, and ripped it clean off the hinges. As he threw it over to the side, he yelled at the attendant, "We won't be paying for the parking or for this gate! We're leaving, so *you* better step aside!"

Watching Jim's Incredible Hulk move from a front-row seat and Deputy Fife's shocked reaction, we stopped laughing and our mouths fell open. While it was very hard to do, the guy had pushed Jim's launch button and the show was officially over. *Put the bullet back in your pocket, Barn.* (Fitting that the most rock-and-roll thing the band ever did came from our chill, quiet bass player!)

Another really funny thing about Jim was that he often

wouldn't recognize someone famous. And over the years, we were around quite a few legends. One day, while sitting in the Memphis airport, there was a group of guys nearby that were obviously a band because they all had on matching tour jackets. (Our inside joke when we see this is they are either a band or a bowling team.) Jim was sitting the closest to one of them and they struck up a conversation. While looking on, we figured out the guys were Jerry Lee Lewis's band.

After they had talked a while, Jim asked, "So, what do you guys do?"

The man answered, "We're in a band. We're touring."

"Oh, cool, what band?"

"Jerry Lee Lewis."

"Oh man, that's really awesome." Then Jim asked, "Well, what do you do in the band?"

The man smiled, and said, "I'm Jerry … Jerry Lee Lewis."

They say everyone looks different in person than on TV or the stage. That's Jim's story and he's sticking to it.

CHAPTER FIVE

When Twist Comes to Shout

Movin' like a fast train
Callin' it the wild thang
Hopin' that you don't say
Well, I've been denied

—FROM THE SONG "When Twist Comes to Shout"

WHEN BOBBY CAME BACK to Nashville from LA, we talked everything out and got back on the same page. No matter what, all of us loved each other like brothers. The foundation we had built early on was still very much in place.

After looking at all our options for a record label to call home, I had an idea of what I thought would be the best path forward for the band. But what I envisioned as a great fit didn't exist yet, so I began making some calls to test the waters. Let me explain ...

While in Hollywood, I had paid attention to the fact that Dick Whitehouse at Curb had been the only guy who had *not* stayed at me about a deal. He just wanted to talk music. When I wasn't ready to take anyone's offer, the others were hammering me about a contract. So Dick's approach made him stand out in the crowd and set him apart. I liked him. Using the tortoise and the hare analogy, Dick was the tortoise. While all the other record execs were in bunny mode, he just slow-rolled and constantly proved his passion for music. I liked that.

But because Curb was strictly a production company at that time, I knew they would need a solid partner for marketing and distribution. While we would need all the aspects of a record label to be firing on all cylinders, having people in our corner that I knew I could trust was crucial. Contracts are important, but the people who have signed them is even more vital. So I called Lynn Schultz at Capitol and asked if they would consider a joint venture with Curb. Up to that point, Curb had worked with MCA, RCA, and CBS Records on other country artists, so I knew they already had a successful template for how to make a partnership work.

The good news was Capitol and Curb were not only on board with the plan but excited about the possibilities with us. On the other side of *Star Search*, just as I had hoped, everything was beginning to fall into place.

The day I walked into the legendary Capitol Records tower in LA to meet with Don Zimmerman, the president, I was one hundred percent on board. But first things first. After some small talk, I said, "Look, Don, you have to know there are some things I *won't* sing about. I'm not gonna do cheatin' songs. I don't drink, so I won't sing drinkin' songs. I want to play country music, but I have to draw the line for me personally. I want to be up-front with you about that *before* we sign." (For the record, Bobby didn't drink either.)

Don smiled, then responded, "Mark, you don't have to worry about that. You can sing anything you want. You didn't do songs like that on *Star Search* and America loved the band's image, so no one is going to ask you to change what has obviously been proven to work."

When all the Capitol and Curb teams came to Nashville for our big signing reception, there was a point when everyone was called together for a toast to the success of the band. Of course, at an event like that in the entertainment industry, the champagne was flowing. As everyone was gathering around, Don walked over and handed me a champagne glass with water in it. He smiled and winked at me as if to say, "I remember. I'm your guy. I got your back."

We were assigned to the LA office of Capitol, not Nashville, and, at that time, Curb was also based in LA. (Mike Curb eventually moved his company and his family to Nashville in 1992.) Don loved the band, to the point that he would come out on the road and stay with us on our bus. He would go out with us to just hang. Once again, this was an example of how the power of relationships is vital. When we were in LA, Don would have us all over to his house for dinner. He was an incredible advocate for the band. With both companies, we had a great team around us.

Everyone involved in our career agreed that we didn't need to waste any time releasing our first album. We had all seen other artists drag out the launch process and miss their window where people are still paying attention. We needed to come in hot off our momentum from the show.

Randy Scruggs was chosen as our producer, and we recorded at his studio in Nashville. That said, regardless of who was chosen for that role over the years, I have always co-produced and am very hands-on in the recording process. Our self-titled debut album *Sawyer Brown* was released in the fall of 1984, eight months after winning *Star Search*.

During the mid-eighties, MTV was massive and had made the release of high-value concept videos a must for any artist with a major label deal. The budget for each of our first videos was $150,000. Running that through an inflation calculator to compare to today brings the number just north of $450,000. On March 5, 1983, CMT—Country Music Television—launched and our genre had its own network to parallel the rock and pop industry. VH1 also played some of our videos. We were such a visually oriented act that videos were the perfect form of media to hear the song and see our energy.

Once the label was firmly in place, artist management was the next piece of the puzzle. There were two guys who had come to those final *Star Search* episodes. They were business partners and promoted all of Kenny Rogers's concerts, as well as BJ Thomas and Johnny Lee. Kenny was as big as it got in the music world at the time, so we signed with them.

For booking live shows, one of our original "off the books" agents, Rick Shipp, who had kept us busy in clubs and was responsible for getting us into the *Star Search* audition, was hired by the William Morris Agency and we went with him. At the time, it was a good move for us all with Rick being our key man there.

Kenny and the Jets

Soon after we signed, Kenny Rogers and his team had scheduled an arena tour. He was one of the biggest artists on the planet at that time, so opening for him was a coveted spot by most everyone in the music world. An up-and-coming country artist was booked to be his show opener but had either gotten sick or injured and wasn't able to make the first two weeks of the tour.

Because we had signed with the people who promoted Kenny's shows, coupled with the fact that we had just come off six months on national TV, they all felt we were a no-brainer to be the replacement and go out for that first run. Plus, Kenny had seen us on the show and liked the band, so we had his approval. (Yeah, our first tour dates were with Kenny Rogers. Talk about starting at the top!)

On the first night out, we played our set and gave the crowd 110 percent. We were going to do everything possible to make an impression with this two-week shot in the big leagues. After Kenny arrived at the venue from the airport, he walked into our dressing room to introduce himself. We exchanged small talk, then I asked him, "Hey, did you see us play tonight?" Looking a little uncomfortable, Kenny confessed, "No, guys, I didn't." I knew I had to make the most of this time, so I said, "Tomorrow night we start at seven o'clock." He didn't say a word, just laughed a little.

The next night in the next city, we were waiting backstage at about 6:55 when the back doors to the arena went up and in rolled a limo. It was Kenny. He got out, walked straight over to me, smiled, and said, "This had better be good." *Game on!* I started praying that this second night would be as good as the first night.

We went out and gave the crowd our very best Sawyer Brown—left it all on the stage. Once we were back in our dressing room, Kenny walked in and said, "Tonight was really good, boys. You can stay out here with me as long as you want." No one ever told us what happened with the original opening artist, but, after that moment, we kept opening for Kenny. We were so grateful to be out with one of the biggest legends in the business.

When Kenny toured, he would do two weeks out and then two weeks at home. We had a lot of offers coming in to our booking agency from the popularity of *Star Search*, so this worked out perfectly for us. We could go play those shows in the two-week blocks when Kenny was off the road.

When the first two weeks with Kenny were done and the two-week break came, we were booked for our first show on our own since coming off *Star Search*. We were scheduled to play a fair in West Palm Beach, Florida. As is often the case with those type of shows, we were supposed to play in a large tent at 3:00 in the afternoon on a weekday. I made what I thought was a safe assumption—this was such a bad time slot that no one was going to show up.

We did our soundcheck at around 10:00 in the morning and *no one* was on the fairgrounds. After lunch, we got ready for the show. The fair organizers had said there wouldn't be a host at our tent, so we just needed to walk onstage and start playing. Mom and Frank had driven down from Apopka, so I knew they were out front, ready to see us. A minute or two before showtime, I said, "Hey, no one is going to be here, but let's at least put on a good show for my mom and brother, okay?"

Walking onstage, just as my Panama hat became visible over the top of the speakers, I heard a roar that sounded like a jet engine. I peeked out to see thousands of people. The tent was packed all the way to the back. Turning around to the guys as they were coming up the steps, I said, "You are *not* going to believe this!"

That was the first time we got the full picture of what *Star Search* had created for us. That first two years, between the momentum from the show and Kenny's tour, we worked nonstop, playing the largest arenas in every major city in the country. Huge artists, along with TV and movie stars, came out to see Kenny. The whole experience was crazy for us. We were living the dream.

At that time, Kenny had three private jets, a home in Bel Air, California, and a home on acreage outside Athens, Georgia. Every night after the show, Kenny would fly home. He wanted to sleep in his own bed and could certainly afford to do that. The next day, he would fly to the next city. If the tour played in the western half of the US, he would fly back to Bel Air. If it played on the eastern half, he'd fly to his home in Athens. Early on, we realized Kenny seemed to enjoy hanging out with us. One night, he asked, "Hey, you guys want to go home with me and then we'll fly to the show tomorrow?" The only possible answer to that offer was, "Yessir!"

As the tour went on, his offers became more frequent and we went with him *every* time he asked. To give you an idea of how incredible his homes were and how many toys he had, we secretly called his Georgia home "Six Flags Over Athens." After the show, we'd all fly to his house, play as long as we could the next day, and then get back on the jet with Kenny to go to the next show. He always made sure we were on time, even though that meant he had to arrive at shows much earlier than he had before, just to accommodate us.

Kenny was an unbelievably gracious host. When he found out Hobie and I were from Florida and that we loved boiled shrimp, he started having a platter added to the already generous table of food and drinks in our dressing room every night. After a while of being on the receiving end of his constant thoughtfulness, one night, I said, "Kenny, you don't *have* to do all this for us. So why do you?"

He smiled, and in his unmistakable signature raspy voice, answered, "Yeah, actually I do, Mark. Back in the early days with The First Edition, we opened for a huge pop act that I won't mention. But let's just say we weren't treated very well. It was not a good experience being on that tour, especially for our first one. So I made a promise to myself that if I ever became the headline act, I was going to treat my opening acts right, the way anyone *should* be treated. I'm just keeping that promise, Mark." Kenny was always a man of his word to us.

But what do you think his answer triggered in me? Yep. I knew right then and there we would someday need to pay Kenny's kindness forward. So when our turn came to headline, we did our very best. I wanted to make sure anybody that opened for us felt welcomed, that we were engaged with them, and they knew they were an important part of the show. I hope any artist that has ever opened for Sawyer Brown would testify that we carried on that tradition. Kenny's level of constant kindness and attention to detail made a huge impression on me and meant a great deal to us in our first experience working with an icon.

When Kenny and Dolly Parton released their duet "Islands in the Stream," a song written by the Bee Gees, it went to number one on the country and adult contemporary charts. The song was a massive global hit. Kenny's team decided to launch a world tour with him headlining and Dolly supporting. And, of course, at a key point in the show, Dolly would come out and sing the hit with Kenny that everyone had come to hear. But someone needed to open for Dolly. Once again, good on his promise—"stay out here with me as long as you want"—Kenny invited us to take that spot.

As if working with Kenny Rogers wasn't enough of a blessing, now we were out with Dolly too. Like Kenny, Dolly was so kind and generous. Her down-to-earth and genuine approach, along with her ability to be spontaneous, was amazing. One night, while playing her banjo on the song "Me and Little Andy," one of her fake fingernails came off while she was strumming. When the song ended, she looked at her guitar player and said, "Can you pick that up? If I bend over, they'll have to milk me to get me back up!" Twenty thousand people exploded in laughter. Dolly was so comfortable in her own skin and taught us to never take ourselves too seriously.

Another amazing talent of Kenny's was that he was also an incredible photographer. He loved taking pictures on the road. He would capture these unbelievable shots of the band—together and also individual shots—then have them enlarged and give them as personal gifts. My mom had an eleven-by-fourteen photo that Kenny had taken of me. He framed and signed it for her. He did the same thing for all the guys in the band. At the time, he was one of the biggest stars on the planet, so for him to choose to take pictures of other artists and place his own camera's focus off himself and onto others was a glimpse into his heart. (Quite a contrast to all the artists who constantly post selfies today.) Needless to say, we had such an amazing and awesome experience for the year and a half we were out with him.

That same year, we were nominated for the CMA Horizon Award. Ray Charles had released a country album and was nominated in that category. John Schneider of *The Dukes of Hazzard* had also put out a very successful country album and was nominated as well. Mel McDaniel ("Baby's Got Her Blue Jeans On") and Eddy Raven ("I've Got Mexico") were the other nominees.

Looking at that lineup, we made the assumption that we didn't have a chance against the competition. So when Janie

Fricke and Lee Greenwood opened the envelope to announce, "And the winner is … Sawyer Brown!" we were all in disbelief. In moments like that, your brain has trouble processing what you just heard. It's so surreal, like a dream. You're thinking, *Did they really just say our name?* When you realize everyone is applauding and looking at you, and suddenly the cameras are in your face, you accept this must actually be happening.

In the speech, while I was working hard to recall everyone we needed to thank, Hobie leaned into the mic and said, "We'd like to thank Kenny Rogers for all his help and for adopting us the last few months." (We were well into his tour at that point.) As I turned and found Kenny to our left on the front row, I looked at him and added, "We couldn't have picked a better *closing* act." Everyone laughed, but no one enjoyed that line more than Kenny.

Winning the CMA Horizon Award obviously offered some much-appreciated validation from the country music community. Quite a turn of events in such a short time. (Side note: after the awards show, when we were back out with Kenny, I started saying to the crowd, "We'd like to thank Kenny Rogers for closing our show." He loved that joke.)

Kenny also took us to Japan on his tour. We played the iconic Budokan where so many artists like Bob Dylan, Cheap Trick, and Bryan Adams have recorded live albums. We heard that Eric Clapton was staying at the same hotel as us, getting ready to play there the next night. When we met him later in the lobby, I'll never forget that he asked if he could have one of our sweatshirts. Of course, we got him one. The next morning, there was Eric Clapton in his Sawyer Brown sweatshirt. That's one of those moments where you just have to smile, shake your head, and ask yourself, *How did this happen?*

When Don Zimmerman at Capitol found out we were booked to play some large venues in Japan, he hired the infamous Elvis Costello to create special remixes of "Step That Step" and "Betty's Bein' Bad." At that time, Elvis had become known for mixing a song in a style that worked well there. They had released them both in Japan to build momentum before we arrived.

Capitol launched a marketing campaign built around us being a rockabilly act like The Stray Cats, and Elvis had remixed the songs with that feel. We didn't get to hear them until we got there, but we loved what he did. We saw billboards with our picture superimposed in front of a '57 Chevy. We didn't change how we played our songs for those shows, but Capitol's promotion helped us develop our own following over there. (The old joke among artists that goes, "No one has heard of me here, but I'm huge in Japan" can actually be true.)

We didn't travel internationally as much as other bands, but when we did, I had a horrible time with jet lag. It would kick my butt. I remember getting to my hotel in Japan, unlocking my room, and then sitting my luggage down in the doorway, keeping it propped open. I walked over and lay back on the bed "to rest my eyes for a few minutes." I woke up the next day to see my luggage still setting there with the door wide open. I had slept there all night fully clothed with my feet on the floor.

While in Tokyo, we realized how much people loved baseball. Someone there connected us to a group of players who gave us a friendly challenge. They thought it would be fun to compete against some Americans. The Capitol Records crew there had a team and played in a league, so they got uniforms for us. Everything in Japan was very formal with a lot of customs involved, whether going out to dinner or playing baseball. Even though this was essentially just a pickup game, we were introduced and had to do the bowing protocol. While none of us had played baseball in years, we're all so competitive that we played hard and beat them. (So much for diplomacy, right?)

Now, to share a few more highlights from the "Islands in the Stream" tour …

There was a string of shows that Dolly couldn't do, so to get a major act to replace her, they booked the legend himself, Ray Charles. That was one of the biggest thrills of our career to get to do some shows with him.

Ray was always a classic acoustic artist. Because he tended to play more intimate venues, he didn't mic up all of the instruments onstage. But this tour was in arenas in the round with an average of twenty thousand people. The first night with Ray was in Chicago. The sound guys, wanting to accommodate him, placed some microphones above the band to try and pick up their natural sound. Well, of course, they couldn't get it loud enough for people to hear and the crowd began to boo. Yeah, it was brutal, except they weren't actually booing Ray, but the fact that they couldn't hear him.

For the next night, no one on the production team wanted to be the one to go tell Ray that they were going to have to mic his band. Finally, when Kenny found out that everyone was scared to talk to Ray, he said he would take care of it personally, out of his great respect, of course. So Kenny went to him and asked, "Ray, do you know how many people are here each night?" He answered, "No, no idea." Kenny said, "Last night, there were twenty-two thousand people. We're going to have to mic your instruments to get you loud enough for the audience to hear you." Ray flashed that huge grin of his and shot back, "Oh! Well, why didn't somebody just tell me! Sure, do what you gotta do!"

On another day, we were setting up our gear onstage the same time that Ray's right-hand man was working on his setup. Hobie was playing his Yamaha DX-7 keyboard, which was the new big-tech toy at the time. Ray's guy asked, "Hey, man, what is that you're playin'?" Hobie answered, "It's a Yamaha DX-7." He then said, "Ray would love to hear that." Hobie, trying to accommodate the legend, responded, "Well, he is welcome to play mine anytime he wants." The man quipped, "Nah! Ray don't play no gizmo!" Famously, Ray only played a grand piano onstage. But from that day on, Hobie's beloved keyboard became known to the band as "The Gizmo."

Once the tour ended, we realized it was going to be hard to find artists we could go out with that would suit us as well as Kenny had for the past eighteen months. The reason was a traditional country artist just wasn't a good fit for us to open. Our style of music and energy onstage was too much of a mismatch. And then, just being honest, some major artists just didn't want to have to follow us. Someone like Kenny or Dolly could walk out and start singing one of their massive hits and the whole place would go crazy. They could follow anyone and kill it. But that wasn't true of many artists. We opened for a few traditional acts and never got asked back, which is fine. I get it. We worked quite a bit with Hank Williams Jr. But, well, he's Hank Jr. Like Kenny, he can follow anyone.

For the past several years in our live show, I do a bit where I talk about how we won *Star Search*, released a hit debut album, and were then asked to tour with Kenny. I tell the story of how as we would come off the stage every night after burning it up, I would see Kenny standing in the wings and think to myself, *Well, let's see the old man follow that.* Next, I say, "Then Kenny would mosey out to the microphone, lean in, and sing, "On a warm summer's eve…" As soon as I finish the story, the guys kick in and we play "The Gambler," leading the crowd in singing the entire song. Our nightly Kenny Rogers tribute.

High-Energy Horizon

Our first single released to country radio was "Leona" in October of 1984. The song broke into the top ten on the country charts. In January of 1985, "Step That Step" was our first number one—the song that Blake Mevis had caught me unofficially cutting as a demo in the middle of the night.

The label wanted to shoot the video for "Step That Step" in LA. They actually shot the entire production on film. If you watch the video on YouTube, an odd cameo that randomly occurred was the comedian Gallagher. We were, once again, staying at the Hyatt on Sunset and, while in the hotel restaurant having breakfast, Gallagher walked in. He saw us and came over to our table. We all introduced ourselves and started talking. Along with the rest of America, he had seen us on *Star Search*.

Gallagher asked, "You guys live in Nashville, so what are you doing here?" I answered, "We're shooting our new music video. Would you like to be in it?" He grinned and shot back, "Yeah!" Just in case you aren't familiar with him, at that time, he was probably the most popular and recognizable comedian on the planet with his crazy hair and off-the-wall antics. He was best known for his Sledge-o-Matic that he used to smash watermelons onstage.

At the shoot, Gallagher showed up in roller skates and kept

them on all day. He's in quick shots throughout the video, doing his goofy, hilarious specialty. The video was already a raucous, fun concept, but he added another great element to the party atmosphere on set that day. Definitely high energy. We had also secured an endorsement with Converse shoes, so that explains some of the close-ups of my feet while dancing on the stage during the last chorus. When "Step That Step" debuted on CMT a few weeks after the single went to radio, the video created great synergy for the song.

Honestly, if you listen to "Step That Step" today, you would likely think, *How in the world did that even make it on country radio, much less go to number one?* Full disclosure—I almost didn't put the song on the record because I was concerned it might be too aggressive. The person who swayed me was Hobie. He put his foot down and told me the song *had* to be on the record. I remember him telling me, "I don't care what people think, Mark. That song is who we are. That's *our* sound. It's going on the album."

Hobie was the champion for that song that went all the way to number one. I think when it got to radio, the tidal wave created on *Star Search* was still sweeping the country, and the momentum, coupled with the success of the video, just couldn't be ignored.

We decided that our third single would be our first ballad— "Used to Blue." The story behind that song was the writer Bill LaBounty had left LA and moved to Nashville. He had married Becky, the singer who had introduced me to the jingle producer. Today, songwriters are just working to get cuts, but back then, they would save their best songs for established artists. I called Becky and asked for a favor. To honor his wife, Bill sent us "Used to Blue" for our debut album. The song became a big hit on both the US and Canadian country charts.

We started working on our second album called *Shakin'* on days off during the Kenny and Dolly tour. Back then, artists were expected to release a new album every year. But, as the old saying goes, "Hindsight is 20/20." Looking back, we went just a little too far on that record. We had pushed the envelope for country music on the first album, but went even further on our sophomore project. That said, the album still peaked at number three on the country charts.

Our next video was for "Betty's Bein' Bad" from that album. The label wanted to shoot that one in New York. We were able to get legendary NBC weatherman Willard Scott to play Betty's bumbling boyfriend. His larger-than-life personality and over-the-top facial expressions made him perfect as Betty's mismatched comedic partner. The single went to number five on both the US and Canadian country charts.

We were starting to see that the "fifteen minutes of fame" dynamic was a very real thing. To keep the momentum going made for hard work into that second and third year. Constantly on the road, our sales were holding strong and bookings were still pouring in. Our fan base was growing more and more loyal, and our reach was widening. In fact, until 1995, we averaged 250 dates a year.

During that season, Capitol moved Don Zimmerman from LA to England to run Capitol Worldwide. With that, they moved us to Capitol Nashville. Jim Foglesong was the head of the label here in town, having signed artists like Barbara Mandrell, Don Williams, George Strait, Garth Brooks, and Reba. They were running hot with a strong roster of artists. Lynn Schultz was still involved, always in our corner, no matter what. He made sure he was in on anything and everything regarding us.

We were also nominated for an ACM Award (Academy of Country Music) that year, but we knew there was no way we would win. When we were asked to be presenters, knowing we would be on camera, we had all bought matching black-and-pink-checked suits. Before the show, rockabilly icon Carl Perkins ("Blue Suede Shoes") came up to us and said, "I absolutely love you guys. I dig everything about your band."

During the broadcast, they had us walk out at the commercial break to get into place. While waiting on the cue from the director, I could see all the veteran traditional artists staring at us with, well, let's just say, varying levels of disgust on their faces. The general consensus appeared to be, *Why are these guys even allowed in here? Who let them in?*

Dave Loggins, whose huge hit "Please Come to Boston," was nominated that year, was seated near the front. Just before the cameras came back live, Dave stood up, pointed at us with both arms straight out, and yelled as loud as he could, "I get it! I get it, man! I get what you're doing! I dig it!" He totally distracted and defused the otherwise awkward moment for everyone. I was thinking that if Dave and Carl get us, the effort was worth it.

Let me explain my motive on decisions like that. At that time, Alabama was huge. And they were so good—incredibly talented. I loved (and still love) those guys. But I knew we could *not* be compared to them. We had to be set apart, and our image was the best way to accomplish that. Like I said before, if Alabama was The Eagles, we had to be The Rolling Stones. For that reason, our style was always as intentional as the music—to the point that when I ran into the publicist at Capitol Records at any awards show, she would take one look at me, shake her head, and comment, "Why are you making my job so difficult? You're killing me here, Mark."

I think some of my inspiration came as a kid watching wrestling on TV with my grandfather. He loved pro wrestling. They have always had clear-cut roles of the good guys and the bad guys. The classic conflict with the image and look being a major part of the vibe. The last thing I wanted to be was vanilla. I wanted people to love us *or* absolutely hate us. Pick a side. And if someone hated us, I never took that personally. It was more like a compliment that we forced someone into a choice. Just like watching wrestling with my grandfather.

I didn't want anyone to casually walk past and ignore us. Like at the ACM Awards, you were either going to be Dave Loggins and yell "I get it!" or you were going to be one of the veterans on the front row in total disgust. If you loved us, you were probably in line to buy a ticket to our show. Right after *Star Search*, it felt like we were America's band. But now, as we were forging our own path in the music business, we had to stay distinct and unique to stand out.

Oil and Water

In September of 1986, we titled our third album *Out Goin' Cattin'*, after an old phrase my grandfather used whenever he went out on the town for the evening. For the actual title cut, Joe Bonsall of The Oak Ridge Boys did a guest vocal with us and was also in the video. With this release, everything was still firing on all cylinders. Everything *except* country radio. We were starting to lose momentum there. So, of course, when something appears to be broken, everyone starts trying to fix it. And when you ask, "How can we fix this?" everyone with a nose has an opinion. And then everyone wants *their* opinion to be the magic bullet. Too many people started speaking into the direction the band should go to course-correct our radio airplay issue.

During this era in music, when any artist would release a single to radio, any station that was always a champion of your music would play it right away. But other stations would hold back and watch to see what happened. By the time the late-bloomers decide to jump on the bandwagon, the early adopters might already be pulling you back on their rotation.

That's why timing is such a crucial aspect of the radio game across *all* genres. That's exactly the reason that some of our highest-impact records didn't necessarily go to number one. Yet, because they stayed in heavy rotation on country radio, and our videos were constantly being played on CMT, to our fans, we may as well have had a number one. They were just loving the song and didn't care about its position on the chart.

In Jim Foglesong's efforts to help us, he wanted to bring in Ron Chancey to produce. Ron had success with The Oak Ridge Boys at MCA. But that sound, style, and direction just wasn't us, it wasn't me. The Oaks are classic and were always amazing at what they do. Absolutely no disrespect to them, and also no fault to Ron at all. We were just oil and water. He was more traditional country, creating the proverbial square peg in a round hole for us.

With everyone putting in their two cents, for the first time, we had external *and* internal crises happening. This season also brought back the tension between Bobby and me. Once again, we had differing ideas about the direction of the band and how to regain traction with sales and charts. Because Bobby also played fiddle and pedal steel, he found Ron's direction toward a more traditional sound appealing. I understood that. But to me, God had already made The Oak Ridge Boys and they were great at being them. We needed to keep being who we had always been.

The music business has always been formula-based, so finding a proven pattern and creating a copy is a constant temptation for the industry in what to do with artists. It was then and still is today. For example, when a country music artist finds success by creating a new sub-genre, you quickly see other labels pop out similar artists. You can play those albums side by side and struggle to tell where one stops and another starts. But, hey, if you're only after a seamless playlist and don't care who the artists are, you're good to go.

So, for *Somewhere in the Night*, released in 1986, Ron and I coproduced the album. There was also a push from our record label to bring in outside songs from established writers. All this drama and politics made it tough for me to focus on the music. For that reason, I wasn't as involved in the songwriting as I had been on previous projects. I made the intentional decision to cooperate and go along with everyone else's wishes. That is, except for one thing—I wanted to get out of Nashville. I wanted to record at the legendary Muscle Shoals Studio in Alabama. Ron had worked there before, so he was good with that.

Going to Muscle Shoals also allowed me to work with Mac McAnally for the first time. Mac is a singer, songwriter, session player, and producer. A highly respected musician's musician. He's in the Nashville Songwriter's Hall of Fame and has won the CMA Musician of the Year award ten times. Mac is also famous for being in Jimmy Buffett's band since 1998. He played acoustic guitar on the record and was the bandleader for all the musicians cutting the tracks.

Yet, in spite of everyone's best efforts, *Somewhere* is the least selling album of our twenty-three releases. One single, "This Missin' You Heart of Mine," went to number two on country radio. The problem was the song created an identity crisis for our fans. No one knew it was us, because the sound was so different. But like always, we managed to motor through, continue touring, and grow our fan base on the road.

Line in the Sand

When we were getting ready to start on *Wide Open*, the label wanted us to use Ron again. Just like before, I disagreed but didn't want to fight them. But I figured if I was going down, at least it was happening on the beach. I chose a studio in Fort Lauderdale in my home state of Florida. Once again, Mac was the bandleader and we brought in some extra players from Muscle Shoals.

Since before I was in Sawyer Brown, songwriting had become a discipline for me. I have always written, which I view as a major part of my job. So by the time we would need to submit songs for a new album, I would have a good number to present to the band. Bobby's mode for songwriting was more on-demand, written after we set the date with the producer and the label to present new songs. For *Wide Open*, I was ready to cut some of my songs again, so I decided to put my foot down on what we chose. The quality of songs and fit for the band was the bottom line. When some of Bobby's songs weren't chosen, he got upset with me.

Ron, my coproducer, probably felt like he was caught between two tornadoes. There were days he should have worn a black-and-white-striped shirt and carried a whistle, because he had to be a referee. But producers often have to play multiple roles when working on an album with a band. The creative process isn't always pretty.

Wide Open released in October of 1988. The highlight of that record was the video for "My Baby's Gone." We shot these really fun scenes with the band in an old farmhouse. Elvis's famous vocal group, The Jordanaires, agreed to sing on the song and appear in the video. People started calling it "the stompin' out the lightbulbs video" or "the light bulb song." In the last thirty seconds, I'm in a room dancing with all these bulbs lit up on the floor. One by one, I stomp out the lights, until the very last one left at the end makes the screen go black. That video was *huge* on CMT, and the song went to number eleven on the charts. We had several videos that charted higher than the songs on radio, once again proving our visual element has always been the most powerful aspect of the band. To us, the energy in the music is everything.

By the time that album released, the conflict with Bobby had spread from just me to the other guys in the band. I want to pause here and be clear that, from then to today, I can honestly say we *all* love Bobby. We never wanted anything to do with the bad-blood band breakups we've all heard about over the years. The best way I can explain the dynamic was that Bobby was always restless. He was spontaneous and dabbled with different ideas. He constantly looked for other things to do. Having worked so long in the entertainment industry, I have seen this trait in a lot of creative people. So in this season when Bobby began to feel like the band was declining and potentially going to disappear soon, the divide grew. That forced me into keeping the peace to keep the band going.

When we returned to Nashville, it was clear that we could no longer make decisions *together*. Something had to change from a business perspective. I know people have differing opinions on this, but from my experience, a band that attempts to be a true democracy won't last.

One night, I called Bobby. "Hey, we need to talk." I met him at 3:00 a.m. at a Krystal that was open twenty-four hours. After we sat down, I said, "First, Bobby, I'll be good with whatever you choose, but I need you to choose now. Here's the options: First, I will leave and you can have the band. I'll go solo. Second, you can leave and I'll take the band. Third, you can stay, but I have control of all the decision-making. I don't want you gone, but I just can't make decisions *with you* anymore. Choose any of the three—I'll go with your choice, but you gotta make the call tonight. One of us has to be the clear leader."

Bobby answered, "Well, I'm not ready to walk away, but I also don't want the band without you, so I agree to you having total control of the band and I'll stay."

By this point, everyone around us seemed to believe that we were on our way out. That is, everyone except Hobie, Joe, Jim, and me. We're survivors and fighters who had each other and we also had our fans.

For me, I was more committed now than ever. With the reins solely in my hands, if we were going down, it was going to be on *my* watch.

Smokin' Hot Wife

I got a truck and some land
And I play in a band with my friends
on a Saturday night
I thank God for the good life
I'm fightin' the good fight
From my porch in the swing
by my smokin' hot wife

—**FROM THE SONG** "Smokin' Hot Wife"

IN 1985, we were invited to perform "Betty's Bein' Bad" on Dick Clark's *American Bandstand*. Of course, when you're on TV, your hair and makeup are done by their people. When we walked in, I saw this really, really, pretty, pretty, pretty girl. (Just making sure you get the picture here.) I made a beeline through everyone in the room straight for her, like I was on the court headed to the basket for a layup with only seconds left till the buzzer.

I introduced myself and she sat me down in her chair to put on my stage makeup. She had been called in as a sub that day. As we small-talked, I knew I was being really obvious but couldn't help myself, because I was already completely smitten with her. I *knew* I was being really awkward.

Since the show taped in the afternoon, I was attempting to ask her out to dinner because we were flying out late that same night. As I was stepping all over my own words, she interrupted and asked me, "Are you trying to ask me out to dinner?" I stopped and answered, "Yeah." And she said, "Okay, I'll go." I introduced myself, working really hard to remember my own name. She smiled and said, "Hi, Mark. I'm Lisa Knight."

After the show was over and I had washed my makeup off, we went out. Lisa and I talked and got along amazingly well. I *really* liked her. Like *a lot*. Being it was the mid-eighties, there was no cell phones, no social media, and no email. The only way to communicate was landlines and mailing letters. And long-distance calls, well, they charged you dearly, by the minute. Unlimited *anything* had not been invented yet.

We began talking on the phone. Every few days turned into every other day. Then every other day turned into every day. Then every day turned into as often as possible. The interesting thing about long-distance relationships, at least back then, was you could really get to know the depths of someone's heart. No FaceTime, only talking. But also after a while, you can actually start to forget what someone looks like. Especially when you only saw them one time.

A month or so into the relationship, I had a couple of rare days off, so we agreed I would fly out to LA to see her. She lived with her mom, so after she picked me up at the airport, we went back to her home. While I was sitting in the living room alone, I began to look around. I saw all these photos of Lisa with Peter Brady of *The Brady Bunch*. At various ages, but in every single picture, the two of them were together. I started to get a bit creeped out, thinking, *This is weird. Like really weird. Is she a groupie? Superfan? Or what?!*

When Lisa walked back in the room, I blurted out, "Okay, so you gotta tell me … what's the deal with all the pictures of you and Peter Brady? You sure seem to know him really well." She laughed and answered with the one option I hadn't considered: "Christopher is my brother. These are just our family pictures." Yeah, I didn't see that coming.

So, if you're a Peter Brady/Christopher Knight fan, I have to tell you, he is a great guy. A wonderful man. And an awesome brother-in-law. What you see is what you get with Christopher. He's who you hope he is. After all these years, we're incredibly close. (Needless to say, we have a lot of his furniture brand throughout our house, because Christopher Knight Home and Christopher Knight Collection are such great products sold by all the major online retailers. And, well, he *is* my wife's brother.)

Lisa and I dated long-distance for about five years. Honestly, I was on the road so much that living in the same city wouldn't have made that much difference in being able to see each other. But because of the separation, we had to be very intentional about the time we spent together. Like I said, when all you have is the phone to communicate, then you aren't watching TV or going to movies or spending time with friends. You talk. You communicate. You can go deep with each other and deal with things some couples who see each other every day don't talk about.

Very successful at her craft, Lisa worked as a freelance makeup artist for ABC doing TV shows such as *The Golden Girls*, *General Hospital*, and *Empty Nest*. But when we finally decided it was time to get married, she made the choice to leave her job and move to Nashville. I had offered to relocate to LA if she wanted to stay at her career. I didn't care where we lived and, by that time,

I had the means to get wherever I needed to be. My job required traveling anyway. But Lisa knew exactly what she wanted, and we've made our home here from our wedding to today.

We met in November of 1985 and were married in January of 1990. Quickly, Lisa loved Nashville and, before long, didn't care to go back to LA, except to see her family, of course. She made the decision to leave her career so we could be together as much as possible. We both wanted to start a family. She soon became pregnant with our daughter, Madison, who was born in 1991. Our son, Gunnar, was born in 1994.

I never would have thought that a country boy from Apopka, Florida, would end up marrying a Valley Girl from California. But God put Lisa and me together. In my line of work, it takes a special partner to be able to pull this off for all these years. I would not be where I am today without her. She has been able to navigate being Super-Mom and Super-Wife, a task that continually amazes me. Lisa has been the one constant for me and our kids, and now our grandchildren, in this crazy, wild adventure of a life.

And did I mention, she is smokin' hot?

CHAPTER SIX

Big Picture

It takes a while to understand
You don't always know where
you're gonna fit in
You just keep on running the human race
Follow your heart and find your place

—**From the song** "Big Picture"

WHEN I BECAME 100 percent responsible for the future of
Sawyer Brown, so many in the music industry were questioning
our direction or predicting our demise. I heard someone make a
comparison of us to The Beach Boys' early days. It's actually hard
to believe now, but a lot of people in the music industry at that
time thought they were just a gimmick. Their label was cranking
out albums because they didn't believe they could last. That
same attitude was in the air about us and I knew it. I felt it. That
mindset certainly didn't hold up for The Beach Boys and, thank
God, it didn't for us either. Yet, at the time, there were many days
I certainly felt that weight heavy on my shoulders.

The media constantly ripped us, especially anyone
committed to traditional country music. With critics and reporters,

it was clearly not cool to think we were cool. ("Haters" were a thing long before social media gave them a name.) With that dynamic always in our face, we had to learn to have really tough skin and just motor through with our heads down. We had to go to work and ignore the noise. What helped us the most in maintaining that attitude was the fact that we were rarely in town. We lived on the road, visiting our homes in Nashville on rare days off to do laundry and pay bills. But our work ethic kept creating a dedicated and loyal fan base that grew in number every year.

Yet, I have never been defensive if someone viewed us in a negative light, because I could see how the band looked like a bottle rocket. Big noise with a huge flash that makes everyone look up and say, "Wow!" But the assumption is after you see the explosion, as quickly as it came, the rocket is gone, totally burned up. But for us, as a band of brothers, we just kept on firing away.

Looking back, while I understand people's perception, all those folks, God bless 'em, just didn't know our hearts. The music business has never focused on longevity. That's the very reason terms like "one-hit wonder" and "sophomore album curse" are so well-known. But our response was to always stay competitive. Our career was launched *based* on a competition! Our goal of sustainability made the band willing to always keep a healthy chip on our shoulder.

I knew from day one that we could never afford to get comfortable in this business. The best analogy to offer is when a basketball team looks up at the scoreboard and sees a solid lead. If they get cocky, start to lay back, and stop being aggressive because they're way ahead, too often they can end up losing badly. I had seen that dynamic play out too many times. That's why my approach has always been all gas, no brakes.

Once again, I want to say how much I *love* traditional country music. We just have never played it. To this day, I love John Anderson. Randy Travis. George Strait. Gene Watson. Vern Gosdin. All the legends that I look up to. I have a passion for the music all those guys gave to the world. But we have always been who we are, just like those artists are true to who they are. We were born as a hybrid of rock and country and have grown up that way. We stuck to our guns, because we saw how we were making an impact.

Around that time, our management team started to get nervous that I was fully in the driver's seat for the band. It wasn't really so much about me having too much control, but more about them not having as much as they wanted. They began getting desperate to find opportunities to show their value. They figured their best play was to try to get us back to where we started—in the media spotlight.

I got a call one day that they wanted to meet. They said they had something *huge* to present to me.

The day I walked into their conference room, after the usual small talk, they launched into their pitch. A US company with a popular, high-visibility brand was ready to sign the band to a million-dollar deal that would include appearances in TV commercials and magazine ads, and offer tour sponsorship. A partnership to yoke up Sawyer Brown with their product to push both.

Their team had been working on and negotiating a contract for months and now it was on the table, ready for my signature. Of course, they were going to make their commission percentage on the total, as always. They were visibly pumped and expected me to join their excitement. To them, this was an absolute no-brainer. And I'm sure to many artists, it would have been.

When they were done, I simply asked, "Who's the company?"

Their answer was a major beer brand.

Immediately, I got that sick feeling in my gut and all the peace drained out of my heart. Although my personal convictions have always been strong and uncompromising, I have never had *any* desire to judge anyone else's decisions or actions. We all have to live with our own choices.

I calmly stated, "Guys, I can't do that. I can't use our platform that way."

They began to repeat how long and hard they had worked on the deal and how we needed a shot in the arm like this to send our career back on an upward swing. They basically said they wouldn't take no for an answer that day. They asked me to go home, sleep on it, think it over, and come back the next afternoon for round two. I went home knowing twenty-four hours wouldn't change my mind, but I wanted to respect them.

As requested, I showed back up at their office the next day. "So, Mark, what do you think? It's a million dollars and a guarantee to be on national TV again. Are you ready to make this happen and sign?"

Once again, I politely answered, "No, guys, I can't. I appreciate all your work on our behalf, but the answer is still no."

The lead manager became furious. He had played nice the day before, but now his patience had run out. He began to yell and pound his fist on the conference table to emphasize his frustration and disbelief that I would pass up a deal like this. He ended with a very loud, "Mark Miller, you give me *one* good reason why you can't agree to this!"

I squared up, looked him in the eye, and said, "I can give you *three.* The first reason is I've never had *any* beer, any alcohol. I've never even *tasted* beer. So, me endorsing *any* brand would be a lie. Second, my mom would be ashamed of me. And the third is I never want to use my platform to promote any product that I have seen destroy lives. Because my faith is the main focus of my life, the *last thing* I want when I get to Heaven is to find out all the damage this did to people. How it devastated lives with addiction, car accidents, and violence. And the kids that come to my concerts, for them to think I'm giving them permission, to tell them it's okay, when I *don't* think it's okay. For those reasons, I *can't* and I *won't* do it."

Those guys had no idea how big of a deal my number two reason was to me. I wasn't going to elaborate with them, but my single mom had raised me a certain way and would *not* have approved of me endorsing alcohol. To be clear, I have no problem with people making the choice to drink. I don't have a problem with beer companies or the good people who work at those factories. But I have my beliefs that I have held to firmly over my sixty-plus years of life. I will only have to answer for me one day, no one else.

That moment of conflict with our management team was the beginning of the end. My no had put us on a countdown and I knew it. While I wish they could have understood and respected my conviction, the relationship was definitely damaged. But I've seen over the years that God uses events like these as tests that, if passed, can create off-ramps to get you where He wants you to go next.

Punk Meets the Possum

In 1989, when the time had come to start work on our sixth album, we decided that Randy Scruggs and I would produce the record at his studio in Nashville. I decided on the title *The Boys Are Back*. The big story on that record was a last-minute decision to cover a classic country song.

While working on the album, the band had to go to New York City for an event. With some time to kill one afternoon, Hobie and I had gone into a little boutique to shop for stage clothes. LA and NYC were always great spots for finding new additions to our funky wardrobe. With the store playing loud music, suddenly we heard this punk-rock song blasting out of the speakers. But the lyrics were oddly familiar, recognizable. I froze to listen. It was George Jones's 1964 hit song "The Race Is On." The band was The Frantic Flintstones, who called their style "psychobilly," a fast, grungy, punk-meets-rockabilly vibe. I remember thinking, *Holy cow! How cool is that? What a great idea.* Hobie and I were freaking out at their version and laughing because of how awesomely fun it was.

When we got back home and were finishing up the record, I couldn't seem to get that new version of "The Race Is On" out of my head. It kept playing on repeat in my brain. (Musicologists call that an "earworm.") On our last night in the studio with all the players there, around 11:00, we had finished the final song. Hobie stared at me a minute, and then asked, "Hey, Mark, I'm looking at you, and I'm thinking, *We're not done yet, are we?*"

I told everyone in the studio about the cover song we had heard in New York, and closed with, "You've got George Jones, the Possum, and then you've got this punk-rock version on the other end of the spectrum. Who best to land right in the middle? Us!"

So the guys worked out their parts, we found a good upbeat tempo, and our cover of "The Race Is On" was born. Pure fun. Ron "Snake" Reynolds, who was notorious for hating everything, was our engineer. After we listened to the playback, Randy Scruggs asked Snake, "Whaddaya think?" He scowled and answered, "Well, if you like this kind of crap, then I guess it's okay." That was as close to a positive review as you could ever expect out of Snake, so we *knew* we were onto something.

Randy went over to the landline, called Jim Foglesong, got him out of bed, and asked him to come to the studio. (Yeah, like right then.) So after midnight, the president of the record label drove to the studio to hear what we had cut. I'm sure he was thinking, *This had better be good!* As we all listened to the final take, Randy, Jim, and I knew we had captured something special. Over the years, the unplanned, impromptu, let's-just-try-this creative moments can end up being some of the most special of your career. The last song cut on *The Boys Are Back* was the one we didn't see coming and that almost didn't make it on the album. The classic "The Race Is On" was about to take on another life and make a huge impact for the second time with the country crowd.

Now, back in the late eighties, Sawyer Brown recutting a George Jones song would have been considered 100 percent sacrilegious. But our version evidently turned out to be distant enough from his, as well as so different, that it never even got compared to the original. We were so far outside the box that a lot of people thought the song was brand new.

Even though the single peaked at number five on country radio, this was another one of our songs that felt like a number one, all because of people's reactions. Another major impact song that got the fans' attention.

To give you an idea of how huge "The Race Is On" became, we went up to Canada to open for one of our heroes, Nitty Gritty Dirt Band, on a two-week run there. On the evening of the first show, not long after the doors had opened, Colin, our road manager, walked into our dressing room with a huge box on his shoulder. He lifted it off, turned it upside down, and dumped out the contents. Suddenly, the floor was covered with Canadian money. Colin said, "Guys, I don't know what's going on, but I just sold *everything* we have." I asked, "You mean everything we had for *tonight*?" He clarified, "No! I mean everything we brought to sell on the entire two-week tour! I'm going to have to get on the phone to see about getting more product shipped up here."

That night, the crowd was incredible, with a whole lot of folks wearing our shirts and caps they had just bought. But when we started the intro to "The Race Is On," it was like the Carnegie Hall show in New York all over again. The place erupted and went nuts. The crowd was in a frenzy—jumping, dancing, and shouting out the words louder than me on the mic. When we ended the song, they started chanting in unison, demanding to hear it again. We ended up playing the song *three times*!

After getting that same kind of reaction with the second night's crowd, Jeff Hanna and Jimmy Ibbotson of Nitty Gritty Dirt Band told the promoter, "Hey, we're going to switch spots for the rest of the tour. We'll go on first and let Sawyer Brown close." At the time, they had a huge song called "Fishin' in the Dark," which was an anthem up there. But "The Race Is On" had caught on like wildfire all over Canada because of the heavy rotation of the country radio stations there.

Six months later, that same promoter brought us back to tour Canada as the billed headliner. That was a great snapshot of how much people loved the song, especially live—and also what *one song* can do for an artist's career, even when it doesn't hit the number one spot.

We released two other singles off *The Boys Are Back* after "The Race Is On." Both "I Did It for Love" and "Puttin' the Dark Back in the Night" peaked at number thirty-three. Those songs' chart positions show you the crazy ups and downs we had with country radio. One huge hit certainly does not guarantee you success with your next single.

Renovation and Revival

As I surveyed the music industry landscape, one thing was starting to become clear to me. I knew we had to go through our first reinvention of the band. I felt like the time had come for a major change. To explain, when you look at artists' careers that have lasted as long as ours has, for the majority, you'll see this cycle can take place several times over the years. Some classic and obvious examples are The Beatles with *Sgt. Pepper's Lonely Hearts Club Band* and The Bee Gees with *Saturday Night Fever*. Reinventions are always connected to a new album with a major change in sound, style, and image.

This dynamic can also take place when new members are added. When Bernie Leadon left the Eagles and Glenn and Don brought in Joe Walsh, the next album was *Hotel California*. When Mick Fleetwood and John and Christine McVie decided to add Lindsey Buckingham and Stevie Nicks after Bob Welch left, their first album together produced "Over My Head," "Rhiannon," and "Say You Love Me." These are always risky moves at the onset, because some fans don't want you to evolve. But if you do it right, you can grow to a new height and create a wider reach.

Well into 1989, with the fallout from me saying no to our

management on the beer company offer, the divide between us was growing wider. Taking care of such an important aspect of our career became my first order of business in our new direction. While I knew I had to replace their roles, I felt like it was time to build our own team. I didn't want to just start interviewing other Nashville country music managers and end up in the same place again. I was ready to surround myself with people I could trust without question. That decision put two guys at the top of my list. One I had been watching and getting to know for a while. The other, although I had always wanted to work with him, I never thought I would have a shot, knowing how much money he made.

The first was TK Kimbrell, who I knew from him being Steve Wariner's road manager. When we did shows with Steve, I always took note of what an incredible job TK did. He was the first person in the music business I had met whose work ethic could go toe-to-toe with mine or—risking his head exploding here but—maybe even go beyond mine. Realizing how much we both loved basketball and how competitive we were, TK and I also started playing ball together when we were both off the road.

I had spent enough time with him that I knew I wanted TK to be the band's new manager. Finally, one day when I felt like the time was right, I asked if he would be interested. He thought I was joking. No matter how much I tried to convince him I was serious, he thought I was kidding. So I had our accountant draw up a formal offer and send it to him. When he actually saw it in black-and-white, he must have finally believed me, because he accepted.

With TK on board, I was able to officially end the management relationship we'd had since we won *Star Search*. My goal of creating a new season for Sawyer Brown was beginning to come together.

In early 1990, with all the changes going on, I was at a place where I really needed my brother for some R and R and some heart-to-heart. The band was going to be parked somewhere in the Midwest for a few days off, so I invited Frank to meet up with me on the road and hang out.

In chapter one, I told you how incredibly smart Frank is. Okay, brilliant. He graduated from college with a computer science degree, but before he even got his diploma, a major software company's headhunter found him and offered a crazy salary. Frank was makin' bank. He was also the only guy in the company not required to wear a suit and tie. With his long hair and beard, they kept him tucked away, working on cutting-edge projects.

When I called Frank to meet up, he said he had ten weeks of vacation coming and was actually ready to take some time off. He was great to spend it with me. When Frank went to his boss to make the request, the guy pulled out the company checkbook, wrote out a huge number, and signed. After he handed it to Frank, my brother asked, "What is *this* for?" His boss replied, "This is a bonus to guarantee you actually come back to work here after your vacation." Talk about incentive!

After Frank arrived, we went and bought all the sports equipment we thought we might want and just had some fun during our time off. But we also had some very serious and honest conversations about life, the kind only super-close brothers can have. After we got back to Nashville, I asked Frank if he would go over all of Sawyer Brown's financial records and do an audit to check on our business. Especially since we were moving away from the other managers and starting fresh with someone new, this was good timing. And Frank knew exactly what he was doing. Like Mom, he has always been amazing with money.

After a couple of days, Frank came to me and said, "Mark, I've found thousands and thousands of dollars owed to you. And I can prove it." Surprised but not surprised, I listened as he showed me everything he had found up to that point. Finally, Frank said, "Mark, here's what I'm going to do. I'll go back to my job in Florida, put in my notice with the company, finish up my projects, then I'm coming to Nashville to work for you." (I can tell you, in case you haven't figured it out already, that the second guy I wanted to work with us was my brother, Frank. But he was making so much money, I thought I would never have a shot.)

Now I was suddenly more surprised at his offer than hearing about the money he found. "But Frank, I can't afford you. We don't have the kind of money you've been making."

As only a brother can do, he looked me in the eye and firmly stated, "Mark, from what I've seen here, you can't afford to *not* hire me!" In other words, he saw enough ways he could pay for himself.

So, by the spring of 1990, Sawyer Brown had its own hand-picked, custom management. TK knew the music business as well as anyone I know, and Frank knew how to make money work for us, while keeping everything in line and in order. Over the years, there have been times when I realized I made a bad decision. I've gone to Frank and asked, "Why did you let me do that?" He's answered, "It's not my job to question you. You've been right more than you've been wrong. My job is to facilitate and carry things out. Sometimes we're going to hit a home run, sometimes we're going to strike out. That's just the way it is." That's my brother's heart.

I think to our fans and people who know us well, Frank is some kind of mythical character. Like Dolly's husband, Carl. You hear about him but never actually see him. Well, in our camp, we got Frank. People will ask, "So, is Frank ever going to come out on the road?" All of us will bust out laughing, because the answer is no. He's back at the office making sure everything you see out on the road is firing on all cylinders.

After I had my dream team in place, the next album was our *Greatest Hits* record, released in August of 1990. After just five years and six albums, to already be releasing a compilation seemed strange. I was actually surprised that we could have one this early in our career. Realizing how many songs we had climb so high up the country charts was encouraging. But there were nine songs taken from our first three albums. No cuts from *Somewhere in the Night* or *Wide Open*.

The only new song we included on that record was "When Love Comes Calling," which Randy Scruggs and I had written. That was the only single the label released to radio. Capitol and Curb's motivation for putting out a greatest-hits package was probably just about capitalizing on the momentum of "The Race Is On"—to push out a quick project in case the band ended before the next record could be recorded. Just another sign of the crazy roller-coaster ride that the music business can be.

If you're young enough to only know listening to music via streaming, you might not understand that back when the CD (compact disc) was king, fans loved greatest-hits packages because they could listen to an artist's most popular songs in one sitting. Otherwise, you had to pop several discs in and out of your CD player. Plus, if you liked an artist but had never bought their music, one purchase could get you all their best songs. For those reasons, they were really popular among consumers and fans at the time.

In and around our heavy touring schedule, we worked on

our next album, *Buick*. Once again this one was produced by me and Randy at his studio and released in early 1991. It turned out as quirky and funky as we had ever been. I was a writer or co-writer on all ten tracks with titles like "Superman's Daughter," "My Baby Drives a Buick," and "Thunder Bay." Not exactly classic country titles. But, in keeping with our ongoing battle, the project was once again just a bit too much for the industry. The charts provided proof that country radio was ready to move on without us. The first single off *Buick* was "One Less Pony" that only got to number seventy. The second, "Mama's Little Baby Loves Me," went to sixty-eight. Not good. That's like getting a participation trophy that says, "Thanks for playing."

But even more change was about to take place.

While we were continuing to work through our reinvention of the band and our brand, Bobby had grown restless again in light of the album's singles not charting well. Likely thinking the end was near, he started putting out feelers in the industry. The Nashville Network wanted to produce a show called *You Can Be a Star*. They offered Bobby the job of being host. He came to us and said he really wanted to accept, while keeping his spot in the band. We all knew that meant anytime the show scheduled a day to rehearse or shoot, we couldn't work.

Hobie, Jim, Joe, and I talked it over and came to an agreement. We told Bobby if the TV show was the direction he wanted to go, then we felt like it was time for us to move on. We were clear that we would not kick him out of the band, but we couldn't afford to put our career on hold for him to essentially be a solo act on TV. So, in 1991, Bobby said yes to the show and the band had the first vacancy in our career.

Moving forward, Sawyer Brown's lineup would be different.

Mixing It Up on Music Row

One day, I had a meeting scheduled with Lynn Schultz at the Capitol Records office to discuss our next album. I was more than ready to put *Buick* in my rearview mirror, literally. As I pulled into a parking space, I looked up to see all these people streaming out of the front doors. Most were carrying boxes. Some of the guys were visibly angry and some women were crying. Deciding that today didn't look like a good time for a meeting, I left and drove back home.

Not long after I walked into my house, the phone rang. When I answered, I heard, "Mark! Bowen here! I need to see you today. You need to come on up to Capitol. I've fired everybody. Cleaned house. There's nobody else in the building, so when you get here, just come on up." That explained the exodus I had witnessed earlier. Even Lynn was let go.

When Jimmy Bowen had taken over as president of Capitol Nashville, he came with a reputation for firing everyone and starting all over. He had done it multiple times at the labels he ran. But I knew what everyone in country music understood—he was one of the most powerful record execs in the nation, for sure in Nashville, because he had been very successful in developing huge artists and selling a ton of records.

On the drive back up, I had resigned myself to the fact that he wanted me to come in so he could look me in the eye as he booted us off his label. Call me in to kick me out. I knew that along with letting staff go, that usually also meant gutting the artist roster. I figured he had probably talked to some of the naysayers, looked at our overall declining chart performance, and was going to fire us too. This was evidently Capitol execution day and I was next.

I pulled back into the parking lot, which was now vacant except for Bowen's car. I walked into what felt like a ghost town, a place normally buzzing with activity. I went up to the president's office, a place I had visited countless times when Jim Foglesong was there. Bowen sat there with the phone receiver in his hand, frustratedly punching numbers on the keypad. He looked up and motioned for me to wait, while he kept pressing buttons and getting angrier.

Finally, I asked, "You know what I would've done if I were you?"

His eyes shot up at me as he responded, "No, Miller, what would you have done if you were me?"

Figuring I had nothing to lose, I offered, "I'd have kept somebody around to show me how to use those phones."

He slammed the receiver back into the cradle, laughed, and blurted out, "Now *that's* funny! That … is … funny." He pointed at me and stated, "I like you!" Bowen motioned for me to sit down, then continued, "I'm sitting here looking at your album sales and I got a question. How the hell do you sell this many records? I'm just looking at these numbers going, 'Oh my gosh.'" Needless to say, I did not see that coming.

He continued, "I don't even know what to call what you do. But obviously people love it. So, here's the deal. You gotta bring me one of these." (He emphasized by pointing at the numbers and dollars on the reports he had been reading.) "I want one of my own. Now that I'm here, make *me* one of those albums! Let's sell a bunch of records. And son, it's gotta be one hundred percent whatever you do. You have to bring me authentic Sawyer Brown! That's what I want! I want a shot at selling *this*," he stated as he poked his finger at the balance sheets again.

Laughing to myself, I answered, "Yessir, I can do that."

Bowen wrapped up, "And don't let anybody mess with you while you're doing this record. You're in charge. But I'm telling you right now, if this is successful, I'm taking *all* the credit. And if it's not, I'm blaming it all on *you*." He ended with a big grin.

I said, "Done deal, sir." I felt like a kid who had just been handed the keys to the candy store.

Betting on Us

Soon after that day, Frank and TK asked to meet with me. "Listen, Mark," they said. "You need a hit and 'The Walk' *is* a hit. We think so. The band thinks so. We *all* agree. We totally understand how you feel and why, but if you will trust us to release it as a single, you have our word that we will do *everything* in our power to make sure the song has the very best chance on the charts. *And* we'll make back every dollar we spend, plus more. This will be an investment in the band's future."

Now, allow me to give you some backstory about this conversation.

First, "The Walk" was on the *Buick* album, the record that the label and I were done with. The marketing and promotion money was all gone, and radio had put the final nails in the coffin on the last two singles from that project. I had just received my marching orders from Bowen to waste no time getting started on a new album.

Second, "The Walk" was deeply personal to me. I wrote it about my relationship with my grandfather. It was the first time a song was connected to someone so close to my heart. It was different. It was about *me*. So, the last thing I was going to do was let radio disrespect my song. I just didn't want to give anyone the chance to pop off with something negative or condescending. Had that happened, I wanted to avoid driving my truck through some station lobby and getting arrested. I'd seen one too many bad country artists' mug shots to do anything crazy enough to get on that list. Plus, I had put "The Walk" out for just one audience—our fans. I felt like they knew me, so they would get it.

So, how could we possibly release that song to radio?

At the time, one of the guys had heard about a pop act that had taken a song from their last record that hadn't performed well, put it on their new album, released it as the first single, and found success. They had believed in the song enough to try and give it a new life on a new album. And it worked. That was our answer.

I was already feeling confident about the new songs I had written for the next record. Including "The Walk" in that mix and releasing it as the first single to radio may have had no precedent in country music, but it was clearly our only option.

So, we all agreed and started mapping out our strategy. When we presented our plan to Jimmy Bowen, we told him, "We're gonna take the risk on this one," committing in the neighborhood of half a million dollars of our own money. We told him that we would bombard country programmers and take full responsibility for the single. Bowen fully signed off with his support.

If other artists had taken similar steps at that time in the music world, I had never heard of it. Today, an artist putting in their own money and using their own people is far more common. I can't say for certain that no one else had ever done it back then, but we certainly weren't following anyone's lead or template. We just knew we had to take ownership of this single.

We hit the ground running and hired *every* single independent country radio promoter in the United States, meaning those who didn't work directly for a label, but would contract with any artist. Our all-hands-on-deck approach was both offense *and* defense. We wanted as many on board as possible, but we also didn't want to leave anyone out there for another artist to work against us. While there were about ten people total, some of them represented a team of promoters. After coordinating schedules, we flew them all to Nashville and got everyone in the same room. We played them the final mix of "The Walk" and made it clear that we, not Capitol or Curb, were taking full responsibility for the promotion of the single to country radio.

With videos always being such a key element for us in adding the visual to our songs, we went to LA to work with Mike Solomon. We had seen his work and felt like he could capture the heart and soul of the song. The fact that this was a ballad required a completely different vibe than most of our other videos. While we had been country-rock since day one, we were ready to show more of the country side of our roots on this new album.

TK and Frank led our team of promoters, working day and night, calling stations. Once the single went to radio and the video was released on CMT, the plan began working and "The Walk" started to climb up the charts.

Late one night after a show, TK called to say that Bowen wanted to talk with me. We arranged a call, and he said, "Mark, here's the deal. You guys have put together an unbelievable promotion on 'The Walk.' You are definitely about to go number one. But I have a song right now coming up the charts with one of my biggest artists. I need to sell *millions* of records to recoup our money. Now, if you say the word, you're going to go in and be number one. There's nothing anybody can do about that. Not me, not anyone. But, Mark, I'm asking you to consider pulling back on the gas to let me take this other song to number one. And if you do this for me, I *will* make it up to you."

I told Jimmy I would talk to TK and get back with him right away. On the phone, I told TK, "Well, you know what we have to do, don't you?" He responded, "Yeah, but the decision has to come from you, Mark." I continued, "Okay, then tell everybody to back off."

First, Bowen's call proved to us that our strategy had worked and the song was going to do exactly what we had planned. But I also knew Jimmy well enough to know, if he said he would make it up to us down the road, then he would. And, as I have said before, at whatever position we landed at the top of the charts, we had already seen that an actual number one wasn't as important as just getting into those top spots. Once again, to our fans and all the new folks the song had introduced us to, whether number one or number five, it didn't matter to them.

The very next week, the other artist went to number one and we peaked at number two. And, for the record, Jimmy did eventually return the favor, just as he had promised. In the end, everybody won.

"The Walk" was an impact song at a crucial crossroads in our career, and we were once again seeing huge success. Within just a few weeks, we were able to recoup our money and saw an incredible return on the investment. In the country radio world, programmers saw that we could bring in a serious song and get the nation's attention once again. TK and Frank had been 100 percent right, which, for me, was amazing evidence that they were the right team for us, brought in at just the right time. Brothers I could trust without reservation.

Now the band had a new momentum, a fresh wind in our sails for a new season in our career.

Studio to the Stage

Now that you know the story of "The Walk," I want to go back and tell you more about our 1992 album, *The Dirt Road*. I had never written a song believing or telling myself that it was a hit. That is, until this album. I knew beyond the shadow of a doubt that I had just written a song that would be huge. The title was "Some Girls Do." I knew I had to give this song my very best shot with the highest level of production it deserved. Also, Hobie and I had written what would become the title cut, "The Dirt Road," another song I believed was key to this new place we were going in country music.

After having been challenged by Jimmy Bowen to make our best release yet, my first call was to Mac McAnally. "Hey, we want to come back to Muscle Shoals to work on our next record." Knowing we were going to need a guitar player, Mac brought in a guy named Duncan Cameron.

One evening, playing pool in the big room there at Shoals, I talked to Duncan about "Some Girls Do." I told him it was the first song I had written that I believed could go to number one. I needed him to give it his absolute best—a big-time hook needs a signature guitar lick. I wanted an opening riff that was fun, grabbed you right away, and was immediately recognizable.

After Duncan had listened to my demo several times, the next day as we were getting ready to start recording the song, he asked, "Mark, what about something like this?" He tore into that now-classic opening guitar line that carries the song over the backbeat of the snare leading into the first verse. I was sitting there in the control room, listening and grinning ear to ear, thinking, *Holy smokes! That's it!*

When we had finished the song and I was listening to the playback, I had that familiar feeling in my gut that something wasn't quite right yet. I know this can sound a bit strange, but it was *too* good. *Way* too good. Too edgy. The last thing I wanted to do was produce the song in a way that country radio wouldn't touch it. Been there, done that.

When we came back to Nashville and Randy Scruggs and I were putting final touches on the tracks, I told him, "We want to recut 'Some Girls Do.' A completely new track." When we were finished with that version and I listened to it, I realized the first one was too hot and this second one was too cold. The first one was too edgy and the second too traditional. Two tries and I had missed the mark. I had to get it "just right." I needed to land on a sound that sat perfectly in the sweet spot for country radio.

For this third try, we brought up Mac, Duncan, and a steel guitar player from California named JayDee Maness. I played all the guys both versions and explained what I was after. I told them, just like "The Race Is On," I wanted it somewhere between punk and Jones. We had to land in the middle.

That day, we created the hybrid version of "Some Girls Do," the one you still hear today. After a lot of hard work and a labor of love, *The Dirt Road* was ready to release to the world. Everything about the album, from the cover shot to the songs, showed a fresh and new Sawyer Brown. With a new team behind us and the breakout success of "The Walk," we were reinvented, renovated, and revived.

The only thing left was to fill our open guitar and backup vocal slot for the live shows.

Duncan Cameron had done an incredible job playing guitar on the record. He came through in a big way for me on "Some Girls Do." I also found out he had played on the road with Glenn Frey back when all of the Eagles members were doing solo records and tours. He also sang backup. After spending many hours with him in the studio, I had taken notice that Duncan was tough. Like, if I was going to get into a fight, I'd want him to back me up. I felt like he was a great fit for us, for the direction we were headed.

Because we had our first shows coming up after the album was finished, I decided to ask Duncan if he would be interested in playing for us. He was quick to say no, telling me that he was a session musician, not a road guy. But he said he liked us and would agree to go out as a sub, just until we could find someone permanent.

Our first two shows were back-to-back dates in Joplin, Missouri. We had sold out the little arena there both nights. But Duncan didn't know that yet.

After soundcheck and dinner, they had opened the doors and the crowd began streaming in. We were all just sitting around in the dressing room when Duncan walked in and said, "Hey, this place is packed. Like to the gills."

"Yeah, we know," I said.

He asked, "What about tomorrow night's show?"

I nodded. "It's sold out too."

Looking a little surprised, he asked, "So, do you do this *every* night?"

"Yeah, we do—*most* nights."

His eyebrows went up and his eyes widened, as he responded, "Huh. Okay."

Waiting in the wings to go on, I could see that Duncan was a little nervous. Being the kind of guy and level of player he is, I was a bit surprised to see him get anxious. But whatever he had in his head about our shows and the rooms we played, he was now getting the full picture, seeing the fans, and respecting what we do.

We played the first night and everything went off without a hitch. Next night, the second show was also incredible.

As we walked off stage, Duncan stopped me. "Hey, Mark, is this job still open?"

I grinned. "Yeah."

He smiled back. "Then I'm in."

The four years from 1988 to 1991 had been a wild ride. We had been in the valley of the shadow of death and up on the mountaintop. But I now had a peaceful feeling that we were finally finding our groove for the long haul in this crazy business.

Bobby

BOBBY COULD PLAY anything—guitar, fiddle, steel guitar, banjo, *anything*. He is very charismatic, loaded with charm, really funny, and always a great hang. At six feet seven and that amazing eighties hair thing going on back in the day, Bobby looked like a rock star when he walked into a room.

I was always amazed at Bobby's musical ability. In those early days, we would all be working so hard to learn a bunch of cover songs, but he could just show up and play exactly like the record. Hobie and I had to stay up late and cram to learn them all, but from Merle Haggard to ZZ Top, Bobby never had to practice. He could just hear a song and somehow play it.

At the point we started, Bobby had been in several bands and played for a lot of artists, having literally grown up playing music. Because his dad played, Bobby got to perform as a kid. That experience was why we deferred to him so much.

Bobby's family was always great to us and very supportive of the band. His dad built our first trailer, handmade with love. Anytime we were near his folks' home in Michigan, we would stay with them. Even after Bobby was no longer in the band, his folks would come out to see us. His dad has passed, but his mom still comes to see us today.

You don't go through the kind of experiences we did together and not become family. And we'll always be family. Even though we all lead busy lives, I still know, to this day, if I need Bobby, he'll be there. And he knows I would be there for him. He was a major part of building this band. We will always recognize everything he did to establish Sawyer Brown.

For years, Bobby has been the band leader at the Orange Blossom Opry, northwest of Orlando. His band opens for all the artists that come in. They also back a lot of the artists, and then have their own featured shows. A few years ago, we played there, doing two shows that night. We all sat backstage in between sets, told stories, laughed for hours, talking about all the crazy, stupid stuff we did in our younger years. That night, after Bobby's band opened for us, he sat and watched our show, even after hearing all those songs for so many years. That says everything about our relationship today and our support of one another.

CHAPTER SEVEN

Blue Denim Soul

He set his mind talkin' about Elvis,
lookin' like James Dean
He said a country boy rockin' ain't all that bad
You shake your leg or you wear you a hat
You bring the house down and
you make all the pretty girls scream

—FROM THE SONG "Blue Denim Soul"

FOLLOWING A SHOW one night, the promoter came backstage to find me. "Hey, there's a phone call for you in the production office." Puzzled because that never happens, I asked, "Who is it?" He answered, "Says he's David Lee Roth … from Van Halen."

My first thought was, *Alright, which one of my buddies is punking me?* I walked to the office and picked up the phone, prepared to bust the prank. "This is Mark."

Immediately, I realized this was *no* joke. I had heard enough interviews and watched enough videos to recognize the raspy, fast-paced, high-energy yet articulate voice on the other end. This was *the* David Lee Roth.

He had found our tour schedule and got someone on his

153

team to figure out how to get through to me late that night. "Hey, Mark, glad I got you. I saw you guys on *Star Search*. I've been listening to you, watching the videos, and I can't figure you out, man, like, are you rock and roll or country? Which is it? Well, it's cool! I'm diggin' it, man! Your sound, it's so unique."

I listened as he riffed on all his thoughts about us, the state of music genres, and the industry. But, the entire time, I was shocked that this huge rock star was obviously buying our records, watching our videos, and was evidently intrigued with us.

Next, he started to ask me questions like, "Mark, explain your sound to me. Who do you guys listen to? Who are your influences?" After about an hour, I had to laugh as he invited us to go 100 percent rock. In his classic hyper style, Diamond Dave said, "Hey, man, you guys just come on over. The water's fine! You can do what we're doing! There's plenty of room!"

My one-time experience with David Lee Roth was over-the-top positive. He was a huge music buff who knew his stuff. That was so encouraging, especially to me as another front man.

So, after forty years, when someone asks me to name the most random things that ever happened on the road, one of my top five answers is the night the original and last lead singer for Van Halen called me. But that experience also showed me you just never know who might be out there paying attention to what you're doing. As with so many of these stories, had you told me just five minutes before what was about to happen, I would have called you crazy!

Signature Song

Over the years, we've consistently seen that a huge part of the draw for folks, whether a West Coast rock star like Roth, a farmer in the Midwest, a factory worker in the Northeast, or a soccer mom in the South, is that we're organic. Always have been. We've been true to who we actually are as people. For example, we said no to cowboy hats, because none of us ever wore one. Boots? Yes. Cowboy hats? No. It has to be true to us, individually and together as a band.

With the 1992 release of *The Dirt Road*, we took everything even further in the direction of full-on organic. "The Walk" had shown our fans, radio, the industry, and the country music community an entirely different side *of* us and sound *from* us. For the album cover, the goal was to show that, at heart, we've always been a working man's band. I traded the rock-and-roll clothes and the Panama for overalls and a ball cap. The guys wore denim, from jeans to jackets. Our image evolved, from a rock look to more country. (Frank and I eventually got into the cattle business together, so that's when things got legit, for sure.)

The largest demographic in our fan base has always been blue-collar folks, and we've never considered ourselves anything other than a blue-collar band. The suitcases in the cover shot were to represent the fact that we were, and still are, essentially a traveling garage band. So our "new image" wasn't really new, because our relentless work ethic had always identified most with working-class middle America.

Now, eight years into our career, we were no longer just wide-eyed boys. We had traveled the world, become seasoned in the music business, and experienced a great deal of life. I was thirty-four and married with a young daughter. We had all matured as men and as a band. We knew exactly who we were, who we *weren't*, and where we were going.

We sent out "The Dirt Road" as a single in November, prior to the release of the full album in January of 1992. Even with the past success of "Step That Step," "The Race Is On," and now "The Walk," we just *thought* we knew what a hit record was until that March when we released "Some Girls Do." And then when the video debuted on CMT, the song exploded. What I had suspected could happen when I wrote the song came to be.

In the music business, an artist's "signature song" is a massive hit that will have to be performed *every* night for the rest of their career. If you think of any major singer or band, you can quickly name *the* song that they became known for and will forever be identified with. For us, "Some Girls Do" was the song that changed everything. The one that strapped our career onto a rocket and made us an arena act. Everything came together with incredible synergy. We had the new lineup and look. The best team with TK and Frank. The right record at the right time. *The* song with a number one video to create the visual experience. All with a fan base that was growing by the week. To use another sports analogy, we now had a completely different ball game on our hands.

In 1992, the CD was king. There was no other competing format. The record labels were killing it with consumers buying physical product in stores at ten to fifteen dollars each. Those were the glory days in the music business, long before streaming. I do believe it's also important to point out that, in this season, Garth Brooks and Shania Twain created such a stir in music, across all genre lines, that everyone in country rode their wave to some degree. They were so huge that, for the first time, *the world* began to pay attention to country music. Those two artists expanded the audience to include pop and rock fans. The old saying "A rising tide lifts all boats" was certainly true in that day.

Just as we were experiencing our greatest success, our original contract was expiring and the time to renegotiate was coming up. One day, Mike Curb called me with an interesting offer. "Mark, I'm ready to turn Curb into a freestanding, independent label. I've already talked to Capitol about taking you. If you'll agree to sign and the band goes all-in with me, I'll leave LA and move my family and the business to Nashville."

Because our original agreement with Capitol and Curb was a partnership, Capitol had only been making half the money from us, half of what they made with all their other artists. That's why there was always a ceiling there with us. They had plenty of successful artists with whom they put in all the money but made *all* the profit. So, Mike's offer would take us from being way down on a label's priority list to the top act on the roster.

With that understanding, my answer to Mike was just one word: "Absolutely!"

He went right to work and did everything he said he would—moved to Nashville, set up Curb as a fully independent label, and signed us as his first act. That opportunity meant so much to us at the perfect time in our career. But our agreement to go with Mike meant a lot to him as well. (We remain close friends to this day.)

Looking back, I always felt like we had to go through everything we did to get where we wanted to be. Because, without that constant struggle, we might not have had the grit and edge we needed at the right moments. The ongoing conflict was also our greatest motivator. One of King Solomon's best pieces of wisdom is found in Ecclesiastes 7:8: "Finishing is better than starting. Patience is better than pride."

La La Land

Because Mike wanted to get a record out on his new label as soon as possible, he asked us to get started on our first project for him right away. By this time, sadly, Muscle Shoals Sound had closed down. So Mac McAnally and I went in together and bought the gear we needed to set up and record at his house, which was also in the town of Muscle Shoals, Alabama.

The plan was Mac and I would write and cut the tracks at his house, then vocals, overdubs, and so on would be done with Randy Scruggs in Nashville. So, once again, we would be the producers and Mac would be the bandleader in Shoals. Throughout the project, I drove back and forth as needed.

From day one, I loved the vibe down in Alabama. Mac and I enjoyed hanging out, writing, and recording there. He became a huge influence on me as a writer, artist, and producer. Our personalities worked great together and, because we had similar backgrounds, I easily related to him.

After the success of "The Dirt Road," and specifically "Some Girls Do," I was feeling pressure to follow up and duplicate the success. There's a concept in music called "the sophomore album," which means after a successful first record, there's a natural demand from both the label and the fans to repeat the magic with your second project. While *Café on the Corner* was our ninth album, because of what we had just experienced, it felt like our second record—the sophomore.

I've seen a lot of artists over the years try to follow up their signature song with what would be called, in movie terms, the sequel. But I didn't want to try and write "Some Girls Do II." As a creative person, I felt the constant need to keep moving forward, to keep evolving. Plus, with each passing year, my own life experiences and the growth of the band brought new things to write about.

I remember talking to Mac about how I was feeling. After hearing me confess all my fears, doubts, and stresses to him, he simply said, "Mark, just figure out what you wanna say and make a record about that."

Breaking down the truth and making it so simple like that was a game changer for me. I got it. I immediately started thinking, *Okay, I can breathe now.* And that's exactly the approach I took on the record. Relax. Create. Say what I *want* to say, what I feel I *need* to say.

Mac's house was built in the late 1800s and sits on a hill off the Tennessee River, close to where Muscle Shoals Sound was located. It's a beautiful, historic home with a huge porch. *Very* classic Southern. We lived at his house during the recording and brought a few players down from Nashville to add to the guys we always used from Shoals.

In most studios, sessions are sold and blocked by the hour. So often, just as you're getting creative and the magic is happening, you might have to leave because your time is up and another artist is ready to come in. At Mac's house in Shoals, there was *no* clock. And because the food is so incredible down there, we would work just long enough to get to the next meal on time. The vibe and the freedom to express yourself, however you wanted, was amazing. That's exactly why we came to call Mac's place "La La Land."

After he had written the song "Café on the Corner," Mac played it for me. He wasn't pitching it to me, just letting me hear it because he was planning on the song being on his next album. David Geffen, the founder of Geffen Records, who signed John Lennon and Elton John, had discovered Mac when he was just sixteen years old. Somehow, as an artist, he always flew under the commercial radar over the years. Because Mac had such a strong fan base, Geffen never released singles to radio, but they still sold a *lot* of records to his fans. I really liked "Café on the Corner" and, eventually, was able to talk him into letting Sawyer Brown have it.

By this time, TK had also started to manage Mac's career. One day when TK and I were driving to Shoals for us to record, he said, "Hey, check this out. I want to play you a song Mac wrote." Immediately, I loved the song and felt like it fit us and my voice. When I asked TK what our chances might be to get it, he said, "No, you can't have it. Mac's gonna put it on his new album."

The song was "All These Years."

While in the middle of recording the album, I still wanted to cut the song. Now, I'm a *huge* Boston Celtics fan and so is Mac. One day, while I was watching a game, I knew he would be too. So right at halftime, I called him. "Hey, let me record 'All These Years.'"

Mac responded, "No, Mark, you *don't* wanna do that." I ended with, "Well, please just think about it. I'll call you back when the game's over." Right after the final buzzer, I hit redial. "Okay, are you going to let me record the song?" Again, Mac said no, so I pressed him, "Why? Just tell me *why*?" He answered, "Because if you record it, then you'll want it to be a single, right?" I said, "Yeah, exactly." Mac continued, "Mark, you're on a roll right now in your career, and radio will *not* play that song." Now I understood his reasoning. His no was just trying to protect us.

Mac paused for a second, then asked, "Well, if I *did* say yes, how would you cut it?" I responded, "Exactly the way you did. Acoustic guitar, some strings, and vocals." Without skipping a beat, he said, "Yeah, Mark, they won't play it." I pressed harder, "But I want to cut it." Finally, Mac gave in, "Okay, but you're crazy. You're gonna blow it. You've got everything going for you right now. If you release the song with that arrangement, it'll be a mistake. Mark, I just don't want to be responsible for that."

With his warnings in mind, we cut the song the way Mac did and released it as a single to radio. But he turned out to be right, to a degree. The song stayed in the forties on the charts for about a month. But it just kept inching its way up slowly. There were several times we thought we were going to lose it. Finally, the song made it into heavy rotation and peaked at number three in the US and number two in Canada.

What we eventually discovered is that you have to listen to the entire song to understand the story. You don't have it figured out by the chorus. So that's why "All These Years" was such a slow burn as a single. Enough people finally heard the whole song that, once it broke through the top twenty, it went up like a rocket. The nature of the lyrics affected radio airplay, but didn't stop it.

But the story of why Mac didn't want to agree to us recording the song tells you everything you need to know about his heart. He would choose to protect our career over him making royalties on a single and an album cut. This is one of the many reasons that Mac has been the invisible sixth member of Sawyer Brown for years.

Even with the laid-back pace, we managed to honor Mike's request to get the record out as quickly as possible. In fact, there was only eight months between "Some Girls Do" and when the first single off *Café on the Corner* went out in August of 1992 with the release of the album. In that era, songs went up and down the charts a lot faster. Today, someone might have a hit a year and a half after a record comes out. Back then, we could release four singles to radio in a year. The cycle was much shorter and far faster.

Money on the Table

In our relationship with Mike at Curb Records, we never felt any pressure from him. We always put enough on ourselves that no one else had to. From my early days of being a staff writer, my work ethic drove me to constantly keep writing. I have always been a closer. While a lot of songwriters will have a bunch of half-finished songs, I need to see something all the way through and complete what I work on. Plus, we were always so busy touring that I couldn't afford to waste any time. When I sat down to write, I had to know there was a solid idea with a great hook for a new song. I was always writing for the current or the next Sawyer Brown album.

With the heightened success, we were doing as many as 275 dates a year. Looking at our hit songs and videos, I kept running the numbers on our live show guarantees and feeling like what we were being paid to play wasn't matching up. Every time I would ask our booking agency about the offers coming in, they would tell me we were maxed out on our price. They couldn't get any more for us.

There's a term in the booking and promotion business called "papering the house," which means the last day or so, if the show isn't going to sell out, the promoter might give away or heavily discount tickets to make the room look full. But when I was given that as an answer—"Mark, they papered the house"—considering where we were, that just didn't make sense to me. Surely, our massive increase in sales and airplay would also translate into selling more tickets. That's just the way this business works.

I knew it was time to take my concerns to TK and Frank. We had recently expanded our team by bringing in Curt Motley. I went to the three of them and said, "Hey, I'm tired of feeling like we aren't making the money we should be for where we are in our career. I believe we're selling more tickets than what we're getting paid for. I don't want anybody to take advantage of us, and I feel like the agency is letting that happen. So, here's what I want to try. Let's choose five markets around the country where we know we've done well. Rent out the building, promote our own show, do everything ourselves. Once and for all, prove who's right—them or me."

The guys immediately agreed, choosing the first venue in St. Joseph, Missouri, which held five thousand. We had always had a positive experience there and sold out our shows. TK said, "Well, we're all here. Let me just call the venue right now." He dialed their number and put the call on speaker for all four of us to hear the conversation.

After TK got the building manager on and introduced himself, he said, "Hey, we'd like to come in, rent out your building, and promote our own show. Can you get me the cost?" The manager asked, "Okay, when do you want to do the show? I'll need to check the calendar." After TK answered, the guy came back with, "Well, wait, why don't you just let me buy the show? We'll be the promoter." We were obviously surprised at how quick this was happening. How fast the middleman was being cut out of the picture.

TK asked, "So, what would that look like?" The manager

said, "Let me look up the last time you guys were here and see what you did." After we waited for him to pull up his records, he stated, "Okay, I got it in front of me. I can give you a guarantee and then an 80/20 split after we recoup expenses."

Now, let me stop here and tell you that our agency had been getting us *half* that amount. And telling me there was no more money to be had. In a matter of fifteen minutes, my gut had paid off again. I *knew* the band was worth a lot more than we were getting paid. The promoters had been booking us at bargain prices and killing it on their profit. To be clear, I want the promoters who bring us in to make money. But at the same time, the artist needs to get what they're worth. That one call provided us with the proof that our agency had been leaving money on the table.

That was the day we started our own in-house booking agency, so with booking and management now under our control, we were fully self-contained. In a very real way, we simply hired ourselves. Curt became our agent, working under the guidance of Frank and TK. (Curt went on to become a major player in the booking world, and he's still our primary agent today.)

Of course, as headliners of our own promoted shows, we wanted to take out strong up-and-coming country artists as our openers. When the agencies started figuring out we were doing our own thing outside the system, most of them stopped working with us. They refused to book their artists as our opening acts. We had to find fresh, young talent that wasn't signed to a major agency yet. But here are some of the incredible artists we had the privilege of taking out with us: Chris LeDoux, Kenny Chesney, Tracy Lawrence, Mark Chesnutt, Toby Keith, and Alan Jackson. We also worked with some amazing female artists like Lorrie Morgan, Suzy Bogguss, and Patty Loveless.

Blue Denim Soul

In 1994, we took out a young artist who had just released his second album on our label, Curb. His current radio single at the time was "Indian Outlaw." One night, we were in South Bend, Indiana, at Notre Dame. I stood in the wings to listen to this guy's set. When he sang "Don't Take the Girl," I went straight to the phone and called TK. "Hey, we gotta book this Tim McGraw guy right now for as long as you can, because he is gonna blow up!" And, of course, as everyone on the planet knows, Tim did exactly that, reaching superstar status.

Toby Keith was out with us for a year and a half. He had a record deal, but once he spent time with us and saw what a great job TK did, TK became his manager too—and still is today. We intentionally took out opening acts that were more traditional than us. Our goal was if you were a country fan, we were going to make you happy.

Wherever we play and whoever may be on the bill with us, I want to give them all a run for their money. For example, on the day of a country festival with a full lineup, my goal has always been for everyone to have to compare their performance to ours. When the crowd leaves, I want us to be the band they're talking about. That level of personal pressure and expectation has kept us hungry and made us work hard any and every time we hit the stage.

Working Man's Band

By the mid-nineties, from the band to the office to the road crew, we were set—prepared for whatever came our way. Not many artists in that day were taking care of everything in-house, but that's where we have always been unorthodox in our approach.

165

I've been very hands-on with all aspects of the band, because I believe God gave me a natural business sense, along with the musical ability, and my responsibility is to make the most of both. We work so hard out on the road and in the studio that I feel like I need to steward what we do very well to honor our team's trust and commitment.

Too many artists have gotten into trouble when they, first, hand everything they do over to someone else without paying attention, and second, start getting crazy when they begin to make the big money. I always wanted to protect us from that. We never flew first-class. We've never stayed at five-star hotels. We really have been a working man's band. Even anything we did that could have appeared to be extravagant was actually very practical. For about three years, we had a jet. But we were doing so many dates that there came a point, like we had learned from watching Kenny Rogers, where we could actually maximize our money and time with an investment like that.

For example, one summer, we did a tour with The Beach Boys. Those guys were always a hot ticket from Memorial Day to Labor Day. With the jet, we could double up a day—do an opening slot with them and then fly to our own headline show the same night. We had backline—rented gear—at the first show and then our crew would have our production at the second show. We had an inside joke back then that we needed to figure out a way to do a morning set somewhere, just to say that we had done the whole day—breakfast, lunch, and dinner shows.

Our very first show on The Beach Boys tour was opening for them at the University of Iowa. When we went on, they weren't there yet. But halfway through our set, I looked over and saw Mike Love, Carl Wilson, Bruce Johnston, and Al Jardine standing in the wings watching. That was one of the most surreal moments of my career, because I have always been a superfan of those guys.

For some strange reason, that was just one of those freak shows where some girls started diving over the barriers, trying to get to the stage. That was *never* the norm for us. But it definitely happened there. While the security guys were catching girls and tossing them back over or escorting them out, all The Beach Boys were doubled over laughing. They were having the best time watching the show. When we ended our final song and walked off, we could feel a respect from those guys, which began a lifelong friendship. We always loved any opportunity to work with them and hang out. In 1995, it was such a thrill to be invited to be on a compilation album of Beach Boys songs. We did "I Get Around" and also performed the song with them on an awards show in 1996.

Now, back to the jet. Here's the really crazy part—Duncan was also our pilot. Yep. Licensed and experienced, he would fly us to the show, play guitar, and fly us home. The only way for a jet to pay for itself is to keep it flying, so the last year we had it, we leased it out to several other country artists.

But that brings me to our favorite mode of transportation over the years—our bus. Even today, I would much rather be rolling down the highway than flying on a plane. From the start, we have always owned our own buses. And, once again, we have Kenny Rogers to thank for that. He had a bus built by Liberty, a company that only built yachts. The first bus they ever built was for Kenny. Typically, artists name their buses. This one was called The Gambler. Perfect, right?

That first year, when we were out on tour with Kenny, since he was flying everywhere on his jets, he let us ride in his bus. At the end of the tour, Kenny gave us The Gambler. Technically, we did pay him some token amount, but the price was so ridiculously low that it's closer to the truth to say that Kenny gave it to us. The blessing was that it helped us stay in our own bus, because we always had something to sell to put into the next one when the miles got too high.

Our first driver for The Gambler was Hoot Borden, an old-school legend with a lot of rules of what you could and couldn't do on "his bus." His way of letting you know that someone had messed up was leaving a bullet sitting on the table with your name written on it. That was his warning to toe the line. We all knew he carried a handgun, but fortunately we never saw him use it on anyone. At least, not on any of *us*. "Hooter" taught us a lot about the road and all the things we would need to watch out for. Our last bus that we sold in 2021 had 1.8 million miles on it. Today, we're on our thirteenth bus. But it all started with Kenny.

Now, back to our records. With a lot of hard work, Mike Curb's commitment from the label, and following Mac's advice to "figure out what I want to say," *Café on the Corner* ended up a success and a strong follow-up to *The Dirt Road*. The title track peaked at number five in the US and number two in Canada. "All These Years" was number three in the US and number two in Canada. And "Trouble on the Line" was number five in the US and number seven in Canada.

But even with the "sophomore album" being a success, that didn't really ease the feeling of having a chip on our shoulders. From then on, *every* album still felt like our sophomore album, because we were constantly having to prove ourselves to radio. We never had an automatic song that we knew would just sail to the top. We haven't experienced what a lot of artists have where you get on a roll and everything you touch just turns to gold. That's not how our career has ever gone. No complaint, just a fact.

The other side of the coin is that caused us to never rely on a formula. Because we never wanted to duplicate what we had done before, we couldn't allow ourselves to get complacent or comfortable. Whatever we did next had to be special. We had to be unique. But that was just our blue denim soul showing—a relentless work ethic as a band that has always kept us committed to our amazing fans.

The Joes

Joe-Joe

As I MENTIONED EARLIER, when Hobie and I first started with Don King, he hadn't locked in on a drummer yet. He had hired several different guys for various shows, but for different reasons, no one had worked out. But when a big festival was booked in Myrtle Beach, South Carolina, Don told us he had a drummer named Joe Smyth coming to play. He hadn't ever rehearsed with the band, so that show was the first time any of us saw or heard him.

Because I was the crew guy, I had to help him get his drums set up. The first thing I noticed was Joe-Joe had a setup that was more like Alex Van Halen's kit than any country drummer's. He was covered up and surrounded by drums and cymbals of all sizes. Working hard for two hours on the maze of percussion, I was thinking, *After all this, you had better hit every one of these! This better not just be for show!* But as soon as Don's set started, we all saw that Joe-Joe was unbelievable. There were guys in other bands coming out to listen to him.

Here's Joe's backstory: Joe-Joe went to the highly respected Berklee College of Music in Boston. Now, if you aren't a musician, just know that Berklee is a very serious school that turns out some of the best musicians and artists on the planet. He went on to get his master's degree in percussion performance and composition from the University of Miami. Being classically trained in timpani, drums, and mallets earned him positions with the Miami Philharmonic, the Miami POPS, and the Brookline Symphony. Today, besides playing with us, Joe-Joe is one of the head music professors at Brentwood Academy, one of Nashville's top private schools. (Yeah, with that resume, none of the typical drummer jokes will work for Joe.)

For a while, just like Jim, Joe-Joe was a really quiet guy. He was an anomaly, because he looked and acted like a college professor, but then he would get behind his drum kit and just kill it. After getting all his degrees, like the rest of us, he had come to Nashville to give music a shot. He was just trying to make a living like thousands of other musicians. When Don ended the band and let us all go, obviously we wanted Joe-Joe with us. But he is so humble. I recall him telling us, "Hey, I can fill in, but if you guys want somebody else, that's fine. Whatever you want."

Well, we've wanted no one else but Joe-Joe for forty years!

Because my mom was a teacher, I have always had such a deep respect for anyone who put in the work on their education—and that was Joe. That kind of dedication should be honored. The fact that guys with this level of education and skill were up to touring at the level we have for so many years proves, one, how tough they are, and two, how special our situation is.

When we first started out as Savanna, Joe-Joe had a panel van to carry his drums. So guess what vehicle the band used to get to gigs? We put a lot of miles on his van with the little trailer behind it that Bobby's dad built. We would all sleep on the floor, taking turns driving. But Joe-Joe had the most job security of any of us, because he owned the transportation!

The Joes

One of the things I most respect about Joe-Joe is how gracious and appreciative he is. He has gotten the worst of me over the years onstage, because the groove, the beat, the tempo is such a vital part of what I depend on as the front man. Being the drummer, he has had to deal with my intensity more than anyone else in the band. But as challenging as that has been, he always just goes with me, *every* night. He can take it, because he's tough. He just rolls with it. There are many nights where I'm sure he has wanted to throw a stick at me, and I wouldn't blame him. That's where we're like brothers.

To speak to Joe-Joe's toughness on another level, about twenty years ago, he was diagnosed with cancer and went through full-blown chemo and radiation treatments. But he would not, and did not, miss a show. There would be nights that it was brutal for him to get through, yet he would be back there, doing his thing. Sometimes, we wouldn't have him do soundcheck to be sure he had enough energy to get through the show.

The crazy thing is he didn't even tell us he had cancer until he felt like he had to. When he finally came to us one day to share everything he was going through, of course, we were all in shock. We had no idea. Before he told us about the cancer, I was getting mad at him onstage. I would give him "that look." When he finally broke down and told us what had been going on, man, I have to tell you, I felt absolutely terrible. I should have known something was up when his normal stamina wasn't there. Like anyone you love, watching Joe-Joe suffer through that was tough.

Joe-Joe has a relentless work ethic. He sits back there and gives it his all every night. His heart and attitude speak so highly of his character.

Joe Erkman

For the past thirty-plus years, Joe has been a sixth road band member. There are only so many hands that can play all the parts on the records. He covers everything we need with strings—mandolin, acoustic guitar, and electric guitar. Joe is incredible at his craft and one of the best-disciplined performers I've ever known. We have played the same songs thousands of times, and every night Joe plays them with precision and perfection.

CHAPTER EIGHT

Soul Searchin'

When we go, what we have we leave behind
Oh, but who we are will be ours for all time

—**FROM THE SONG** "Soul Searchin'"

FOR THE 1993 *Outskirts of Town* album, I decided to go with the age-old wisdom of "If it ain't broke, don't fix it." We went back to Mac's house, aka La La Land, for more music, even more food, and *way* too much fun. But we did make one major change. I felt like it was time for Mac to join me as coproducer.

Randy Scruggs had been very influential and incredible to work with over the years, but the time had come for a change. And Mac had certainly earned that role. My comfort level with him and the connection to Muscle Shoals just felt like home in every way. Freedom and creativity seemed to hang in the air down there, and I could breathe easy in spite of the pressure that always comes with a new project.

We all felt like "The Boys and Me" was going to be the big song on that record. Everyone loved the way it rocked. As always, I ran off a rough mix of the songs we had tracked to listen to as I drove around, to see how they felt. We knew that "Boys" would most likely be the lead-off single, that is, until something really interesting happened.

One day as we were driving around playing the songs, my daughter, Madison, was in the back, nestled into her car seat. When the tracks finished, she kept asking me to play one song over and over again—"Thank God for You." By her constant "Play it again, Daddy," that was clearly her favorite.

Soon after, I was on the phone with Mac. His three girls were all little at the time too. I told him, "I know we're going to lead with 'The Boys and Me,' but my daughter keeps wanting to hear 'Thank God for You.'" He responded, "Well, that's interesting you bring that up, because that's the same song my girls want me to keep playing too."

The great thing about the innocence of kids is they either like something or they don't. And they have no problem giving you the unvarnished truth. All our girls liked the other songs, but not the way they did "Thank God." They *loved* that one. Out of the mouths of babes, as they say. We literally switched the release order of the singles and led with that song, moving "The Boys and Me" to second. And thank God for little girls, because our paying attention to their favorite helped us get to number one on both the US and Canada charts. So if someone asked about our demographic testing on that song, our honest answer would be that it ranked high among preschool girls.

One of the things all the success had brought was being able to up our game in the production for our live show. We designed a stage that had conveyor belts going in two different directions to get me quickly from one side to the other. (We actually picked those up from Madonna after one of her tours.) We also had a slide that went from the risers to the floor. (Yes, like a playground slide, but a really nice one for grown men.) Every night, I would appear onstage by being shot up through the floor—a concept borrowed from Michael Jackson's Super Bowl performance in January 1993.

Before we changed the order for the single releases, we had already set up "The Boys and Me" video shoot, so we decided to show off our new stage show with the band in action. We shot it at a venue in St. Joseph, Missouri, that we had chosen for tour rehearsals. The upscale production became a reflection of what we had always done—just have fun with the crowd for a power-packed ninety minutes. The sound, lights, and props were all designed to create an entertaining, we're-going-to-give-you-your-money's-worth evening for our fans.

To quickly get out a video for "Thank God for You," we shot that on a set back in Nashville. One major memory from that day once again involved my daughter, Madison. In the many videos we had shot over the years, I never had a "love interest." I had done dance routines with female partners, but never acted out anything even close to a love scene, which was actually very common for artists to do in videos at that time.

Because of "Thank God" being Madison's favorite song and the fact that we were shooting in town, Lisa brought her to the set to watch. While singing in one scene, I flipped over the back of a couch and landed very close to an actress and sang a line or two to her. Then I jumped up and moved on. That was it, no touching or other contact. Well, when my daughter saw me make that move and sing to the girl, she got really upset. Too young, of course, to understand that Daddy was just acting. Let's just say that I had a little "'splainin'" to do afterward to her. But at the same time, it was really cool for us to see her be so protective of her mom and dad's marriage.

One of the reasons that Madison didn't yet understand what I was doing is because, in our home, we never made a big deal out of "what Dad does." I never wanted that. I also never displayed any awards or gold records on the walls, where my kids would constantly have to walk by and think, *Oh, I'm going to have to beat that. This is what I have to live up to.* I knew my kids were going to inherit some level of my competitive DNA. The "Thank God" video shoot was the first time Madison had seen me do anything other than sing onstage. Sure, my kids listened to the songs, but connecting all the dots to the entertainment industry was a different matter, especially navigating things like acting and the perception of fame.

Even when my kids were in school and I would go to their events, it just wasn't a big deal to us that I was in a band. Whether Madison was in a play or Gunnar in a basketball game, my kids were *the only thing* the night was about. That has always been what life is about to me. I was very sensitive to that dynamic to protect them. I just wanted to be Dad, because that has always been a far more important role to me than music.

Working at La La Land, with as many songs as Mac and I wrote, I don't think we ever just sat down and pounded one out the way most writers work. We would pass an idea back and forth until we felt like the song was finished. Mac knew me and the band so well that he always had the right ideas that would work for us. And while he was *never* going to dance like me, he could write songs that *I* could dance to. Another cool thing about our connection to Mac was he countered the way we were viewed by so many people in the industry. We were the butt of a lot of jokes over the years, and his close association with the band gave us a certain amount of musical integrity.

But with the consistent radio success from *The Dirt Road* to *Café on the Corner* to *Outskirts of Town*, people were starting to take the band seriously. We were gaining legitimacy and definitely seeing a corner turned in the industry. Booking our own headlining shows and touring nonstop with the huge stage production, we were gaining traction and adding fans by the night. Our tours were some of the highest-grossing for country artists during this era.

We skipped a record release in 1994, and Curb put out our second greatest hits project in January of 1995, covering our charted songs since the last hits project in 1990. We recorded two new songs for that album—"This Time" and "I Don't Believe in Goodbye," both of which were sent out as singles and made it into the top five on the charts.

In August of 1995, we released *This Thing Called Wantin' and Havin' It All*, our eleventh studio album. We stayed with our winning strategy back with Mac in Shoals. The title cut was the first single to go to radio in July, before the album came out. "Round Here" went out in November, "Treat Her Right" in March of 1996, and then "She's Gettin' There" in the summer. We were now staying consistently at the top of the charts, although none of these went to number one. (As you've probably already picked up by now, getting a number one is a you-gotta-move-heaven-and-earth effort. The jump from two to one is the biggest leap on the chart.)

The Godfather of Soul

After a few hit songs, you just never know who may call you. To set the stage for this story, I need to tell you that TK, Curt, and I are all pranksters. So when something ever sounded even a little outrageous at all from either or both of them, my guard was up immediately.

One day, Curt called and said, "Mark, you're not going to believe what I'm about to tell you … but, please … *don't* hang up the phone. Okay? I'm serious."

Already smiling, I responded, "Alright, what is it?"

"James Brown—*the* James Brown—wants you to play at his birthday party."

I rolled my eyes and hung up the phone. *Nice try! I'm not waiting around for that punch line. But bonus points to him for going big.*

Curt called right back. "Mark! Man, I am serious! I swear! James Brown wants you to play his birthday party. He loves y'all."

I said, "No, no, you're not serious." And I hung up on him again.

He called right back, and this time he was frustrated. "Mark! I am *dead* serious. James Brown requested you play three specific songs at his party for more money than you have ever been paid, *especially* for a fifteen-minute set!"

I kept asking Curt if he was for real, and he kept assuring me it was an actual offer. After I finally decided to believe him, he added, "There is just one other thing he wants."

"Okay, and what is that?"

"He wants you to wear the yellow suit that you wore in the 'Hard to Say' video."

I laughed. "Okay! I'm in! We'll do it and I'll be happy to wear that suit."

James Brown had rented out an arena in Athens, Georgia, to celebrate his birthday. In the center of the floor, close to the stage, they placed a huge La-Z-Boy recliner for him to sit and enjoy the show. The intimate group of people he had invited made the massive venue look empty. Besides us, the other artists that played were Bootsy Collins, Isaac Hayes, and Kenny Wayne Shepherd.

Afterward, James came backstage, thanked us for coming, and talked for a while. He really did speak the way you always heard him onstage. That's exactly how the Godfather of Soul really sounded. I was also surprised to see that he was actually a really small guy like me. We hung out with him and the other artists, staying until the very end.

This was another one of those incredible opportunities we had to meet one of our heroes. And it made it even more sweet that, just like the late-night call from David Lee Roth, James Brown was listening to our music and watching our videos. Moments like that were always very surreal and humbling.

Oh, and the three songs that he wanted to hear us play? "Thank God for You," "The Boys and Me," and "Some Girls Do."

Cash Cow

Being with Mike Curb on an independent record label fit my personality and style perfectly. The freedom he allowed to create was incredible. While the buck clearly stopped with him as the founder and president, we had such a great working relationship.

When the time came to start looking at the renegotiation of our contract, my attorney called me and said, "Hey, because we're on the last album of your deal, I reached out to Mike about a new contract, and I think it may have hurt his feelings a little. He said he thought just the two of you would sit down and figure it out over lunch."

So, having no problem with that request, I scheduled a lunch with Mike. During that season, if we set a meeting, I would block out four hours, because time with him was so fascinating. He's produced everything from the Osmonds to Hank Jr., so he has this incredible music background, all the way back to his days with Mike Curb Congregation. I have always loved hearing his stories.

After eating, we finally got around to talking about our next deal. Mike asked, "Okay, Mark, what do you want?"

I was ready. "Well, I want to be paid like a pro ball player."

Mike looked puzzled. "What do you mean?"

"A ball player gets paid on what you *think* they're gonna do. You don't pay 'em on what they've done. In the music business, everyone pays big *after* you've done something big. But I believe we've reached a certain level where I think you should be confident enough to know what we'll do in the future. We have a solid track record now."

"Okay, Mark, so what does that look like?"

Without flinching, I told him what I wanted and, let's just say, it was an optimistic amount of money up-front for each album.

Mike was visibly troubled and a bit in shock. "How do you justify *that*?"

"I don't have to, Mike. You asked me what I wanted, and I told you what I want."

Mike sort of smiled, obviously letting what I said sink in. So I continued ...

"Let me give you an analogy here. When my brother and I decided to get into the cattle business, like everything else we've ever done, we went all in. We wanted to do it right, so we went to the biggest cattle sale in the country. There was this *one* cow that everybody knew was the *best* cow at that auction. By the end of the day, my brother and I owned that cow. Now, did we overpay for that cow? Yes, yes, we did. We overpaid by a *lot*. But at the end of the bidding, we owned the cow that everyone knew was the best one there. And everybody there also saw that the Miller brothers were serious about the cattle business. So, Mike, you have to ask yourself ... are *you* serious about the *music* business?"

He just stared at me with a blank expression, then said, "I don't like that analogy."

"Mike, you gotta re-sign us, but you gotta buy the cow."

He just kept shaking his head. Then he added, "Well, is there *anything* else?"

I said, "Yeah, I would like a membership to the Golf Club of Tennessee."

He didn't say another word, but I could see the wheels turning in that brilliant mind of his.

When I got in the car, I called my attorney and explained what I had asked for. He started laughing and then responded, "Well, Mark, you're not going to get that, but if you get anything even close, it's a home run."

In about an hour, my attorney called back. "Mark, you're not going to believe this. Mike said he would do it. He's going to give you everything you asked for. And I really didn't understand this but he said to tell you that he's going to buy the cow. I assume you know what that means?"

Mike and I had talked a lot over the years, ever since we signed with him and Capitol. He knew our very first deal was not good. At one point, he had asked me if I ever felt like I had been taken advantage of. Was I ever upset about what we had signed?

THE BOYS AND ME

I answered honestly, "Not ever, not one single time. Here's the deal. I was a big boy. I knew what I was signing. It was explained to me. I knew what I was in for. But whatever path it took for me to get to where I am right now, sitting here with you at this table, I'm totally fine with. So, no, absolutely not. I wasn't ever upset with you or anybody else about a deal that I signed."

Today, I can look back, forty years later, and know that in reality, it was *the* best thing for the band. *All of it.*

Regardless of how my negotiation might sound to someone, Mike would look at how I presented that argument as a compliment to him. He revered the band and always saw us as more rock than country. That was his perspective, coming out of the music scene in LA. What a great relationship we have had over the years, to this day.

Classic Covers and Classic Cars

In 1996, we began working on our twelfth studio album that would be released in April of 1997. The title cut was "Six Days on the Road," a cover of the classic Dave Dudley hit from 1963. Again, Mac and I coproduced the album, recording at La La Land in Shoals and various studios in Nashville. With this being the first album in our new contract, I wanted to make sure Mike was happy with the direction, because he had put so much money up front in the advance. It was important to me that he was pleased with what he was getting for his investment.

After we had cut the track and done a rough mix of "Six Days," I decided I should drive back to Nashville and get his temperature on the song before moving forward. Besides being the president of the label, he has always been a great A&R rep. He knows music so well. I wanted to run the song by him before making a final decision.

After the two-hour drive from Shoals, I walked into his office and said, "Hey, Mike, I want to play you a new track, just to get your opinion on this song." He popped it in his player and turned up the massive speakers in his office. After only a few bars in, he walked back over to his stereo and cranked the volume to ten. Then he opened his office door all the way. Now "Six Days" was *blaring*!

By the end of the first chorus, people were running down the hall to his office to see what was going on. By the final chord, the doorway was crowded with Curb employees. I could tell they were all into the song.

Mike looked at me, then pointed to everyone standing at his door, and said, "*That's* what I think about this song! Mark, you've got a smash here."

Done deal. I was so glad I had taken the time away from the project to drive up and play the song for Mike. What I had not expected was, due to Mike's response, everyone at the label was now pumped about the new album. (Remember, this was back in the day when you couldn't email or text someone an audio track. Had I been able to do that, I would have never had that experience with Mike and his staff. There's still something to be said for meeting face-to-face.)

Before I left Mike's office that day, I said, "Hey, I've always wanted to recut 'This Night Won't Last Forever.'" He responded by looking down at his desk, thinking, and then stating, "'This Night Won't Last Forever.' 1979. Michael Johnson. Number five on the AC pop chart." Moments like that were when you could see Mike's brilliance. Just like that, I pulled a random song out of the air for him and he gave me the history. To this day, Mike can tell you every Sawyer Brown song, when and where it landed on the charts too.

Surprised but not surprised, I responded, "Yeah, well, I just didn't know about having two cover songs on the same album."

After I had been back on the road to Shoals just a short while, my phone rang. It was Mike. "Hey, Mark, you know what you said about 'This Night Won't Last Forever'? That's not a bad idea." I asked, "Are you saying you want me to cut it?" Mike answered, "Oh, no, no, no, I'm not saying that. But, you guys are always different because you take ownership of a song. So I'm not afraid of that. If it's a hit, it's a hit." I knew that meant he wanted me to cut it. When I hung up from him, I called Mac and told him that "Six Days" was 100 percent approved and we were also cutting "This Night."

Both songs ended up being hits.

By this time, we had found our groove with video director Mike Solomon. We had come to trust him to the point that we would just show up on the first day of the shoot with no idea what he had planned. No advance info, no storyboards, no nothing. We were like, "Just tell us what to wear, where to stand, and what to do." Total trust. He knew us all so well and was a perfect fit. Of all the things I eventually led in our career, our videos were one aspect I always left alone. I knew that Mike knew best.

The visual experience of a song had become just as vital to our career as radio airplay, if not more so. We put the same amount of effort into the quality of our videos as we did the singles. Even though our shoots got more and more expensive, Curb knew the value of the marketing they created with CMT being the primary media outlet for country music. In 1993, 1994, and 1995, we won the Video Group of the Year award. At one point in our career, we had done more videos than any other artist in country music.

So, for the "Six Days on the Road" video, Mike decided he wanted to shoot in Miami. He told me he wanted to find a really cool vintage car. But going down there was a budget-killer, so buying a prop like that was going to be a trick. The good news is I have always been a car buff. If you ever saw my bunk on the tour bus back in the pre-internet days, there would always be *AutoTrader* magazines stacked up on my bed. I *love* cars, especially the classics.

When I asked Mike to get specific about the car he envisioned for the video, he said, "Some funky old station wagon. The concept is the band traveling from show to show in this old wagon." I looked through a current *Autotrader*, starting my search for a classic *for cheap*. Finally, I found an old Buick "Woody" for five thousand dollars somewhere near Charlotte, North Carolina. The car would still run and it looked perfect. Because Frank and I were in the cattle business, I had all kinds of trailers. I called my cousin Jason and hired him to drive my dually pickup with a long trailer to North Carolina, pick up the wagon, and deliver it to where we were going to shoot the video in Miami. Yeah, Nashville to Charlotte to Miami and back. I told Mike to just trust me that I had found the right car for his new Sawyer Brown storyline.

So we were in Miami shooting scenes when here comes Jason driving up in the dually, hauling the Woody on a farm trailer. When I saw that rig, I immediately thought of that first plane ride from Nashville to LA when we were headed to *Star Search* and *The Beverly Hillbillies* theme song was playing in my head. That wagon not only made it in the video, it also made the album cover. (Hey, let's get the most out of our five grand and the cross-country haul, right?)

We loved the vibe Mike created for that song, and we had so much fun driving down the back roads in that old wagon, acting crazy. (Well, that's not really acting for us.)

For the second video, "This Night Won't Last Forever," because we had spent so much on "Six Days," we went low-budget. I don't think CMT had done this before at the time, but we recorded the song live in the big room at Ocean Way Studios in Nashville with an audience surrounding us. Mac and Steve Wariner joined us on guitar and backup vocals. We created the MTV *Unplugged* look, which worked great for a mid-tempo pop cover ballad. The wide shots of the room with the red backdrop and the candles were beautiful. Even though part of the goal was to save money, it offered a cool departure and contrast from the "Six Days on the Road" video.

But just when I thought we were finished with the album, there was one more song left in the grand plan. A song that would be written out of relationship and reverence but would become an anthem of both grief and grace for an entire state.

#18

At a show at Kansas State University, we were at a meet and greet with the fans. As I glanced down the line, I noticed this one young man that was a good foot taller than everybody else. He looked like a movie star, really good-looking kid, big and strong. As he got closer to our table, I kept thinking, *I don't recognize him, but this guy has to be a pro athlete or something.*

When he was finally standing in front of me, I said, "Okay, big fella, what's your story?" He grinned ear to ear and said, "I'm a *huge* Sawyer Brown fan!" I responded, "Well, that's really cool. So, what do you do?"

He answered, "I play football for Nebraska! I'm a freshman. I play quarterback."

Still amazed at this kid's looks, I smiled and said, "Well, but of course you do. Look at you! They wouldn't let you play any other position. Because that's sure not the face of a linebacker. Of course you're a quarterback. So, what's your name?"

He answered, "Brook ... Brook Berringer."

From that moment, Brook and I became really good friends. Over the next four years, every summer when he wasn't working, Brook would come out on the road with us. He was a great athlete and a great basketball player too. Having a guy out on the road with me who can play ball anytime fit right into my plan.

Another cool thing we didn't see coming was the whole band got introduced to Nebraska football. Now, I grew up in Florida, so I'm a big Florida State fan. Because of that, I thought I knew college football. I thought I knew what Saturday afternoons on a football field were all about. But no. Not until I got introduced to *Nebraska* football. It's like a religion in that state.

For the four years that Brook was quarterback at Nebraska, we were *his* band. We started going to as many games as we could at Memorial Stadium in Lincoln to watch him play ball. He would leave us tickets at will call. We even sang the national anthem at a couple of games. Down on the field at kickoff, it was like watching titans clash on the battlefield. When they hit each other running at full speed, you could hear the crack of the shoulder pads all over the stadium.

We not only became major fans of Nebraska football, but also of Coach Tom Osborne. He's bigger than life, both as a coach and in his character. In 1994 and 1995, Nebraska won back-to-back national championships. There were kids who had full scholarships to other schools that would opt to walk on at Nebraska because it meant that much to them to play there. They would give up a scholarship at Colorado or Kansas or Missouri to walk on and have a shot at playing for Coach Osborne.

In 1996, they were planning a ring presentation ceremony for the players in front of sixty thousand people at the stadium. Brook had an idea that he presented to the coach and athletic director. "Hey, wouldn't it be cool if we brought in Sawyer Brown as surprise guests? After we give out the rings, they can come out and do a concert?" Brook had so much charisma that he convinced everyone to pull this off.

After everything was set up for us to play the event, they acquired a major production company for the staging, sound, and lights. As the ceremony got closer, Brook called one day to ask me if I would write a song for the event. I answered him honestly. "No, Brook, I can't do that. We're really busy and I have to stay focused on writing for our album, not for a one-off concert. I'm sorry, I just don't have the time."

But, oddly enough, within a few days, I began to get inspired with a melody and words. I knew Brook's story, how he was from Goodland, Kansas, and his life's dream was to play football for Coach Osborne in Nebraska. So I ended up writing what I simply called "The Nebraska Song." After knowing Brook for four years and watching him play so much, it came out naturally. But I decided not to tell anyone I had written the song.

The day before the big event, Brook called me. "Hey, Mark,

will you let me get up onstage tomorrow night and sing 'Some Girls Do' with you?" I laughed and said, "Absolutely! The winning quarterback for Nebraska in his own stadium in front of sixty thousand fans? You are more than welcome to get up and sing with me."

Then he asked, "Well, did you write the song?"

I paused, smiled, then answered, "Yeah, Brook, I did. I know what I told you, but this one just came out."

He went ballistic. "Oh! My! Gosh! I gotta hear it. I gotta hear it right now!"

I responded, "Brook, no. I'm not going to play this song for you over the phone. You can hear it tomorrow when everyone else does."

But as he kept insisting and I kept saying no, he finally gave it one last shot. "Mark, I am not hanging up until you play me that song!"

So I gave in, grabbed a guitar, lodged the phone between my shoulder and my chin, and played him "The Nebraska Song."

When I was done, he freaked out, going on and on about how great the song was and how everyone was going to love it. And then he said, "Alright, Mark, I'm picking you guys up at the airport tomorrow myself. I can't wait to see y'all there. I'm going to run now. I've got a flying session scheduled."

Brook had been taking flying lessons, because another dream he had was to become a pilot. He was working on getting in his training hours for his license. The NFL draft was just two days away, and he was definitely going to be signed by a pro team. At just twenty-two years old, all his dreams were coming true.

That night, before the big surprise concert in Lincoln, Nebraska, Lisa and I were eating out with friends. My cell rang. It was TK. I answered and he asked, "Mark, where are you?" I said, "I'm at a restaurant." He said, "I need you to step outside."

I knew his request was kind of strange, but I walked out of the restaurant and said, "Okay, I'm alone. What's up?" TK said, "Mark, there's no easy way to tell you, but … Brook died in a plane crash today."

I couldn't believe it. That was one of those surreal moments when your brain can't possibly process what your ears just heard. And your heart refuses to accept it. "TK, I just talked to him a few hours ago. He was going to pick us up tomorrow. He was so excited about the concert. This cannot be happening."

But it was true. He had mentioned he was going flying as soon as we got off our call. Obviously, the school canceled the ring ceremony set for the next day. Everything had changed.

Brook's funeral was held in Goodland, Kansas, where he grew up. Hobie and I flew to Denver and then drove from there. When we got to his mom's house, the place was packed. We had gotten to know his sister but had never met his mom. When we were introduced, she was so appreciative and gracious that we had come. Then she asked, "Mark, is there any way you would sing a song at the funeral?"

I was not at all prepared mentally or emotionally to sing. I loved this kid, and his death was so tragic and sudden that I didn't think I could get through it. Thoughtfully, I said, "Mrs. Berringer, I just don't think I can. Brook meant too much to me. I don't think I could get up there and get through it." She smiled, put her hand on my arm, and assured me she understood.

I walked straight out the front door to have a talk with myself, knowing that God would be listening. *Okay, every now and then you just have to man up. This is something that would mean a lot* to his mom or she wouldn't have asked. She's hurting so badly right now. She knows it would have meant a lot to Brook. And then, doing this would also mean something to us. We're here, so I gotta do this.

I went back in and found his mom. "Okay, ma'am, I'll do it. I'll sing."

They already had a piano onstage at the Civic Center for Hobie to play. Five thousand seats, and not a single one empty, with people standing everywhere. We did a song Duncan had written called "I Will Leave the Light On."

Just before the memorial service began, Coach Osborne came in leading the entire coaching staff and the football team. They had traveled together in buses. Coach spoke, along with two of his assistant coaches. I was blown away. I was already a proud Nebraska football fan, but those three men sounded more like pastors than coaches. The level of Christian integrity and maturity they expressed that day was incredible. No wonder they had been such an amazing influence on Brook as a young Christian. In that moment, I thought that if I had a son who wanted to play football, I would certainly want him to be here, under the influence of these men.

When the service was over, I rode with the other pallbearers to the graveside service. The cemetery was about ten miles from the civic center. When the lead limousine stopped at the gravesite, there were so many people coming that the line of cars stretched all the way back. There were still people who hadn't even gotten out of the parking lot yet. Now, that's the sign of a life that made a difference to a lot of people.

Another incredibly touching aspect was that as we drove to the cemetery, at all the houses in the town that we passed, people had come out and lined the road. Men stood at their mailboxes, holding their Nebraska hats over their hearts. We had the privilege of witnessing this moment of Americana that people rarely get to see—amidst this awful experience of recognizing a young life cut short. While football may have been the catalyst, that moment was actually about people coming together in an amazing display of community and unity.

The Song No One's Heard Me Sing

As we were finishing up the *Six Days on the Road* album, I made the decision to put "The Nebraska Song" on the project. This was during a short season in the reign of the CD when artists were placing "hidden tracks" on records. Sometimes, the track was literally hidden and the only way you knew it was there was to let the CD play to the end. When the listed songs had finished, that track would play. Another trick was to put silent tracks between the final song and the hidden one. So the CD player would read the track number, but there was no sound until the actual hidden track played.

We decided that, following the twelve songs on the record, we would place four-second blank tracks from numbers thirteen to seventeen, making "The Nebraska Song" track eighteen—Brook's football jersey number. It was the thirteenth song, but the eighteenth track on the CD. I had no plans to ever sing the song live. I wanted the one and only time I had sung it to be to Brook on the day that he died. But I also wanted to share the song on our album with our fans and all the good folks in Nebraska who love football and loved Brook.

A short while after "Six Days" came out in April of 1997, Brook's mom called me. She said that Coach Osborne was leading an effort to establish a scholarship to Nebraska in her son's name. She asked if we would do a benefit concert at the university arena and said the school would match the money raised. Later, Coach also called me to discuss the details. Of course, we were 110 percent on board to do anything to honor Brook's memory and legacy. Tickets for the event sold out quickly.

On the day of the benefit concert, following our sound-check, Mrs. Berringer came to our dressing room. She politely asked, "Mark, are you going to sing 'The Nebraska Song' tonight?"

I did my best to explain my feelings to her. "Ma'am, the only person who ever heard me sing the song in person was your son. So I planned on never singing it live again. I decided the best way to share it with everyone was to just put it on our new album."

She smiled and responded, "I understand, Mark, but I think Brook would want everyone to hear the song tonight. I think that, of all places, this would be appropriate. Would you please consider just doing it this one time?"

I promised her I would think about it. But in my heart, I decided I couldn't.

When we went out and started the show, the crowd was incredible. And, of course, everyone knew the story of why we were there and the purpose—another amazing celebration of Brook's life. I will never know if it was just an emotional response or what, but in that moment, I began to feel I was supposed to do the song.

At what I felt to be the right spot in the show, I did my best to share the story with the audience. I was very emotional, having to fight back tears the entire time. When I grabbed an acoustic guitar and started playing the song, from the very first word of the first verse, all twenty thousand people began to sing along with me at the top of their lungs. They were far louder than my vocal coming through the sound system. They sang *every* word with me.

Coach Osborne was sitting on the front row where I could see him in the spillover from the spotlights on the stage. While he had done an amazing job of keeping his emotions in check during the funeral, on this night, hearing all those Nebraska fans singing about Brook wanting to play football for him, he broke. That amazingly strong man finally allowed the tears to fall.

When the song ended and everyone was standing and cheering, Coach came up on the stage and wrapped me in a huge bear hug. I knew, once again, that Mrs. Berringer was right. Doing the song here was the absolute right thing to do. And I could just see Brook grinning ear to ear.

Another incredible story connected to that song was, somehow on a certain day, every single radio station in Nebraska had coordinated to play "The Nebraska Song" at the same time. No matter where you were in the state, if you had a radio station on, you heard it. No matter where you were on the dial, there it was—everywhere. What an amazing idea. Whoever ran point on that endeavor did a superb job getting everyone to agree to play the song, regardless of genre or format, to honor Brook and their beloved Nebraska football.

Over the years, to this day, when we play anywhere in Nebraska, they won't allow us to leave until we play the song. And they all know it's coming, right after "Some Girls Do." I go off stage and then come back with a guitar and sing "The Nebraska Song."

But the coolest part is I still don't think anyone has ever heard me sing the song live other than Brook. Because at *every* show, the audience sings much louder than I do. And I wouldn't have it any other way.

Duncan

DUNCAN CAME to us after playing with Glenn Frey, one of the founding members of the Eagles, The Amazing Rhythm Aces, and the Muscle Shoals Rhythm Section. But he was with us throughout our heyday, our prime years. Every night he hit the stage with us, I felt like we had one of the best guitar players in the world. Duncan was also a great singer. He sounded just like Don Henley, with a really cool texture in his voice that I'm sure was a part of Glenn hiring him.

On his first weekend out with us, we were all together in the back of the bus when Duncan looked at me and said, "I'm gonna produce the band's records from now on." I replied, "Just so you know, this is my band and I'm the producer. You will *never* produce the band. Know that going in right now." Duncan just shrugged and responded, "Okay. Well, I *had* to try." That's just Duncan. He would push on a door to see if it would open.

In my experience, pilots are very confident, sometimes to the point of being arrogant. Duncan had that air about him. But for my pilot, my doctor, my attorney, that is exactly the kind of man I want. I loved that about him. Did he try me at times? Absolutely, but it was worth it.

Duncan is a warrior. He can handle the pressure. I always knew, no matter the situation, he was that guy I wanted in the trenches, in the fox hole, with me. He's going to put his back up against yours and fight. You can depend on that. Every night when we walked out onstage, Duncan was going to bring it.

In all the bands he had been in before, he was what we call in the music business a stand-and-burn player, meaning you're so good that you don't have to do anything else. He was that guy with Frey, with the Aces, and at Shoals, of course. But when he came into the band, we required some flash. Even though it wasn't in his wheelhouse to have that kind of animation onstage, he was able to literally flip a switch and become an entertainer too. He can rock. He did what the job called for. He got it and understood, *Okay, this is what I need to be in this band.* He's a competitor like me. From the very first day he was in the band, he was aggressive.

On the day we were playing a sold-out show at the Delta Center in Salt Lake City in front of eighteen thousand people, Duncan and Hobie had gotten into a debate about something. The two of them were still a little on edge with each other at showtime. Onstage, when Duncan stepped up to play a solo on "Six Days on the Road," I went over and stood by Hobie. While Duncan was absolutely shredding and wowing the crowd, Hobie looked at me, smiled, and said, "That's why we put up with him!"

One time when we were reminiscing about his glory days of playing, he gave us a very humbling compliment: "I had been in these stand-and-burn bands where everyone is in one spot on the stage and plays incredible. But when I came into this band, I saw how relevant you are and how the show affected the audience in such a great way. I wanted to be a part of that."

CHAPTER NINE

Going Back to Indiana

*"When you step on the court,
you play to win."*

—LARRY BIRD

IN ALL OUR YEARS playing as a band, not only have we never canceled a show, but we have always started right on time, with only one exception. The night of May 25, 1987—game five of the NBA playoffs, the Boston Celtics against the Detroit Pistons.

When we were on the road, we would have someone record the Celtics games for us to watch later. Sometimes we even got a local sports bar to record a game on their VHS player. After the show, we would get the tape and watch the game on our bus. We made sure no one told us the final score. We wanted to experience the game without knowing the result.

But for that particular game, it was so amazing and so close that I held our start time off for thirty minutes, so I could watch the action in real time. When we went onstage, I confessed to the crowd and apologized. But our fans totally understood and we went on to have a great night.

What sealed my decision that night to delay the show and keep watching the game was when Larry Bird stole the ball and passed it to Dennis Johnson to score with one second left on the clock. Boston for the win, courtesy of Mr. Bird's miraculous save—one of the most revered plays in pro basketball history. I'm confident I have made it clear just how passionate I am about basketball, but this chapter will certainly drive that point home to a new level.

One really interesting thing I have learned throughout my career is that a lot of pro athletes secretly want to be music artists and many music artists want to be pro athletes. It's some kind of crazy "grass is greener" thing. I've had the great privilege during these four decades to become friends with many of my favorite pro athletes. Some of my closest in that group are (in alphabetical order to avoid any fights from breaking out): Troy Aikman, Damon Bailey, Charles Barkley, John Daly, Jim Farmer, Ryan Klesko, John Kruk, Kyle Macy, Greg Maddux, Karl Malone, Eric Montross, Craig (Noodles) Neal, Clifford Ray, Keith Smart, John Stockton, Rick Sutcliffe, Kurt Warner, Mitch Williams, and Ben Zobrist.

One thing all these guys have in common—whether pro football, baseball, basketball, or golf—is they're just regular guys who are some of the best athletes in the world, and you'd never know it if you were hanging out with them. But when you're as amazing as they are, you don't have to blow your own horn about your accomplishments. Your career highlights speak for themselves.

That said—sorry, gentlemen—but my coolest story is when I met my all-time sports hero, Larry Bird.

If there's one thing that is widely known about Larry off the court, it's that he's an introvert. Even more so than I am. Yet, I get him, because there are parts of our personalities that are exactly the same. We would each prefer to just be a ghost in the corner in any social setting.

In the mid-nineties, we were booked to play the Hulman Center at Indiana State University in Terra Haute, where Larry played college basketball. A native of Indiana, Larry owned a hotel there named Boston Connection, which was, of course, because he played for the Celtics. With the date coming up, I told our road manager I wanted us to stay at Larry's hotel.

When we arrived, I got off the bus and saw a guy by the hotel entrance. *Oh my gosh, that's Larry Bird!* But as I got closer, while I could tell it wasn't him, it was definitely someone with an amazing resemblance to my basketball hero. When the man saw us coming, he broke away from his conversation and headed toward us. He smiled and reached out his hand to me. "Hey, my name is Mark Bird. I manage the hotel. It's an honor to have you guys stay here." I was trying to figure out how to ask him, "So, uh … are you …" He smiled and said, "Yeah, I'm Larry's brother."

After talking for a while, we invited Mark to our show. Later that night, when we returned to the hotel, he hung out with us in the restaurant. During the conversation, I brought up that I was from Florida and that I have a place in Naples. Mark said, "That's where Larry lives in the off-season. I know he's a big Sawyer Brown fan. You ought to call him sometime when you're down there. Let me give you his number."

So now, here I am with my hero's phone number. But I'm just not *that* guy. I am not about to call Larry Bird and say, "Hey, I got your number from your brother. Can we meet?" Not gonna do it.

But the next time we were in Naples, the landline phone rang, I heard Lisa answer, then say, "Yeah, he's here. Hang on."

Holding the receiver, she said, "Hey, Mark. It's Larry Bird." (Now, let's get something clear here. My wife doesn't necessarily keep up with the who's who. Elvis could have come to our front door and she probably would have asked him to take his shoes off first.)

My first thought was, *This is Frank. He's totally messing with me.* I took the phone from Lisa and said, "Yeah, wha-duh-ya-want?" Like really sarcastic. When I heard, "Uh, hey, Mark, this is Larry Bird," I immediately knew that the voice on the phone was *not* my brother or anyone else I knew, having watched plenty of interviews over the years. This was actually *the* Larry Bird!

Immediately changing my tone, I perked up. "Oh man. Hey, Larry, how's it going?" He said, "I wanted to see if you'd like to go golfing tomorrow." Now in full-on disbelief, I answered, "Sure." He said, "Great. I'll pick you up at ten in the morning."

At 9:59 a.m., I was waiting outside when Larry pulled up and got out. After we made our introductions, he grabbed my clubs, put them in his trunk, and off we went to the course, which was about twenty minutes away.

I sat there, respectfully waiting for him to open up the conversation. But Larry drove in total silence, staring straight ahead. He didn't say a word. Nothing. (Did I mention he's an introvert?) But, like I said, being one, too, I wasn't that unnerved by the quiet. And then, believe it or not, Larry had the radio on, and what song did the deejay play just a few minutes into our drive, as if on cue? "Thank God for You." Larry looked over at me, kind of half-smiled, and just shook his head like, *Can you believe that? What are the odds?* But he still didn't say a word and neither did I.

When we arrived at the golf course, I met the two guys we would be playing. I quickly realized that they were obvious extroverts, or they were really nervous about playing with Larry, or both, because they talked nonstop. Even when we broke for lunch and they pounded him with questions, Larry said very little. A few times he answered, but most of the time he didn't. But that didn't stop these guys.

Because I didn't feel the need to chime in and change the dynamic, I didn't say much either. But when "Bert and Ernie" found out that I was a country singer, they started calling me "Ferlin Husky," a legendary artist from the 1950s. I have to assume he was the only name they knew.

In eighteen holes of golf, there was zero chit-chat with Larry. Occasionally, because he had played the course a lot, he would tell me what was coming up or give me some course navigation, like "Now, Mark, there's a bunker up here on the left" or "You got water to the right that you want to stay away from."

But, because Larry wasn't talking, I finally made the assumption that the problem must be me. He must have felt like his brother, Mark, had set him up and he wasn't having a good time. Like, "Hey, do me a favor, bro, and go play golf with this guy. I like his band." Maybe he was just doing a favor for his brother? Maybe he was miserable?

When we finished the game, we drove the entire way back in silence. Not a word. And, no, there was no Sawyer Brown song on the radio for the return trip. But there was a surprise coming. When we got out of the car to get my clubs, Larry said, "Hey, man, that was fun. You want to go again tomorrow?" *Say what?!* "Sure, Larry." He and I went golfing *five days in a row.*

One of those days after we finished playing, he asked, "Hey, would you want to go to dinner? You and your wife with me and my wife?" Of course, I agreed. Larry talked a little bit, but his wife is more outgoing, so she and Lisa kept the conversation flowing. One thing that Larry's wife divulged to Lisa—that Larry would *never* admit—was that he was a big fan of the band. Evidently, his favorite song of ours is "The Race Is On." His wife said when the video came out, he asked her to record it on CMT, so he could watch it whenever he wanted.

On one of the days, Larry had told me he had to take the next day off to take care of something. But later that night around 10:00, he called. "Hey, is there any way you could play tomorrow? I have to do a favor for these two guys from Indiana. I really don't want to have to talk to them. Could you come play and ride in my cart?"

I hung up the phone, thinking, *I guess this week I'm Larry Bird's go-to guy, because I won't talk on the drive or the course. I don't need to have a conversation. We can just hang. I guess he likes that.*

Over time, we got to know each other well and became friends. Our backgrounds are a lot alike. How we grew up, and how our work ethic got us both where we ended up. We had a lot in common, but the biggest connection was my love for basketball and his love for music.

The thing about hanging out with Larry in public is, while I can be fairly inconspicuous, he's six feet ten and no one on the planet looks like him! He is so easily recognizable. To merge his fame with his personality, one decision he made to create boundaries is that he will sign an autograph or take a picture with a kid or an older person, but not anyone else. He's had to set some kind of guidelines in public, and he's really good at it. With that level of public recognition, it's the only way to survive and have any sort of normal life.

One of the things I learned early on in being around

celebrities of any kind is you have to get good at reading the room and allow things to be on their terms. And that's okay. For example, Larry is the most comfortable around a team, whether on the court or a golfing group of a dozen guys. I have to say that hanging out with him in Boston is seeing life on an entirely different level. He is absolutely revered up there, to the point that people didn't bother him at all, much less ask for an autograph. But I can tell you for sure, Larry Bird is the *king* of Boston.

For the most part, for me, the old saying "Never meet your heroes, because you will likely be disappointed" has not held true. Yet another aspect of life I am grateful for.

Fast-Break with the Fury

In the fall of 1996, my worlds collided when something happened I had always dreamed about but assumed my day had passed. Many times I have publicly stated that I consider myself a better basketball player than a singer or artist. I always stayed in shape and in playing form. On days off from the road, I'd often go to one of the local universities, Belmont or David Lipscomb, and take part in pickup games against the players on their teams. Then whenever those guys put together a game, they would often call me too.

Our manager TK had a cousin named John Kimbrell. Because of his size and ability on the court, they called him Big John. In 1986 at Lipscomb, John led the team to their first-ever number one ranking. Lipscomb went on to capture the national championship with John named the MVP, beating out Dennis Rodman and Scottie Pippin. He was also Lipscomb's first

All-American. In 1987, John was inducted into the Tennessee Sports Hall of Fame.

Although he was drafted by the Milwaukee Bucks, John ended up signing a deal to play ball in Europe. Fast-forward to a few years later, he left the pros to teach and coach. So, anytime I was asked to put together a team for a benefit game, I always invited John to play. He and I connected really well as point guard and center. Some of my other regulars I played with were Damon Bailey, Jim Farmer, John Kruk, Kyle Macy, and Rick Sutcliffe. Over the years, we raised a lot of money for school sports programs in Tennessee and other great causes.

One day, John called me. "Hey, Mark, I want to give the NBA another shot. The Fort Wayne Fury is in the CBA, so I want to go up to Indiana for their open tryouts."

Now, allow me to explain. Borrowing from baseball terms, the Continental Basketball League—CBA—was essentially the minor leagues for the NBA. One path to the pros would be to make it onto a CBA team, get yourself in strong playing form, and then hopefully become a transient player that goes back and forth onto an NBA team. Okay, back to John's call to me ...

"The Fury's tryout is in Fort Wayne, a six-hour drive. Mark, would you go up with me to play and get me the ball?"

In open tryouts like that, no one *passes* the ball; they shoot. Everybody's wanting to show off what they can do with what little time they have to impress the coaches. So if you're a center, it's going to be tough for you to get the ball, because the guards are all wanting to show their stuff. I was confident enough in my ability to know I could keep up with those guys. I also knew I could get John the ball. So although I was just a little north of the age range, I agreed to go and we started working out together more regularly to get him ready for his big day.

At the tryout, John made certain he and I got on the same team. Being in such a competitive environment getting to make a go at my passion, I felt like I was having some kind of out-of-body experience. I played better than I had *ever* played, against the best competition I had ever faced in my life. As promised, I got John the ball a lot. But I also hit a decent number of my own shots. By the end of the tryout, our team won the tournament. In fact, I actually hit the three-pointer to win the game for us. (You're welcome, John.)

In the tryouts, John was amazing. So I had no question he was going to make the team.

I was standing courtside, toweling off sweat and catching my breath, watching a coach talk to John, when a lady came over to me. She started asking for a lot of personal information, filling out a form on a clipboard. When she got to my social security number, I said, "Whoa, wait … now *what* is this for?"

She paused, a little surprised at my question. "Well, you made the team." (How many times have I told you I did not see something coming? Okay, add another one. A major one!)

As I was processing what she told me, a distinguished-looking man in a tailored suit walked up. He smiled and asked, "Hey, can we talk a minute?"

"Uh, sure."

"I'm Jay Fry, the owner of the Fury. Mark, I know who you are. I know who Sawyer Brown is, so I recognized you. Our coach has *no* idea what you do, but he *loves* you as a basketball player. So, is there *any* possible way you could play for us?"

Not believing the answer I had to give, I stated, "No, I don't think so."

Jay continued, "Man, it would be the coolest thing if we

could figure out a way to make this work."

Not sure what he actually meant by "make this work," I asked, "Well, what would that look like ... exactly?"

Jay answered, "We have a mandatory camp for two weeks in October to learn the system—offense and defense. After that, we could treat you like we do our NBA players—a transient that comes and goes on the games where you're available. Once you know our system, we would just take whatever you could give us."

Now, even though the year before, we had cut back from 250 shows to about 175, we were still very busy on the road, and by this time, I had a daughter and a son. Still, freaking out that this could even be a possibility, I asked the owner to give me a few minutes to make a call.

I went straight to phone Lisa. "Hey, I ... uh ... I made the team."

"What?! Are you kidding me?!"

After I told her the whole story and the conversation with the owner, Lisa had the greatest attitude. She immediately said, "Well, you *absolutely* have to do this!" So, at thirty-nine years old with no sports agent, I signed a pro contract to play basketball.

I know there have been some pro athletes go into country music when they retire, but I'm fairly confident I'm the only country artist to ever navigate both at the same time.

At the two-week training camp in October, the team worked out five days and then had the weekend off before the second week. Fortunately, our schedule allowed me to be at the camp. But I was also able to get to our shows on Friday and Saturday with no problem and then get back to start again on Monday.

A really beautiful part of the story for me was that our coach, Gerald Oliver, never had any idea who I was. And he didn't care.

He just saw me as another player on his team. Not the lead singer for Sawyer Brown who was also playing ball for him as a novelty. Obviously, the marketing angle for the owner was great, but none of that mattered to Coach Oliver. He just wanted to win games. And that's all I wanted too.

But here's a really crazy turn of events—John Kimbrell and I weren't teammates for long. He got traded, sent to Connecticut, while I stayed in Indiana.

Damon Bailey and Keith Smart were also on the team. So these two Indiana basketball legends became great friends of mine. Another obvious aspect of this adventure was that all these guys had the ability to go to the NBA. I knew I only had the skills to get to the Fury. So the entire time I played, I just looked at it as an opportunity to live out my dream and have a blast. I never felt any kind of pressure to get to the next level like the rest of the guys. Because of that fact, I actually played really well.

I wanted to be like any other player there, with no special treatment. Some of the team knew who I was and some never did. But none of them ever questioned me, as in "Who's this guy and why is he here?" That was such a cool feeling that I was accepted as a basketball player at that level with such amazing players. Because I was so dialed in when I was there, I learned so much more about basketball than I had ever known before.

Each game was scheduled down to the minute as far as who played when. The coach would say, "Mark, at ten minutes, you go in and replace so-and-so and give him a five-minute break." After you were given your game assignment, you didn't ask the coach; you just got up and checked in at your slot.

As I mentioned earlier, at this time, we had a private jet and two tour buses to allow the band to do more shows. So transportation for me to get to games quickly was not an issue. Whenever the schedule worked with the band, I brought one of my buses, because the ones the CBA provided weren't great. When I was able to bring both of them, the guys loved it, because they could split up, lay down in the bunks, or hang in the lounge, rather than just sit in a seat on long rides.

At one particular game, we were told that Coach Oliver's wife had gotten really sick and she needed to be taken somewhere specific for medical care. I went straight to Jay, the owner, and told them I would make arrangements to fly them both wherever they needed to be taken. I was grateful in moments like that to be able to use my resources to help people I cared about.

I played with the Fury for two seasons. With our heavy touring schedule and the age of my kids, to no surprise, the logistics just got too hard. Still, I am so grateful for that time with the coaches and players and the incredible comradery we formed, a bond that has lasted for many years. I got to live out my original dream, the one I had long before music ever entered the picture, with men who gave me an incredible experience and became great friends.

And I'll say this once again—being in a band is just like being on a team.

The Sawyer Brown All-Stars

Up through the age of fifty, I put together and played on the Sawyer Brown All-Star Basketball Team. Every year, we would go play various college teams for their exhibition games. We won some but lost a lot because I was always just throwing a team together for each game we scheduled. We never had formal practices. But I had access to all these really good players going against very organized college teams. Usually by the end of the game, they would fast-break us, because they saw we were starting to run out of gas.

One time, we were playing Florida Southern—a really high-powered team that year, and one of the highest scoring teams in Division II in the nation. Toward the end of the game, they were 125 to our 107, clearly beating us. When one of our guys was at the free-throw line, a young guard who had played really tough the entire game, said to me, "Hey, I saw in the program that you played at UCF." I said, "Yeah, I did." He continued, "So, when was that?" I just started laughing and answered, "Man, it was a long, long time ago." The kid pressed me, "No, really, *when*?" I said, "Well, I'm fifty years old, so ..."

He looked at me, looked up at the scoreboard, then back at me. "Well then, we're really not doing *that* good, now are we?"

Suddenly, the eighteen-point lead had a very different perspective to that young college basketball point guard. Just as the free throw ended, he said, "Man, I am *tired* of chasing you all over the court."

I laughed. Grateful I could still give this kid a decent run for his money.

Ain't That Always the Way

ONE NIGHT, our booking agent, Curt, had booked us to play a show at the Las Vegas Hilton. When we arrived at the venue, the building manager came up to me and said, "Mr. Miller, we wanted to let you know we'll accommodate whatever time you want to put on the suit. We've got everything ready for you."

I had no idea what he meant and didn't know how to respond, so I just told the guy, "Okay, thanks." Then I forgot about it.

A while later, he came back to find me. Again, he said, "Mr. Miller, we have the suit ready. If you could let us know when you want to put it on, we can get your photo."

Now very puzzled, I said, "Hey, I really don't know what you're talking about. Can you explain what you're asking?"

The manager looked confused, then answered, "Well, it's in your contract for tonight. Your agent, Curt Motley, said you would only do the show if you could put on one of Elvis's jumpsuits and have your picture made in it."

He pulled out the contract and, sure enough, right there in legal black-and-white, Curt had sold them on the ridiculous idea that the only way that I would perform was if I could try on one of Elvis's jumpsuits. All as an elaborate prank that he had waited months to hatch.

Here's the backstory ... The Hilton is the iconic hotel where, from 1969 to 1976, Elvis performed 837 consecutive sold-out shows (two a night) in front of a total of 2.5 million people. The hotel had partnered with Graceland to house an exhibition of The King's memorabilia. One of the highlights of the presentation was a huge display of his legendary one-piece jumpsuits. Curt knew that bit of trivia and decided to use it to his advantage—and likely just to see if they would even agree to it. (Now you see why I didn't believe James Brown had called us to play his birthday party?)

But like they say in those bad infomercials: but wait, there's more.

We were booked to play for a private event at Opryland, a theme park in Nashville at the time. Hometown shows are rare, so it's nice to be able to leave that morning, play a show, and sleep in your own bed that night. As we were getting ready to go on, I noticed that both TK and Curt had shown up. That was a bit unusual, even for us playing in town. I should have been suspicious that something was up, but I dismissed the fact that they were there.

We hit the stage hard and I was dancing like I always do. As I looked past the lights into the crowd, the first thing I realized was they were all men. *And* they weren't reacting to the songs at all. The first time I stopped to talk between songs, they showed no expression. No response. No laughing. Dead.

Somewhere around the fourth song, I glanced over at TK and Curt who were doubled over laughing, having a great time. Immediately, I started trying to figure out the joke. Finally, Curt cupped his hands over his mouth and yelled, "They're all from South America! None of these guys speak English! And they don't know who Sawyer Brown is!"

I was out there working my tail off to win over a crowd that had no idea who we were or what I was saying. Afterward they told me that the sponsor who bought the show just wanted a "popular American band" to play for them. Of course, TK and Curt didn't want me to know that intel beforehand so they could have a front-row seat to the train wreck!

CHAPTER TEN

Tryin' to Find a Way to Make It Last

*I talked to an old man and
he'd been down on his knees
Said he learned who to turn to
and where it all leads*

—**FROM THE SONG** "Tryin' to Find (A Way to Make It Last)"

EVERY ARTIST in any music genre aspires to get to the arena level. In the US, performing where all the pro basketball teams play is the pinnacle. While these certainly are not the best venues for sound, it's the only way to get fifteen to twenty thousand–plus people in the same room, singing the same song together. By the mid-nineties, we had arrived in that space.

What took years can appear to happen overnight to the public when you suddenly find yourself on everyone's radar. The whole experience was very surreal to us, because we still considered ourselves a garage band—guys who are most comfortable in the blue-collar grassroots zone. To this day, we are still amazed that people just keep showing up.

By this point in our career, we were touring with a high level of production. We were now up to four buses, several semi-trucks loaded with crazy-expensive gear, and upwards of forty people on the road. This created a well-oiled machine where all of the songs had to be pre-planned because of the level of automation onstage. While the music was still just us, there were now a lot of visual elements involved in the show. We had to consider things like timing and safety while performing. Sure, a lot of this was fun, but I had grown frustrated with the limitations put on what I wanted to be able to do on any given night. The toys impacted the level of personal touch in creating a different show every night.

Before, I had been free to direct the evening, like a conductor of a symphony—or the ringmaster of a circus is probably a better metaphor. I wanted to go back to the days of allowing the fans to take the show wherever they wanted. By watching and reading them, we were able to add, cut, or change the order on the fly. During our early years, the guys had always done such an awesome job of following my lead that we were able to flow with the energy of the crowd. That dynamic had really established our brand and connection with our fans. And I wanted that back.

Doing the show with conveyor belts, a slide, catapult, lifts, backlighting, and an ominous show opening was really cool in one sense, but I finally told everyone I couldn't handle being on autopilot. I also no longer wanted to be held captive to a set list. Hearing my concerns, Frank decided to do a survey of the fans to ask what *they* enjoyed most during an evening with Sawyer Brown. His results were really interesting, but not that surprising. One thing was very clear: people didn't care about the production.

There were two consistent answers. Number one, they "love that the band sounds like the records." And number two, they "love to watch Mark dance." Those were the two key reasons people bought tickets to see us. After gathering this new intel, Frank told us, "Well, boys, that settles it. All the stuff's coming home. It's official. You're a garage band."

So, as soon as possible, we got rid of the bells and whistles, culling everything down to the necessities for a Sawyer Brown show. We went back to a drum riser, a good light show, and a great sound system. That's it. The toys worked for a time and are great for other artists, but we had to get back to basics. Our focus returned to the original mission—to absolutely *bring it* every single night.

My personal philosophy as a front man has always been if you've never bought a ticket to one of our shows, then you can't know what we should do for the fans. Over the years when I've had various music execs try to tell me what people want, I've asked, "Have you ever bought a ticket to one of our shows?" When they answer no, I politely let them know they don't get a say.

I pride myself on the fact that I have always kept my finger on the pulse of what's going on out in the crowd. I'm going to let the audience lead me to what happens next in the show. When we lock in with them, that dynamic is pure magic. And that experience is never going to repeat, because that *exact* group of people will never be in front of us again. For that reason, *every* night is special.

Because we have fans who have seen us over a thousand times, they obviously know every little detail of our show. If something new happens one night, rarely is that planned. If the spontaneous works, it can stay. To the contrary, there have been things I have come up with that I thought for sure were going to be so funny, or powerful, or whatever. In my mind, the idea was amazing. But in reality, in front of a crowd, it created crickets. I have even started laughing at myself onstage when I realized something didn't work. That's why the flexibility is so important. Aside from those years with huge production, we have not had a set list onstage. I go with the crowd, and the guys go with me.

In all the years of being on the road, I never went to other artists' shows. There was rarely an opportunity. But one day, Frank told me he was taking me to see The Bee Gees. No discussion. On that particular tour, they had the Tower of Power horns and more production than most shows were taking out at that time. I have to confess, the experience was magnificent. But the most incredible part for me was when everyone left the stage, except the three brothers, Barry, Robin, and Maurice Gibb. For about half an hour, with Barry playing acoustic guitar, they sang in their trademark harmony—so simple, but showcasing their incredible talent. That night, I heard something that cannot be replicated or replaced. Just authentic God-given voices. Further evidence to me that you don't need all the tricks when you have talent.

For forty years, I have always wanted to be certain that I connect with the people in the crowd every single night. No exceptions. Thank God, early on I learned my lesson on that principle. We were booked to play at a casino in Nevada. The shows there can be at crazy hours because so many gambling venues are open all night. Our last set was at 2:00 a.m. (Yes, I said a.m.) When we were about to go on, I looked out to see only eight people in the audience. (If you're able to easily do a head count, you know it's a small crowd.) So I made a decision I never had before—I just went out and got through the show. I did what they call in the entertainment industry "phoning it in." I sang the songs with no real effort. Fulfilled the contract. That's it.

The next day, little did I know that a music critic was one of those eight people. He published an article with this punchline: "This band has incredible potential. But it didn't show onstage last night."

When I read those words, I knew the guy had simply written the truth. I wasn't mad at him. I was furious with myself. Whether 2:00 in the morning, 2:00 in the afternoon, or 9:00 at night, it doesn't matter. Whether eight people or eighty thousand people, you go out there and leave it all on the stage like it's going to be your last show—ever. So I called the guy. I'm sure he was ready for me to scream at him, but I simply said, "Hey, thank you for your honest review. You were right. But I just want you to know that if you ever decide to come see us again, you will never see *that* again." From then on, I have never forgotten the commitment I made to that music critic.

And as if I needed one more reason never to cheat an audience out of our best show, here it is . . .

In the previous chapter, I told you about my friendship with Larry Bird. Years after he and I had become friends, we had ended a day of golf with ten other guys. Larry was busy tallying and comparing the scores. (It's important to note here that he has an incredible memory for details.) Meanwhile, one of the men asked me, "Hey, Mark, have you ever played Reno?" I thought for a second and then answered, "Reno ... No, I don't think so." Larry never looked up from the scores, he just said, "Yeah, you played Harrah's in Reno. Like June or July in 1984. And you got a terrible review the next day."

Suddenly, the memory of *that* night, at least a decade before, came rushing back to me. I said, "Oh, yeah, it was the final show of the night at like two o'clock in the morning. There were only eight people in the audience."

Larry said, "Yeah, my wife and I were *two* of the eight."

Then it hit me. The one night I had decided, *This show at this time with this crowd isn't worth the effort,* my all-time sports hero had been there! He had won the championship that year.

Like I said, I had already allowed that show and the reviewer's painful truth to impact my attitude going forward, but then, after finding out Larry had also been there, I added another layer to my hard-earned lesson: You never know *who* is going to be there on *any* night, so you better bring it!

Reflecting back today, after six thousand–plus shows, trust me, you can put it on automatic pilot if you want. There are certainly many tough, sick, exhausted, and lonely days when the temptation is there. But the night won't be special and *no one* will have any fun. What I absolutely love is that, for many years now, our fans will not let us put the show on cruise control. That's one of the many reasons I have worked so hard to stay in shape, because I want to be the same guy at sixty-five that they saw at twenty-five.

Go, Tell It from the Fourth Row

In 1997, we recorded our first Christmas album. Every year, artists release "holiday albums" that are mostly traditional standards, which is fine. But the direction we chose was to make this record our first faith-based project. For me personally, my faith has always been best expressed in how we lead our lives and treat people, and the message of the songs we record. But the unique aspect of our Christmas project was that the majority of the songs were originals that we wrote. There were only two classic covers.

Most artists do the opposite—a song or two as originals, but they rely on the standards. We wanted to be clear that the songs were about Christ. There's nothing wrong with a winter wonderland or reindeer, but for us, our album needed to be Jesus-focused, about the celebration of His birthday and Him being our Lord and Savior.

To support the record, we planned a Christmas tour. Because of the focus everyone has around the holidays, people tend to only want to hear Christmas songs between Thanksgiving and the big day. Then by New Year's, everything goes back to normal. So we booked a tour to play eighteen cities in those three weeks. While getting the new show ready, we decided to play through the entire album and then do a few of our hits. After all, it's a Christmas tour from a Christmas record during the Christmas season, right?

The first night was at a theater in Wheeling, West Virginia. The songs were going well and the crowd was very polite, appearing to enjoy our new Christmas music. But, of course, it wasn't at all the usual vibe of us coming out of the gate and burnin' the barn down. About three songs in, this young country boy on the fourth row evidently "had all he could stands, he couldn't stands no more." He stood up and yelled out, "What are y'all doin'?! I didn't come to hear this s***! I want to hear 'Six Days on the Road' and 'Some Girls Do'!" Then he just stood there with a troubled look on his face and his arms out in frustration, waiting for a response. Like, if something doesn't change fast, I'm headin' for the truck!

Now, I know there are artists who would have been offended by that outburst or had security escort the guy out. But remember my philosophy: the show belongs to the audience, not to us. When we all busted out laughing, the crowd started laughing too. You know the unspoken rule: when one person speaks up, there are likely nine others who wanted to. So, I'm sure there were people whispering, "Thanks, cowboy, because we were all thinkin' it!"

Still smiling, I looked at him and said, "Buddy, I'm gonna make a deal with you. Let us play a few more of these Christmas songs and then I promise we'll get to the ones you came to hear, okay?" He nodded in agreement and sat back down, willing to give us another chance. We went back to the Christmas set but made an immediate adjustment to get to the hits sooner than planned.

As the tour went on, we realized that, once again, no matter what month our fans come to see us, while they were good with a few Christmas songs, they expected to hear the hits. By that last week, I started coming out onstage and saying, "Hey, our present to you is we're not going to just play our Christmas songs tonight." We started with our usual high-energy openers, then did several of the Christmas songs, transitioned in and out with a couple of the ballads, then took the horse to the barn full speed the way we always have.

Since then, if we do a show around the holidays, we play "Hallelujah, He is Born" and "Glory to the King," because those rock like people are accustomed to us doing. I'm grateful those original Christmas songs have stood the test of time. Mark Hall (from the band Casting Crowns) and his wife, Melanie, say they listen to our Christmas album all year long. I love that the record helps people celebrate the reason for the season. That was our goal.

But as strange as it may seem, that young cowboy's gut-level honesty taught us a valuable lesson about what our fans have come to expect from us.

New Millennium Milestones

Our sixteenth album was released in 1999. Hobie and I had written the title cut "Drive Me Wild" with Mike Lawler. When we recorded the track, with Mac McAnally and me producing, everyone was pleased with how it came out. But as I was driving around listening to the rough mix in my car, I started singing a new section at the end of the chorus. I called everyone and said, "Hey, I don't think we're through with the song." In all my years of writing and recording, I had never done that before. Yet, on this song, I clearly heard more.

But here was the challenge: we had finished recording the entire original version of the song. To recut would be costly and time-consuming. This was in the day when digital editing on a computer had been introduced to the recording industry, but I had not yet used the technology. Mike, our cowriter, was also a music programmer. So at his suggestion, we went in and recorded only the new section of the song. Mike then edited it into the master. Honestly, I was thinking to myself, *I'll go along with this, but it's never going to work.* When I heard the final version, it was seamless, and I was sold. Realizing the possibilities blew my mind.

Even though I knew how the recording world was changing, I still preferred the analog tape sound, especially for vocals. For a long time, even though we were recording digitally, I would still run my vocal across the tape. There's just a different sound with analog, warmer and more natural.

Once the new version of "Drive Me Wild" was done, I thought there was no way it actually had a chance. Once again, I had pushed the limits of country. Here was another song I had produced that was just way too far outside the box. When I turned the project in to Mike Curb, we hadn't decided on the title of the record yet, so I placed that song last in the album sequence.

The next day, Mike called. "Mark, you are brilliant. Absolutely brilliant." Not completely sure what he meant, I responded, "Thanks. So, you like the album?" He continued, "You put the smash last! You made us all wait until we got to the final song. And then we hear the hit!"

I just laughed and, tongue-in-cheek, said, "Yeah, that's *exactly* what I intended to do, Mike. I'm really sorry I made you wait through the other songs." That goes back to something I said earlier—when I write, I don't have any idea if something is a hit or not. "Some Girls Do"? Yes. Everything else, including "Drive Me Wild"? No. I did not have a clue.

For the video, we went to LA to shoot with Mike Solomon again. As always, we had a blast. The main shots were a major eighties vibe. Then we dressed like The Beatles in one scene, The Beach Boys in the next, and finally, The Jackson Five, toward the end. This song is a perfect example to show that you can listen to our music, but watching our videos is really the best way to understand who we are and what we do. (A first for me was that, even though I had been shaving my head for a while, I had always worn some kind of hat. But, for this video, no hat, bare head.)

After the video shoot, we had kept all three sets of those costumes. That Halloween, we were playing a show at a theater in Indiana. We decided it would be funny to wear the sixties Beatles outfits—wigs, suits, ties, and all. (Larry Bird was actually there that night, since he's from Indiana.) We told the promoter that in his introduction we wanted him to say that Sawyer Brown couldn't make it. In their place was a band called The Fabulous Four.

We walked out and started playing "I Saw Her Standing There." As we're into the song, I was looking at the audience and realizing they had no idea who we were. And they were *not* liking it. I could see some of them were starting to get angry. As soon as we finished the song, I called out, "Boys, go into 'Six Days on the Road'! And take those wigs off!" Our Halloween joke backfired on us. Talking about the crowd's reaction is funny now, but it wasn't then. Those good folks in Indiana didn't pay to see a Beatles cover band. But we still had to do the whole show in those outfits.

While "Drive Me Wild" went to number six, "I'm in Love With Her" peaked at forty-seven, likely because it was just such a sad song, far too sad for radio. "800 Pound Jesus" got to number forty, but was obviously just a stretch too far, even though it was such a quirky, cool song. After I first heard it, I called Paul Thorn, the songwriter, and asked him, "How do you come up with an idea like that?" He answered, "Well, my dad really did have a huge statue of Jesus right outside our house. So, it didn't take a whole lot of imagination."

"800 Pound Jesus" became an anthem to our fans. Even though some nights we don't have time to play it, we get requests for that song as much as any other. Once again, even though radio didn't play the song, it made an impact and became a fan favorite. That's why the ultimate measuring stick for us began to be more about our fans' reactions than radio.

When discussions began about our next album, Mike told me, "Mark, the live show is your thing, so let's cut a live album." He of all people knew our track record on the road, so he wanted to try and capture the energy of our show. It made sense to me.

But I knew we didn't have a live album in our record contract, only studio releases. That's a very different project. So I went to Mike to talk over how we could approach his idea. When he asked me his usual question of what I wanted, I knew. My own studio. I was ready to produce on my own—my own dime, my own schedule, and close to home. That created a trade-off between Mike and me: I'd turn in a live album in exchange for the budget to put in a studio on my property where future records could be cut.

Recording a live album can put a ton of pressure on an artist when one or two nights are chosen to set up and capture a performance. Honestly, because the focus becomes getting the right take on a song instead of entertaining the crowd, it's hard to not cheat the audience. While I wouldn't necessarily recommend this approach either, we decided to record the next twenty-two shows. Back at our office, we set up a whiteboard with a graph of each city and a list of the songs. But as we listened through each show, it became really difficult to choose one performance over another.

What became so funny was there would be a night where you thought, *Man, we killed it*. But then when we went back to listen, we realized we couldn't feel the energy, or there would be some other issue. So I began to pay attention to the consistency of a song, as in the tempo, feel, and crowd response. We ended up choosing from several different nights and crediting that city following the song title. The coolest was "All These Years," recorded from a night at the historic Ryman Auditorium in Nashville. Several songs came from the Delta Center in Salt Lake City, at a venue that was our first headline date and a really special place for us. So the live album ended up being from shows all over the country.

Curb released a live CD and also a DVD to listen to *or* watch our first full-length recorded concert. That album was a big seller for us, at a time in the music business when no one was doing live albums. Once again, Mike's gut was right. His idea worked. We released a cover of "Lookin' for Love" as a live single, but it didn't fly at radio. Still, another huge-selling record allowed us to keep winning at the game.

On 2002's *Can You Hear Me Now?* I had the privilege of working with Dave Loggins. (Yes, the same guy who stood up at the ACM's and yelled out, "I get it!" about our crazy outfits.) To this day, I still think the title cut is one of the best songs I ever produced. That album was really special for me in getting to work with Dave. We spent a lot of time together on the project, and I saw firsthand that he is truly a musical genius. He is simply brilliant and was really inspirational to me. There are three guys I've worked with that I feel are on that same level—Mac McAnally, Mike Lawler, and Dave.

Dave and I first got to know each other when he wrote "(This Thing Called) Wantin' and Havin' It All" for us. He pours everything into a song, all his energy, his whole heart and soul. When he pitched it to the label, he said, "Hey, I've written your boys a song. I'm gonna put it in Mark's mailbox. Then I'm going to have to go recover for a few days from writing it." We had no idea what he meant—yet.

When I got the message, I ran to the mailbox and got the CD out of the package, along with the handwritten lyric sheet. As I walked back to the house, I started looking at the *five* legal pages of words. I called Mac and said, "I just got the longest song I've ever seen. This thing must be like ten minutes." But when I got in the house and put it on, I realized why it had so many lines. It's a rapid-fire song that tells a story. That's why Dave told Curb he needed to go recover. (Sidebar: anytime we did a show that had sign language interpreters for the deaf on that song, it looked like something out of the Pentecostal church I grew up in, with hands flying everywhere.)

Like me, Dave is really competitive, so the thing I hated about this project was that it got no attention at radio. Two songs in the forties and one didn't even chart. With the fact that all of us felt like we had such a great record, the lack of airplay was really frustrating, simply because I wanted Dave's work to get the attention I felt like he deserved.

The New Guy

Previously, I told you that for those three years we had our jet, Duncan was also our pilot. He was so good that we were *never* concerned about our safety when he was in the cockpit. Over the years, he would tell us how he was being certified on different aircraft. And I noticed the planes kept getting bigger.

I'll never forget the day he told me he was going to get his certification to fly 737s. I had learned enough from him to understand that the process was very expensive and they don't just let anyone try their hand at that level of aircraft. So my response to his news was, "Okay, so once you get this certification, who's going to say, 'Hey, Duncan, want to take my 737 out for a spin?'"

What I soon found out was that he had made several buddies who flew for Southwest Airlines and they had told him the company was hiring new pilots. So, I was not that surprised when Duncan came to me and said, "Hey, Mark, I've been offered a job to fly 737s for Southwest. What do you think?"

When anyone who's been in our organization has come to me to discuss leaving for an opportunity that I thought was bigger than us, my response has always been, "You gotta take it. But if it doesn't work out, you can come back." Of course, this move was going to be different than most other positions, because we would have to get a new permanent guitar player. I knew how much Duncan loved playing. I knew how much he loved our band. But I also knew how much he loved to fly.

As we discussed his opportunity, I told him, "You know, if you get to do one thing in life that's always been your dream, then you're a blessed man. But if you get to do *two*, then, my friend, you are double blessed. So, I'll support whatever you want to do." One thing I knew for sure, if he left, we would have some big shoes to fill, both personally and professionally.

Duncan soon made the decision to take the offer at Southwest, but he graciously left his end date with the band open to give us time to find the right replacement. Now faced with this reality, I knew I didn't want to have an open audition, running through a cattle call of guitar players trying to impress us. I did *not* want that. So I started asking around to a small group of people I trusted. Because of what we had with Duncan, I wanted someone with the skill level of a studio player but also touring experience. And then, a huge dynamic was someone who would fit with a band of brothers who had been together forever. The "new guy" would be joining a family that had no friction. We all knew how to stay out of each other's space and be ourselves. Finding someone that would fit well inside our mix was going to be a massive challenge.

But then, some kind of strange musical miracle happened. I ended up asking five different people in the business from managers to friends, "Hey, you know a guitar player that might fit

THE BOYS AND ME

us?" Each one gave me the *exact same* answer: "Yeah, there's this guy named Shayne Hill." *Every* single one of them. I called Hobie and asked if he had ever heard of him. He hadn't but told me that two people had suggested him as well. I said, "Well, this is crazy, but everybody is bringing this guy up."

After talking more with those folks, it was obvious Shayne was a great guy. Everyone highly recommended him as a man of integrity. I also heard enough to know that his faith matched ours, which was really important. I got his number, called him, and explained our situation. Shayne responded, "Yeah, I'm interested. Let's talk."

When I invited him over to my house, one of the things I wanted to cover was that I had found out, like so many people in Nashville, he had come to town to try and make it as an artist. As a good-looking guy who sings great and was obviously an incredible player, that made sense. If he had his eyes on a solo career, I knew that becoming a band member wouldn't work. But it sounded like he was at the point where he was praying for God to show him a clear direction.

In the conversation, we were both able to be very honest. I told him that we were at the point where we had no idea where our next record would lead with the label and radio. I was clear that this album might be the end. We were at a place where I couldn't make any guarantees about our future. I wanted no misconceptions of where the band was. Shayne was working with artists like Rascal Flatts and gaining a high profile within the industry as a player, which is why five reputable people had recommended him to me. He deserved the truth, to make the best decision possible.

Shayne's answer was clear. He felt right about us and wanted to commit to the band, however long it lasted. But at the end of the conversation, he gave me what has to be my craziest small-world moment ever. Shayne said, "I want you to know that Bobby Randall actually brought me to town. He had seen me play in my family's band and invited me here. It's going to be a little weird for me to tell Bobby that I'm taking his old job." (Crazy, right? Bobby was actually responsible for providing us with our final guitar player, after being out of the band for a decade.)

Because we had released a live album/DVD, Shayne would be able to hear (and see) every song, exactly the way we perform them live, exactly what Duncan played and sang. For an audition, he and I went to my studio. The engineer pulled up each of the live tracks one at a time and muted the main guitar out of the song for Shayne to play the parts. He got out his guitar and we plugged him up through our speakers. As he began to work through the songs, I was amazed that he already knew them all and was able to play along perfectly from start to finish. I could quickly tell that Shayne was fierce. Energetic. As good as Duncan. I quickly thought, *This is our guy!*

Shayne later told me that his family's band had played some of our hits as covers in their shows. Regardless, he nailed every guitar part on the live album.

For years, one of the band's running jokes has been, "Mark, you know you can't get rid of any of us, because then you'll have to rehearse." Yeah, I hate it. Because the band is so good, whenever we want to put in a new song, everyone will learn their parts on their own, then we run it at soundcheck, and play it that night. From there, we just tweak it over the next several shows. Shayne definitely made this transition really easy for me.

For him to be a great guitar player and singer in replacing Duncan was a given. But I have to quickly add that Shayne is also an incredible person. At the point he joined the band, right before *Mission Temple Fireworks Stand,* he fit in so well with us, particularly at the place we were in our career. Also with him being ten years younger, that made for a lot of great generation-gap jokes. Especially when he would say, "Yeah, I don't know who that band is," or "I've never heard that song." We mess with him a lot, but that's also been so much fun for us all. Shayne is a bit more traditional in his musical background, but he can rock and bring it with the best of 'em.

Aside from his playing, the main reason Shayne has been such a great fit is because he is so even-tempered. We always felt so fortunate to get Duncan, but we feel the same to have Shayne onstage with us every night. And now he's been in the band longer than Bobby or Duncan.

From 2004 through today, it's been so easy on the bus with everybody, which is such a huge blessing when you have to travel as much as we do. With so many bands, there's a dynamic that exists where everyone is a great player, except for one, who's just there because he's a good hang. But I love that I can say every guy in our band is both—a great player *and* a great person.

Catch & Release

By 2003, after Curb put out a faith-based compilation project of some past songs, I was starting to feel like we were being overlooked there. We had become like the old piece of furniture in the living room that you just keep walking around, but never sit on anymore. It's there. It's comfortable. But it's probably time to move it out. While I know Mike loved us and we loved him, he had signed a lot of huge artists, like Tim McGraw, Jo Dee Messina, and LeAnn Rimes, who were rightly getting the attention. But when you sign with Mike, his attitude is, you're in for life, so I knew it was time for me to be honest with him.

In 2004, I went to Mike and said, "I really think we've done everything we can do here. I don't feel like we mean what we did at one time, but I believe we still have something to say." Gracious as always, Mike listened intently, then asked, "Well, what do you want to do?" I answered, "Let me out so I can go try to get another deal." Mike agreed to my request. I could tell he felt bad that I thought the label hadn't delivered on the last record. He realized the lack of attention was an issue. But we walked away on great terms. And our friendship has never been in question, regardless of business.

Disney had a country label that was going strong in Nashville called Lyric Street Records. Randy Goodman, who had been at RCA, was the president. Doug Howard was the head of A&R. He and I had worked together back when I was a song-writer in the pre–Sawyer Brown days. I knew those guys well, so I wanted to try there first. When I walked in, both Randy and Doug were available. "Hey, Mark, great to see you. What's up?" I simply stated, "I'm off Curb." They looked at each other, then back at me. "Really? … Well, let's talk." After about an hour of discussion, I walked out of there with a new record deal and hit the ground running.

I would still go down to Muscle Shoals to write with Mac, but now with my own studio, I began producing our records myself with no coproducer. With a new label and a fresh team, I was super-excited to start working on the *Mission Temple* record. Well before the album was to be released, we sent the first single out, called "I'll Be Around," a song Doug had found. It was not received by country radio, but because we were still working on the project, we had time to adjust.

When I had completed all the songs, Doug and Randy invited me to play the album for the Lyric Street promotional staff. Now, having been in the business for a long time, I'm pretty good at reading a room. I was watching everyone's facial expressions and body language as they listened. As the songs played, I began to think, *They don't get it. They don't get us at all.* That's when it hit me: I had just left the one guy who *always* got us—Mike.

When the album finished playing, Randy and I went back to his office. Immediately, I said, "Hey, I read the room and they don't get it." With his head down, he tried to reassure me, "Mark, your album's great. But yeah, you're right. They don't. I could tell too." Deciding to put us both out of any further misery, I simply asked, "Would you please give me the album back?" Randy sighed and said, "Okay, let's talk about how we can work that out financially."

With the CD that I had played for Lyric Street in hand, I went by Mike's house on my way home and put it in his mailbox. I hadn't even gotten home when my phone rang. "Mark! This is fantastic! Can I have it back?" Mike got it, like he always had. After I answered with an easy, "Yes," he said, "Well, welcome back." Yes, just like that. That's what years of right relationships produce.

A connecting sidebar—when Bucky Covington came off *American Idol* with a great deal of buzz in the music industry, I began working with him. After a lot of hard work and negotiation, I was able to get him released from *Idol.* I walked into Randy's office at Lyric Street and asked, "Hey, would you be interested in Bucky Covington?" He answered, "Of course, but he's signed with 19 Management." I smiled and said, "I got him out of the deal and I've signed him." Randy smirked. "Well, but of course you have, Mark." I left with a deal for Bucky and produced his first two records, with the first going gold.

This is yet another example of why you never want to burn bridges. Relationships mean everything. Integrity means everything. Everybody that I've ever dealt with, I've been straight with them and most everyone has been straight with me. The proof of that was Lyric Street had given me a huge budget for Bucky. We had cut the record, done the photo shoot, and the album release was slated. One day, Randy called me and said, "Hey, uh, Mark, I realized we never signed Bucky's contract. We should probably get that done." I called Bucky and we went down to their office and made everything official.

Back at Curb, Mike immediately gave us a large marketing budget to shoot the video for "Mission Temple Fireworks Stand." We hired Mike Solomon again and made another really creative project. The song was so much fun because not only did we love it, but we were able to get pedal steel guitarist Robert Randolph to play on the track and appear in the video. He added some vocals, too, since he's such a strong, soulful singer.

Robert grew up in a church that couldn't afford a Hammond B3 organ, so as he was learning to play pedal steel, he figured out how to get a B3 sound out of his instrument. He created his own style that no one else can emulate. Robert became a six-time Grammy nominee that has played with greats like Eric Clapton and Dave Matthews, having been ranked on the list of the top one hundred guitarists of all time.

I loved everything I had heard Robert play on the pedal steel. He was an unbelievable musician. Plus, I knew about his faith and that he would track with the message. I sent his team the song, along with a note: "Hey, we would love for you to come in and play on this." The next day, Robert called. "Dude, I'm there! This rocks!"

When Robert came into the studio, I wanted to be as accommodating as possible so I asked, "Hey, do you need a chart? I can have the band leader write out either a letter chart or the Nashville number system for you. Whatever you want." With a big grin, Robert just said, "I just need you to turn it on!" Impressed with his attitude, I responded, "We can do that." Back up and let the man play!

"Mission Temple" became a huge song to our fans. A big moment for us was being invited to play it on *The Tonight Show*, back in the Jay Leno days. We asked Robert to join us. Having him perform with the band on national TV made the song so much more fun. Just as Jay Leno was getting ready to introduce us and the curtains were about to go up, I looked at Hobie and said, "Dude, we're from Apopka, Florida, and we're getting ready to play *The Tonight Show*." I tend to get anxious and nervous whenever we do live TV, because the footage then lives out there forever on video, especially today with YouTube. But I also cut my teeth doing that exact thing on *Star Search*.

Released in August of 2005, the *Mission Temple* album was our last noble attempt at keeping the label and radio connection going. There was a song called "They Don't Understand" that got airplay on Christian radio and actually went to number fifteen on that genre's chart. We also included another cover, "Keep Your Hands to Yourself," the classic song from The Georgia Satellites. But overall, the album was another swing and a miss at radio. After none of the songs charted well, we finally asked ourselves, "Why are we beating our heads against the wall? We had such a great ride at country radio. We're still selling out shows and gaining fans of all ages, so let's stop the game here and now." We had been blessed with so many hits, so many great songs.

I was actually relieved to stop fighting that battle. I was grateful to get out—to be able to just focus solely on our fans at live shows and not be required to jump through the label's radio hoops, to let go of the politics. That said, over time, I have been blessed by some lasting friendships with radio deejays, programmers, and directors all over the country—great people who I have played golf and basketball with whenever the band is in their town. For a while after we were off the radio, I would see some of these friends while on the road and they felt like they had to apologize to me. "Mark, I wish I could still play your records." I'd just smile and say, "Hey, I know you do, but that door is closed and we had some great years together. Just glad we can stay friends." I think the older we get and the wiser we become, the more we realize the value of relationships over business.

I was absolutely set free by the decision to let go of radio. It was a huge relief, like a ton of bricks had been lifted off my shoulders. One thing I didn't want to be guilty of was just being greedy in trying to get that "one last big hit." We had seen our day for much longer than most artists get to experience. And after twenty-one years, it's ridiculous to say you stopped because you failed. It was time for someone else to take our spot on the wheel. To let other artists tap in and take the ring for the fight.

We were good now. That was the end of an era and, certainly, the beginning of a new day. Even more than I realized at the time.

Transistor Rodeo

And they dance and they dance
And they dance real slow
At the transistor rodeo

—FROM THE SONG "Transistor Rodeo"

ONE NIGHT, we were playing The Grizzly Rose in Denver, a huge venue with a cowboy clientele and a Western saloon vibe. The night was sold out and, knowing we always had a lot of fun there, I decided I was going to wear a full-on eighties outfit.

Just as I was getting off the bus to head to the stage, there was a cowboy walking through the parking lot with his girlfriend. As he passed by me, I half expected some kind of sarcastic remark, or even a threat to beat me up because of how I looked. But instead, he said to his girl, "Now *that's* the Mark Miller I came to see!"

Yeah, that's how we roll, cowboy.

CHAPTER ELEVEN

Glory to the King

And when we sing, we sing for You
We sing to You
We sing glory, all glory to the King

—**FROM THE SONG** "Glory to the King"

FROM DAY ONE, Lisa and I had decided we would be present in parenting our kids. We agreed that being a mom and dad is a 24/7 job where you never take a day off. By 2002, with Madison about to hit her teens and Gunnar being around eight, I wanted my kids to have a present dad in those critical teenage years. I was ready for the music business to take a back seat to my family. I felt strongly that it was time to redirect my energy toward Lisa and our kids.

Frank and I sat down for one of our brother-to-brother talks. He assured me that, as an organization, we were financially sound, and backing off on touring was absolutely possible. I remember him telling me, "Mark, there's no need to keep touring at the pace you always have. It's a good time to slow down. We've done well and you're certainly not extravagant with your lifestyle. Backing off the road and spending more time at home is great." Once again, we were on the same page.

I vividly remember every time we made the decision to cut back on the number of shows we did a year. With my work ethic, I always struggled at those points in our career. The first big cut we made was in the mid-nineties, and then again in the late-nineties when we went down to 175 shows a year. I always felt when someone called to offer us good money to play somewhere, we needed to say yes. In my mind, if I'm getting paid to go sing for an hour and a half, making more than my mom made teaching school for the entire year, it just felt arrogant to say no.

Here was the battle going on in my head: *Are you serious, dude? You're gonna turn this down, when your mom and everyone you grew up with, your blue-collar buddies, can't imagine making that in one night! Just because you don't want to get on a nice tour bus and ride twenty hours?*

That conflict has always run deep inside my heart. That's why I struggled to turn down any show. Plus, in the music business, it's easy to have the mindset that it's all going to come crashing down any day now. Most artists think *this* year is the *last* year, because there is *nothing* stable about the music business.

Over the years, I had heard all the horror stories about artists who weren't good stewards of their money and posses-sions. I always wanted to provide for my family and, just like every parent, make sure my kids had it better than I did. From a young age, God placed a deep desire in my heart to work hard. That's just what I do. So I struggled with guilt anytime we cut back.

With this new decision, Frank's suggestion was to drop from 175 to 125, half the number of shows we had done at our peak, the least we had ever done in any year. When the slowdown caught up with our calendar, I had some days when I was sitting in my house, thinking, *What am I doing?* During the day while the kids were at school, I could only play so much golf.

With the opportunity to connect in deeper ways with my kids, I got more into Madison's horse competitions. With Gunnar, it was … *wait for it* … basketball. I started coaching him and my nephew when they were in middle school. We put together an AAU (Amateur Athletic Union) program as a faith-based mission, and one of the seniors in that group needed someone to take him on a visit to Flagler College in St. Augustine, Florida. A teammate of mine from UCF, Bo Clark, was the head coach there, so I volunteered to go.

I was standing courtside while my player talked with a coach when this really cocky kid named Chase Tremont walked up to me. With an obvious attitude, he said, "My coach says you're really famous. But I've never heard of you."

Not one to shy away from hardwood trash-talk, I came right back, "Well, I *am* really famous. And if you've never heard of *me*, you must live under a rock. Because buddy, I'm *really* famous." I started laughing to signal an end to the joke, but he just kept going, "So, you're in a band, huh?" I answered, "Yep, I'm in a band."

Chase was not going to let up. "The best band in the world plays at my church in Daytona Beach." "Well, then," I responded, "I would love to hear the best band in the world. I want to hear what the best band in the world sounds like, because I thought *I* had the best band in the world." I really liked this kid. We hit it off and kept talking. Finally, he went over to his gym bag, came back with a homemade CD, and handed it to me. "This is my youth pastor and his band. He writes all his own songs."

I looked at the CD and, with a Sharpie, someone had written

two words on it: "Casting Crowns." I asked, "What's your youth pastor's name?" Chase answered, "Mark Hall."

I thanked Chase and put the CD in my backpack, where it stayed hidden for the next several months.

At a Crossroad

One weekend, Madison and I were driving to one of her competitions, still with many hours on the road in front of us. I remembered the conversation with Chase and said, "Hey, look in my bag. There's a CD in there. Grab it and let's listen, just to see what it's like. This kid at Flagler said it was his youth pastor."

The first song we heard was "If We Are the Body." I was immediately blown away by the integrity of the songwriting and this guy's voice. Mark's number was on the CD case, so I called him. "Listen, man, I don't have anything to do with Christian music. I don't know much about it, but I just wanted to call to encourage you. This is really, really good stuff. I'm friends with Steven Curtis Chapman and Michael W. Smith. Our kids go to school together. I would love to play this for them. But I just had to let you know I like what you're doing."

After Mark told me he knew about Sawyer Brown and who I was, he said, "Thank you so much. That means a lot. But I know the whole artist thing has passed me by. I'm thirty-four years old with a wife and three kids. I'm a full-time youth pastor. I just left Daytona Beach and moved to McDonough, Georgia, to serve at Eagles Landing First Baptist Church. Some of the band moved here with us. But if you could maybe play the songs for some of those artists and they might record one, that would mean so much to me."

At the time, I thought that would be our only conversation. I just knew I was supposed to encourage Mark.

For several years, Steven Curtis Chapman, Terry Hemmings, my brother, and I, along with our families, would go on spring break trips together. We'd play golf and hang out with our families on the beach in Florida. By our next trip, Terry had become the CEO of Provident Music, Sony's Christian label. While golfing, he said to me, "Mark, I want to give you your own Christian label imprint." I started laughing and said, "Terry, you and I are close, but buddy, you ain't gonna hang onto that job very long if you do stupid stuff like that. I know nothing about the Christian music business. Getting me involved is the last thing you need to be doing."

But Terry was on a mission, literally. "No, I'm giving you your own label. You know music as well as anyone I know. And I don't know *anyone* who has more Christian integrity than you." I thanked him for the generous compliment, but just shook my head and laughed.

The next day as Terry drove the four of us back to the golf course, I took out the Casting Crowns album and popped it into the CD player. I said, "Tell me what you guys think of this." After "If We Are the Body" finished playing, Terry said, "That's your first artist to sign." I responded, "Really?" Never taking his eyes off the road, he told me, "Sign 'em, Mark."

When we got back to the hotel, Steven asked, "Hey, can I get that CD and listen to it?" The next morning while we were all at the beach, he said, "Mark, I listened to those songs and there's something there. The guy's voice, there's something there." Terry chimed in, "Call him up and offer him a deal."

Later, I called Mark Hall. "Hey, I'm not sure how to explain what's happened here, but I just got my own record label under Provident that I'm calling Beach Street Records. I'd like to sign you."

Silence.

When I got through explaining everything, he said, "That sounds great. But I just have one question and—this is a deal breaker. Am I still going to be able to be a youth pastor?" I laughed and answered, "You can be anything you want to be. These are great songs you've written. We're going to make a record and, as far as I'm concerned, you can stay a youth pastor as long as you want."

To repeat, I didn't know the Christian music industry, but I knew how powerful Mark's songs were and that people needed to hear their message. Couple that with the fact that I had my own studio and felt like I knew how to make a great record.

Over the next several months, Frank and I took everything we had learned from setting up Sawyer Brown and applied that to Casting Crowns. Mark Hall and I had so many parallels—he was the leader, the lead singer, the front man, the spokesman, and the songwriter. Casting Crowns is the Christian music version of Sawyer Brown. And there is *no* difference in our commitment to Christ.

Frank and I went down to McDonough and spent three days doing "band camp" with Crowns. In our first meeting at the church, I could tell Mark was really uncomfortable with the whole idea of being established as the leader. He's such a humble, unassuming guy. With the entire band in the room, I could tell from their facial expressions and body language that every possible feeling was represented, from scared to skeptical.

I had one of those moments when God puts the words in your mouth right when you need it. I told everyone, "Hey, when we finish this meeting, let's all go eat lunch. I want you guys to decide where we're going and I need to know in sixty seconds." Then I just stopped and watched as Mark looked on.

They started to discuss/argue over where to go. At one minute, I said, "Time's up. Tell me where we're going to eat." Silence. No answer. So I stated, "Guys, there are going to be big questions asked of this band. But you can't even figure out where to go eat. Here's the deal. You all followed Mark here from Daytona. He's your leader. When it's time to make decisions, I need to make *one* phone call. I need to talk to *one* person. There's a reason every single one of you is here. Because you trust Mark. And he's the one I want to deal with." I smiled and finished with, "Nothing against any of you … but you can't decide where to go eat."

They all started laughing. They got it. They knew. Mark was their leader. Twenty years in, Mark is still their leader.

While we were getting ready to start recording, I got a call from Terry. "Hey, the band Third Day is not going to make the deadline to turn in their record, so their slot for the marketing department to push an album release is open. Can you have your album done in two and a half weeks?" I didn't even flinch, I just said, "Absolutely!" Now it was game on.

One day in the studio, just as I was about to press the record button for Mark to sing "If We Are the Body," he walked out of the vocal booth. "Hey, I forgot … I've got this other song I haven't played for you that I've been writing." As he began to sing it, I immediately got chills. The song was amazing. He said the title was "Who Am I." (Since then, I've learned that if Mark suddenly switches channels, you better just let him go and follow. The trip will absolutely be worth it.)

By using my own studio and calling in some favors from

some musicians, I was able to get the album done for around $20,000. I made sure we had enough money left over to go to a music store and buy the band the gear they needed to play live. Regardless, this was a fraction of the record budgets I was accustomed to at Curb, but I made it work.

By the grace of God alone, we got the album done by the deadline. Ten songs. I recall asking one of the Provident label execs, "So, what's the expectation on sales for this first project?" He answered, "If you sell forty thousand records, we'll be happy and want a second one."

Now, understand that in the country music world, forty thousand is just a starting place. I was having a crash course in learning to live in this alternate universe that I always knew was there but had zero experience in. I understood how to navigate being a Christian in mainstream music, but being a country music producer in the Christian music industry was an entirely different world.

To date, that first album has sold over two million units. An important note is, of the handful of Christian artists that have sold more, all of them had crossover success in mainstream that helped their sales. Crowns has accomplished that number being solely on the Christian charts.

Now, remember when Frank and I talked about our pull-back on Sawyer Brown's shows? Well, here's the connection ...

Voice of Truth

My wife, Lisa, had grown up in California around show business. (Remember, her brother is Peter Brady.) She became a Christian after we started dating. When she said yes to Jesus as an adult, she became an on-fire believer. Christianity has never been just a Sunday-morning thing to my wife, but an all-day, everyday, seven-days-a-week lifestyle.

During the time I was fully focused on getting Crowns' career launched, one morning I was sitting at our kitchen table. Lisa walked out of the laundry room, pale white with a very serious look on her face. She asked me, "Has God ever spoken to you?" I answered, "You mean like in an audible voice?" She said, "Yes."

Seeing how something very real had clearly just happened to her, I immediately got goose bumps. Lisa said, "He just spoke to me." I responded, "Okay. Well, what did He say?" Carefully, she repeated what she had heard: "He said, 'I took it all away so he would be able to have the time to do this for Me.'"

Then Lisa explained why she felt she had heard that message from God. "I know how hard you worked to get Sawyer Brown another hit. I was praying for you, for another hit to come. This is an explanation of why He didn't grant that. God wanted you to have the space and time to take on Casting Crowns."

In that moment, with Lisa being obedient to hear and share what she had heard from the Lord, that's when it all connected.

What if we had seen another round of success with radio?

What if Frank and I hadn't agreed to cut back on shows?

What if I hadn't started the basketball program with Gunnar?

What if I hadn't had the time to take that kid to Flagler?

What if Chase had not found out who I was and brought up his youth pastor?

What if I had thrown that CD away and never listened to it?

What if Terry hadn't insisted I take on a new record label?

In those moments of realization is when we better see how God has been working behind the scenes to bring about what *only He* can bring about.

Another truly amazing part of this story is that God just kept blessing Sawyer Brown with our one constant—touring to be with our fans. To this day, that has never faltered. We tour at the same level we always have. So, after twenty-one years, when He took away the radio success, He gave me Casting Crowns. But He allowed me to keep the most important part of Sawyer Brown—playing live.

Being involved with Mark Hall and the band has been, and is, one of the greatest blessings in my life. I can say with all certainty that the last time I walk off the stage for Sawyer Brown, I'm going to be okay, because that has never been my plan, my dream. I am so appreciative and I love the fans, but the music business is *what I do*, it is not *who I am*. I'll even go as far as to say if the only reason for Sawyer Brown was to get me to the place where I could answer God's call to help Casting Crowns, I am good with that.

With both of us knowing that God has a will and a plan for our lives, Mark Hall and I laugh about our relationship all the time—a singer in a country band who produces this amazing Christian band. If someone knows about my faith, that I produce Crowns, and they ask me, "So, when is Sawyer Brown going to do a gospel album?" I always answer with, "We're not a gospel band. We're all Christian men, but we're a country-rock band." I don't need to confuse anybody with what we do. We each have our own calling.

And by the way, the one thing Elvis and I have in common (besides my short stint at his racquetball facility) is that we both won just one Grammy Award. Not in our genres, but in the Gospel category. My *only* Grammy is from Casting Crowns.

One thing I know for certain—God put me in Mark Hall's life. I have learned how to be involved in his creative process. When to chime in and when to stay out. But I love being there to remind him how special he is. That God gave him a gift. Mark is bold in his lyrics and his message. That's why when I stand in the back of an arena while he is sharing the gospel onstage, I can easily be overcome with emotion.

Before the first album came out, Provident had done some testing on "If We Are the Body." Terry called me and said, "We've been talking about Mark's lyrics. We don't think you can say that about the church. ... What are your thoughts?" With knowing nothing about the politics and diplomacy inside Christian music, I answered, "Terry, the last time I checked, if something has this much controversy, then it's going to have that much impact. We may not go to number one on the charts, but everyone is going to know this band will be different. I don't want to change anything that Mark has written."

When the single went to Christian radio, it did meet with some resistance at first, but then it took off. But when "If We Are the Body" hit heavy rotation, everything changed. When God speaks, when God decides to do something, it is going to happen. The song was number one for several months with a message that was desperately needed at the time.

There have been moments over the years when Mark has wanted to try something and I will just remind him that we're not here to be cool. I remind him that he's here to be him, because no one else can be. While I've been able to speak into his song-writing, I don't write with him. As his producer, I always want to stay objective, so I never have any of my songs on the table. No conflict of interest. I just help him make records out of what he wants to say. That was the same thing Mac McAnally had done for me. It's that simple.

Whenever I'm asked about the production of any of the Crowns songs, how we did this or that, I simply state that my main goal is to just make sure you can hear Mark. The win is hearing him and that big ol' thunderbolt God gives him, the one that strikes when he sings and speaks.

The most incredible thing about Mark's story is we are twenty years in with their career and he is still the full-time youth pastor at his church. That goes back to the first question he ever asked me before he signed our record deal. He has stayed true to that calling, and I have done my best to protect him in that. Mark has always been as committed to being a youth pastor as he is to making records and touring. If you ask him what he does, his answer will not be a Christian music artist. Or a songwriter. Or a Grammy Award winner. He's a youth pastor.

A great example of this is once when we were in my studio in Franklin, Tennessee, just south of Nashville. We were on a major time crunch to finish a new record—a deadline I was barely going to make. Mark was in the vocal booth singing when suddenly he walked out and said, "I didn't realize what time it is. I'm supposed to take the youth group to the mall tonight. I gotta go." And he walked out the studio door.

Stunned, I realized what he said and went out after him. All I saw was the back of his car leaving my driveway. Freaking out, I called him. "Hey, man, why can't somebody else take the youth group to the mall?" Mark answered, "Nope. That's what I do. I have to be there." Trying to reason with him, I continued, "But we have to get your vocals done. I'm on a deadline." He said, "I know.

I'm sorry. I don't know what to tell you. I have to go." Record or no record, he was headed back to McDonough, Georgia, to take the youth group to the mall.

Knowing I had to figure out a plan, I walked back into the studio and said to the team, "Alright, let's pack up some recording gear, boys. We're going to Georgia." I called Mark again and told him, "When you're done at the mall, I'll be set up in the basement of your house to record. We have to finish these vocals." We grabbed microphones and everything we could pull that we might need, threw it into my truck, and hit the road, a half hour behind Mark.

We eventually put a studio in the basement of Mark's house in Georgia just to make recording easier in circumstances like that. But that is the perfect example of how committed he is to his first calling. To Mark, there's no difference between playing to twenty thousand people in an arena and teaching his youth group on a Wednesday night. He is impacting lives in a positive way every day. I 100 percent believe that is why he's still able to write the kind of anointed songs that he does. They come out of real life. They aren't formulated in a record label's writing room to just get on Christian radio, but born from a heart that loves Jesus and loves people like Jesus does.

Trusting God with Blank Pages

Because of my relationship with Terry Hemmings and Provident, I have had the opportunity to write and produce three feature films, all faith-and-family based. My first experience was when I was asked to score the soundtrack for *Facing the Giants*. After I wrote the script and agreed to produce the 2013 film *Ring the Bell*, I wanted to include a Casting Crowns segment where Mark speaks and does an altar call (like they do every night), along with two songs.

To allow for the time in the film, I left eleven pages blank. I didn't want Mark to have to memorize any lines, plus I knew whatever I wrote was not going to be anything as good as what God would give him in the moment.

One day, the folks at the film company called. They wanted me to know they were really uncomfortable with the blank pages for the Crowns' segment. They said, "Mark, you're going to have to script that scene." I said, "Boys, that's a deal breaker. That ain't gonna happen. Whatever I write is not even going to compare to what Mark Hall will do, what he does every night in any arena." They pressed, "Well, we're very uncomfortable with this, to the point that we don't think we can sign off on it." I responded, "Okay, understood. Thank you, guys." And I hung up the phone.

To me, it was done. About a half hour later, they called back. "Hey Mark, we've been talking … we really like this story. We want to move forward, but we just need to go on record with saying that we're uncomfortable with the blank pages." I said, "That's fine. You can be uncomfortable."

For that particular scene, we filled up a local theater by going to all the area churches and giving them free tickets to a Casting Crowns mini-concert. On the day of the shoot, the place was packed. I told Mark before the band went on, "You'll do two songs, but there are people here who need to hear the gospel." To Mark, he was just coming out to a crowd of people to sing and preach. Once we got all the cameras in place and were ready to shoot, I told them we had one take to get what we needed.

After the first song and Mark's incredible message, we had

scripted for fifteen "actors" to get up from their seats and come down front for the altar call. Everything went off exactly as planned, and Mark and the band did an amazing job. But when we went back and watched the scene through the playback, there weren't fifteen people who came down front; there were *eighteen*. Three people came to know Christ that night. Three of the invited people heard the authentic message of the gospel, and movie shoot or not, they responded.

While the band was onstage, I was going around checking the shots. There were a couple of cameramen from LA who were crying as they watched and listened to Mark's message. Every morning before we would start to shoot, we would do a devotional and pray. One of the camera operators was a well-known and respected guy from Hollywood. A couple of weeks in, one morning, he asked me, "Would you mind if I did the devotional?" Of course, I agreed. He shared about how inspired he was by being a part of the team and what he had witnessed. He said he had never experienced anything like this on any set. Touching lives was what those films were all about, whether the lives of the people on the set or the people who saw the film. Thank God we accomplished both.

With Sawyer Brown, God has given us the gift of offering people the chance to have fun, to laugh, to cry, to feel all these emotions through the music in those two hours with us. I get to go out and witness that every night we're on stage. We are given some "blank pages" for everyone, me included, to forget about our problems and enjoy life.

As Mark and I were working on their tenth album, I was reflecting on what my band does every night. Then I told him how much satisfaction I have received from knowing all those nights that people come to hear Casting Crowns and receive the message of eternal life in Jesus. The God who allows us to have a fun, clean evening with folks is the same God who shows up to touch and reach people through their anointed band.

In Him, there is no dividing line between the sacred and the secular. He's in it all. And for that, I am grateful.

The Walk

'Cause I took this walk you're walking now
Boy, I've been in your shoes
You can't hold back the hands of time
It's just something you've got to do

—FROM THE SONG "The Walk"

ANYONE INVOLVED in the entertainment industry has to make huge sacrifices in their personal lives. That just comes with the territory. The worst part is missing out on things like birthdays and key family events. As I said in the last chapter, by 2002 when we cut back our tour schedule to where we still are today, a huge part of my time and energy was poured into my family. That allowed us to forge incredible bonds, also strengthening Lisa's and my marriage even more. But then, there was a point when we thought our family was complete but God had a surprise for us.

I'm going to share about my kids in birth order and then I'll close like I started my story, with my mom.

Madison

My daughter, Madison, is quite competitive, a multitasker, an eternal optimist, and *really* bright to boot. Sounds like someone else we know—my mom. And just like Mom, Madison is a whopping five feet tall with a giant personality and a smile bigger than Texas. She has the power of persuasion with just about everyone, except her mother. Her senior year, she was the student body president. One time, I had asked her high school principal about an upcoming event. He laughed and said, "Why are you asking me? Madison runs the school!"

While I was on location in Florida shooting *Ring the Bell*, I asked Madison to skip her college spring break and come down to play a really difficult, quirky role. She had been in some plays in school but had no real interest in acting. Needless to say, she wooed the cast and crew with her performance.

Remember when I said she was a multitasker? While we were shooting the movie, Madison had a college internship with a NASCAR company. At the time, the Daytona 500 was running and she asked if I could take her over to the race. When we got there, I assumed she had lined up getting us the proper credentials. She had me drive to the tunnel gate and, while pulling up to the attendant, she informed me that she had made no prior arrangements to get in.

I said, "Madison, this is the Daytona 500! They are not going to let you through without a pass." She said, "Oh, we won't need one. We'll be fine." So I rolled down the window and just pointed at her. She broke into a huge smile and began to tell the gate-keeper all about her internship. Talking really fast, she finished off with, "And I'm supposed to be in the pit, I promise!" He burst into laughter and said, "Little lady, if you promise, then it *must* be true." We managed to make it through two more checkpoints and somehow got into the infield. Just as my daughter had predicted, before long, we were strolling into the pits, with Madison looking like she owned the place. Yeah, it's a gift.

Madison has always had a love for horses and started riding at a very early age. I have a high school buddy, Phil Devita, who is a course designer in the equestrian world. He's the architect for jumping courses, such as the Olympics and other international competitions. He was the only guy I knew that I felt like I could trust to evaluate Madison's riding ability, especially since she wanted to jump competitively. Soon, my friend was in Nashville for a horse show, and I worked out a time for him to watch her ride.

After an hour or so of observation, he came over to me and said, "Well, Mark, I have good news and I have bad news." I said, "Uh-oh. Let's hear the good news first." He answered, "Madison is really talented." I then asked, "Okay, what's the bad news?" He smiled and said, "Madison is really talented." Then my buddy explained, "This is not a sport for just anyone. This is a sport of kings." Then he laughed and said, "I think you *know* what that means."

Phil found her a trainer, and the plan was to be able to start competing at small shows after the first year. But within only a couple of months, Madison had advanced rapidly. The Winter Equestrian Festival in West Palm Beach, Florida, is an event where amateurs and professionals compete on a national level. Now we had a new plan. The trainer thought it might be a good experience for her to go see what she would be up against with no expectations of winning.

In her first event, there were riders and horses from all over the country. But she shocked everyone by winning third place out of twenty-one entries. That first season she would go on to win other competitions and be named champion multiple times.

Madison was incredible on a horse. Riding was to her what basketball is to me. This was her sport. During the winter seasons, we kept going back to West Palm Beach for jumping competitions. On our first trip, I asked Madison's trainer what time we would need to be ready the first morning. He told me that they would start getting the horses ready around 5:30 a.m. I said, "Great, so Madison will be there at five-thirty." He responded, "Oh, no, no. Someone takes care of all that. You just bring her to the ring when it's her time to ride. They'll bring the horse to her. Then after she jumps, they'll take the horse back for you."

Surprised, I said, "No, that's not the way we do it, so she'll be there at five-thirty, get her horse ready and prepped, and take care of the stall." The trainer responded, "But, Mark, no one *here* does that." I answered, "Well, that's what *we* do." Madison got up early every morning, mucked the stalls, and got her own horse ready. After the ride, she took him back. She wasn't just going to "show up and ride."

But the biggest blessing with this sport was being able to share so much quality time with Madison. For dads with daughters, especially as they start into their teen years, finding a common activity to do together to connect can be a huge challenge. I loved watching her athleticism and skill. As she got better and better, Madison moved up in the competition categories. She was competing in what is known as "hunter jumper." That event is not a race or against the clock; it's about style, grace, and beauty as you jump. I liked that season, because it was much safer.

Then she wanted to advance to "stadium jumping," the riding event you see in the Olympics, where there are higher jumps at faster speeds. With her being just sixteen and me being a *very* protective dad, this was an entirely different ball game—my little girl on a huge horse with way too much room for accidents. (In 1995, "Superman" Christopher Reeve was paralyzed after a jump went wrong while he was competing.)

I told Madison's trainer that we had to find a horse that would keep her as safe as possible. After he located one in Pennsylvania, we all went up for her to take a test drive, so to speak. When we arrived at the course, she had never been on a horse trained for this or gone over any stadium jumps. After she mounted the horse, the trainer talked her through what to do—and what *not* to do. He advised her to go over some small jumps first to just get a feel for the horse.

As she turned to make her first run, Madison bypassed the small jump and went straight for the big one, the one the horse is accustomed to doing. Before we could even shout at her to stop, she went right over. While both her trainer and I were upset, he called out, "Madison, that is *not* what I told you to do!" She went straight for the forgiveness-over-permission approach: "Oh, I didn't know what jump you guys were talking about. I'm sorry."

We left that day with the horse.

Back at West Palm Beach for her first stadium jump event, I warned her, "Madison, I'm telling you right now, you're not going in there to win this thing. You're just going to find your groove with this horse. I want you to get through the course, get comfortable, and be safe. Your mindset has to be learning *how* to do this first." She flashed her TV smile and said, "Oh, absolutely. Got it, Daddy."

As soon as Madison went through the gate, she was

flying. And I was *fuh-rea-king* out. When she completed her run and headed back to her mom and me, I was steaming mad. *Steaming.* "Young lady! I don't think you listened to me!" (Her trainer was upset with her too—again.) "I told you that you weren't in there to win this thing. You were just going to take your time to learn and figure this out!" Madison got off her horse, glared at me, and announced, "Daddy! I'm a Miller! I went *in* to win! That's what *we* do!"

Lisa turned and looked at me a moment, then said, "Well, *Daddy*, what do you have to say to *that*?"

Madison had always wanted to go to Vanderbilt University. To be accepted, you had to begin to build a résumé by the ninth grade. Plus your test scores have to be incredibly high. But she had her sights set on that school and was so determined, even though her counselors told her that might be a stretch. (They knew that Vanderbilt is a very difficult school to get into and were likely working to not set her up for failure.)

But once again, her drive to succeed won out and she went on to graduate from—you guessed it—Vanderbilt. She received a scholarship to Stetson University Law School and graduated with her law degree. Her obviously busy schedule and new focus slowly edged competitive riding out of her life.

Lisa and I knew that she was struggling with a lot of the things that come with being an attorney. Around this same time, I had just shot one of my films and still had a crew together. Madison told me about an idea she had for a TV show that connected places we had been as a family on the road, great restaurants where we had eaten, and interesting people we had met over the years. Her title was "Chasing Down Madison Brown," using her first name and the band's "last name."

On the show, she would visit interesting locations, interview people, take part in the featured activities, and do a cooking segment. (She's a foodie and a great cook.) To shoot a pilot episode, we called our good friend Toby Keith. We took the crew to Oklahoma, where Madison interviewed Toby, cooked with the chef at his restaurant, and went out to ride one of his racehorses—combining all her passions.

I had connected with RFD-TV on my movies, so not long after we shot this first show, they asked if I had any other ideas. I shared Madison's show concept with them. Within a half hour of watching the pilot, they called and ordered twenty-six episodes.

To date, we have done three seasons, seventy-eight episodes, and are about to begin work on the fourth season. The show is now in syndication all over the US. Madison is the creator, writer, producer, and of course, host, and I get to be an executive producer to assist her. My daughter is absolutely fearless with the craziest episode (so far) being at a rattlesnake roundup where she got into an enclosed area with *way* too many snakes!

But for Lisa and me, Madison's greatest achievement and blessing is that she has given us two incredible grandsons, Jack and Eli. It's so great to experience parenting at this new amazing place, through the eyes of our daughter.

Gunnar

Because of how my mom had raised me, it was very important for me to raise my son to be tough, to be a man of Christian integrity. For years, being around families of so many celebrities, artists, and pro athletes, the last thing I wanted was for any of my kids, but particularly my son, to be entitled. (By the way, Gunnar is actually his middle name. His first name is Aden.)

When Gunnar was ten, he became interested in playing the guitar. He wanted a new yellow Fender guitar that we had seen at a local store. I could have easily bought the guitar and just given it to him, but I wanted him to know what it felt like to earn something on his own. For several months I had Gunnar work odd jobs around the house and cattle farm to earn enough money to buy the guitar himself. I knew he would appreciate something so much more if he put in the hours and sweat to earn it himself.

When Gunnar got his driver's license, I wanted to get him a new and very safe car. But he said no. He gave me the specific age and type of truck that he wanted. Of course, something much less costly than what I was going to buy him. When I asked why, he said that he didn't want a brand-new car that would make him stand out at school. Because he was doing exactly what we had raised him to do, we complied.

One time while at his school, the principal asked if I would sing the national anthem. I smiled and said, "No, thank you. I don't think my son would be good with that." He never wanted anyone to make a big deal out of him because of what I did. Again, I admired his maturity.

When I was able to start coaching basketball for Gunnar's middle school team, he and I started the AAU program I mentioned before as a faith-based mission. The goal was to find kids who were good players but might never have a chance to be recognized for their talent or have the money to be in a specialty league. Gunnar wanted to be involved in something that would help guys who might never have the opportunities he had.

Over the years, *every one* of the kids in our program went

on to play college basketball on a scholarship. I have always been really proud that Gunnar and I were able to accomplish that feat together.

In 2022, Gunnar graduated from medical school. So, this crazy traveling musician and his bride produced a lawyer *and* a doctor!

Just like my brother, Gunnar was always smart, really brilliant. When I started coaching his basketball team, he wasn't very good. At the end of that season, he came to me and said, "Hey, Dad, I really want to become a good player." In the moment, I recalled how much work I had to put in to become good, especially with me being small. So I said to him, "I don't think you really know what that means, what it will take." Gunnar stated, "Yeah, I think I do. Dad, I think you actually know what you're talking about, and I'm willing to listen to you now." (With that kind of candidness, no question he is my son.) I smiled at his honesty and then told him, "Well, first, you need to know that you're not very good." He responded, "Oh, I know." I added, "Okay, then we've got somewhere to start."

I have to say, from that point, the amount of discipline he showed was unbelievable. Just like his sister, he had a competitive spirit and worked really, really hard. For any of us, when something we truly want to do is not natural to us, then to be good, we have to work super hard. As a result, Gunnar became a great basketball player. Even better than I ever was. Still, nothing rivaled his academic skill.

But my kids-wanting-to-become-musicians nightmare scenario came back to mess with me once again. Awhile after Gunnar had bought his first guitar, as kids often do, he lost interest and sold it. A few years later, as a teenager, he informed me that not only did he want to take up guitar again, but this time he was serious. Immediately, my first thought was, *Okay, here we go. Help me, Lord.*

Trying to think fast, I walked into the studio, grabbed a guitar, came out, and handed it to him. He said, "Wow, okay! So what do I do now?" I answered, "I don't know." He continued, "Well, am I going to take lessons?" I said, "Nope, I didn't get lessons. If you want to learn, you'll just need to figure it out."

About two weeks later, I was in bed asleep one night. Suddenly, someone was tapping me on the shoulder. I woke up to find Gunnar standing there with his guitar strapped on. Grinning, he said, "Check this out." Then he began to play "Sweet Home Alabama." After *two weeks*. Half-awake but listening, I started to pray, *Please, Lord, no, no, no.*

Fast-forward a few years—like basketball, Gunnar put in the work and became a great guitar player. In fact, a monster player. But while I took note of his progress, I never said anything to him about it. When I started working on my second film, Gunnar was around twenty-one. I knew he had written some really good instrumentals on guitar, so I went to him and said, "Hey, I want to use one of your pieces you wrote for the soundtrack of the movie I'm working on. And I want you to play it."

His performance was amazing. When he came back into the studio control room, I said, "Son, that was really, really incredible." He looked at me and stated, "That's the first time you've ever complimented me on my guitar playing ... and I want to know why."

Well aware that was my first affirmation of his skill, I answered him, "Because every day that I got up as an artist, I had to grind. There were never any guarantees in what I did. No guarantee of the next record. *Nothing* was guaranteed. As your dad, I knew God gave you a gift and that was your mind, your brain. I never wanted you to have to do what I had to do. That's why I've been so careful about encouraging you." I closed with, "I wanted something better for you, son, something that I really felt God had in store for you."

Gunnar responded, "Okay, that's good enough. I get it."

Over the many years he has worked to become a doctor, Gunnar has made so many sacrifices to reach his goal. The level of commitment and application to medicine is really unbelievable. One night at our house, he was studying for a test that he said was a month away. I laughed and told him, "When I was in college, I would just cram the night before a test." He looked up and responded, "I could do that. But I'm not here to be a good test taker. I'm here to become a great doctor."

With that, it's very difficult to put into words how I felt when I watched him walk across the stage to receive his diploma and heard them announce his name and new title: Dr. Aden Gunnar Miller.

JeQuan

When Gunnar and I were putting together a team for our AAU program, a dad came up to me after the tryouts and said, "I can see my son's not good enough to play on this team. But there's a kid in Dickson County who's amazing. You've *got* to see him play. I'd like to bring him here next week. But if he makes your team, he's not going to have a way here every week. I can't bring him, so you'll have to figure out something." I agreed.

As promised, the next week the man brought the kid in. The boy was very soft-spoken and kept his head down. I asked him, "So, what's your name?" Quietly, he answered, "JeQuan Lewis." Because I could barely hear him, I asked, "JeQuan?" He said, "Yeah." I continued, "Okay, JeQuan, let's see what you got. Take the ball. Let's see you shoot."

For the next several minutes, I thought I was watching a miniature version of one of the Harlem Globetrotters. I, along with everyone there, was freaking out at how amazing this kid was. At only twelve years old, JeQuan was already unbelievable. A natural talent.

I told the man who brought him, "Well, he certainly can make the team. In fact, he would *be* the team!" The guy said, "He lives with his grandmother. You can go talk to her." I did just that, and the next week we started picking up JeQuan for practice and taking him back home. I knew when we started this kind of program, there would be some sacrifices along the way.

But then something really interesting happened.

Over the next few months, JeQuan quickly became a member of our family. Being just three months apart and into basketball, he and Gunnar became really close. Madison came to love him like another younger brother. Lisa and I soon treated JeQuan just like our own two kids. He started staying with us more and more, but stayed very close and connected to his grandmother. When he turned sixteen, we bought him a car, just like we did Madison and Gunnar.

From early on and to this day, JeQuan calls me Pops and Lisa Mama. And we all love his grandmother. Every time I see her, she cries, hugs me, and says, "You know, he's your son." I just smile and say, "Yes, ma'am, I do." His grandmother's gratitude came from her knowing that everything we were doing for him was going to change his life forever.

As a Christ-follower, you just know when the Holy Spirit puts someone special in your life for a reason. Accepting that, JeQuan and I developed a true father-and-son relationship. The really cool thing is we have arguments just like biological dads and sons. We will go at it over some issues. But he's told me that he loves that we have that kind of connection because it proves to him how much I care. To him, getting mad when he's done something I disagree with is proof of my love for him as a son. If I *didn't* care, I wouldn't be passionate about communicating with him. He understands that.

As a senior in high school, he had a lot of offers to play ball. He started to be recruited by Tennessee, Georgia, and some of the bigger schools. The coach at VCU—Virginia Commonwealth University—at that time was Shaka Smart, who was already gaining a solid reputation in college basketball, having taken his team to the Final Four. He started coming to watch JeQuan play, and, of course, you didn't have to watch for very long to see how good he was. After Shaka had come to watch JeQuan around sixty times, I could tell he was really disciplined and that his entire program was very structured. And JeQuan has to have structure.

One of the most interesting aspects is that JeQuan is not a basketball fan. So other than the colleges that were recruiting him, outside of the major programs like Kentucky, Kansas, or Duke, he didn't know anybody else. I started to see that VCU and playing for Shaka was where he needed to be. Finally, one day, I told him, "When it comes time to pick, you're gonna go to VCU." He shot back with, "But I don't want to go to VCU." I repeated, "You're going to VCU." He got furious. But here's what I knew:

VCU would start him as a freshman. Georgia and UT had already signed a couple of guards, so JeQuan would only be a backup his freshman year. He had never sat on the bench before and would not do well with that.

When decision time came, I told him again, "You're going to VCU and there's no more discussion." He asked, "Why?" I answered, "Several reasons. They need you. They want you. And you'll go into their rotation immediately. They don't have a football team, so basketball is king there." He finally understood my reasoning.

After high school, JeQuan went to VCU and became a star point guard. Then, after graduating from college, he signed with the Milwaukee Bucks and went to their G League affiliate, the Wisconsin Herd in 2017. From 2018 to today, he has played on the pro level in various international leagues. As I write this, he is playing in Europe. We talk to him every day.

If you ever saw the movie *The Blind Side*, you'll know where I'm going with this part of the story. I told all three of my kids that in college, if they kept their grades up, I would buy them their dream car. During JeQuan's junior year, his coach called me. "Mr. Miller, JeQuan says you're going to buy him a car. You can't do that." I responded, "Oh yes, I can. I'm buying him a car." He continued, "The NCAA is not going to let that happen. The only way is for you to make a case to them that you're his guardian." I said, "Okay, that's no problem."

We had to go through the process of formally proving guardianship of our relationship, from the time we met him at twelve years old, well before he was a college prospect. The point was we had to offer enough evidence that we weren't involved with him just to pay for a Division I scholarship athlete, like a booster for the university. Part of the reason was because JeQuan was such a high-profile athlete. He went to the NCAA tournament every year and he was a standout.

But the clincher that finally sealed the case was not anything we did, but what he did. JeQuan wrote a personal letter to the committee about our relationship with him. After everyone on the committee read the letter, his coach called me and said, "Mr. Miller, we all read JeQuan's letter. I want you to know that everyone on the panel was in tears. You were approved—unanimous. It's clear that, to him, you're his dad and Mrs. Miller is his mom."

Anytime a coach or his agent has wanted to discuss business, JeQuan has always said, "You gotta talk to my dad. I'm not doing anything until he signs off." Even with how close we all are, he has been able to maintain a healthy relationship with his grandmother and his mother. We never wanted to replace his biological family.

The day he graduated from college with a degree in sociology, he had a huge grin on his face, because Lisa and I were there with his mom, grandmother, and his daughter, Jaeonna. No one in his family had ever graduated, but there was JeQuan, walking across the stage to get his degree.

As promised, during his senior year in college, I got him his dream car—a Dodge Charger. One day after one of his games, he said, "Pops, I want to take you for a drive in my new car." As we were on the loop around the city, there was this series of billboards along the way. JeQuan was on every one of them. After he showed me, he said, "I wanted to let you know you were right. I'm famous here because basketball is king, just like you told me." Even in the off-season now, he lives in his beloved and adopted city of Richmond, Virginia.

Our relationship with JeQuan has been one of the greatest blessings our family has ever experienced together. He is so proud of Gunnar and Madison, and they are proud of him. Those three are forever brothers and sister.

My Kids and the Band

When Gunnar was a freshman in college, he called me and said, "Dad, today someone in my dorm was playing your music." Now, Gunnar would never tell anyone who his dad is. He's just not going to play that card. You have to find that out for yourself. So, when we played a show in Kentucky near his college, all his fraternity brothers came. He got them all tickets, but he didn't come.

Because I shielded my kids from the band growing up, now that they're older, they've come to respect us on their own accord. Gunnar is really into music, so I know he's very proud. He loves rock music and has become a Sawyer Brown fan on his own. In recent years, he wrote a really cool song about the band that we recorded, called "100 Miles and Runnin.'" He came up with all the guitar parts on the track and wrote all of the lyrics himself.

Madison will come walking into our house with a vintage Sawyer Brown shirt that she bought online. She once told me, "There was a shirt I liked that was signed by you, but it was a hundred bucks. I wasn't going to pay that, Dad."

With JeQuan playing pro basketball, all the players are really into hip-hop music, but getting ready for a game, he listens to us. His favorite song in the world is "The Walk." While the other guys are into rap, he's listening to his country music.

My Mom and the Band

Early on, Mom became the president of our fan club that we called Sawyer Brown Nation. She was perfect for the job because she was so gracious to our fans. When you met her, there were three things you could count on. First, she was going to ask if you're a Christian. Next, she would offer to cook you a meal. And third, if you needed to spend the night, you were always welcome at her place anytime.

For several years, we did these huge events during CMA Fan Fair in Nashville. That entire week, Mom would have our fans sleeping all over her floor. She loved it and the fans loved her. They had their own relationship outside of us. My mom was the biggest fan in the world, yet she was still my mom with this incredible connection with thousands of people. Because of that, over the years, she led a lot of fans to the Lord. Her optimistic and positive nature led people to connect with her faith. I wasn't privy to that relationship. I always removed myself, for her to be who she was to the fans.

When she passed away in 2019, they put together their own memorial service for her, aside from the private service we had. They planned it all. I was invited but didn't speak. In fact, I sat in the back and just marveled at all these people getting up and giving testimonies about my mom. The impact she had on so many people was just amazing.

Mom had always told me that Marty Raybon from Shenandoah was going to sing at her funeral. Sure enough, right before the service started, Marty walked in with his guitar. I had no idea he was coming, but, of course, I remembered what she had always told me. Marty came up to me and said, "I told your mom that I would sing 'Beulah Land' at her funeral. Here I am."

That day, I heard things I never knew. I saw firsthand how Mom had impacted so many of the thousand-plus people that were there. There was a lot of laughter and a lot of tears, but most of all, evidence of a life well-lived for Christ.

There were also some really funny stories. Everyone knew that Mom loved to cook. She had a special recipe that she called shelly beans, a mix of green beans and pinto beans. One of the fans shared the story of calling Mom. The lady said, "'Jackie, I've tried to cook your recipe and they just don't taste the same as yours. What am I missing?' Then Jackie asked me, 'Well, how many sticks of butter did you put in?' to which I asked, 'What do you mean?' She then told me, 'You gotta use two full sticks of butter.'" Someone else shared how Mom's secret ingredient in coleslaw was sugar. The fans had also put together a video of Mom's interaction with thousands of people from over the years.

After Mom died, because nobody else could do it the way she did, we dissolved the fan club at the level she had run it. Still, to this day, there will be groups of her fan-friends that will get together and come see us. We know them all by name and spend time with them.

In 1987, Mom reconnected with her high school sweetheart, Troy, who was a widower. I remember when he was flying in to visit her when they first started seeing each other. Frank and I happened to be home in Florida because it was Christmastime. She was just like a kid again going on her first date. After we picked Troy up at the airport and brought him back to the house, they sat down on the couch to talk. Eventually, Frank and I went to bed. When we got up the next morning, they were still right there, talking. They had been there all night, telling stories about their lives.

About three weeks later, Mom asked me, "Mark, what would you think about me getting married?" I laughed and answered, "Well, if you don't marry Troy, I'm going to! He's awesome!" She had gone through so much of her life being lonely that Frank and I were 100 percent on board with her marriage. We were so grateful that we got to see her happy.

Because Troy worked in Memphis, he and Mom lived there. When he was ready to retire, I moved them to Franklin, close to us. Today, now in his late eighties, Papa Troy is still with us. He's a big part of our lives. He's my kids' grandfather. They don't know anything else. He has been a true blessing, along with his daughter, my stepsister, Denise. She handles all of our travel and her husband, Colin, has been with us for thirty-plus years. He's an extension of Frank on the road—road manager, production manager, stage manager, merch manager, and, he will tell you, a babysitter. Colin is an incredible human being who loves *and* hates the band, depending on the moment. But every day, he's my fellow sports enthusiast. One of my best friends. I would never want to be on the road without him at the helm.

Terry Henry (my first cousin) is our lighting director and always makes sure everyone can see my dance moves. Kelli, Frank's wife, oversees our office. So, Denise gets us where we need to go, Colin takes care of us on the journey, Terry makes sure the band can be seen, Kelli keeps the office running smoothly, and, like I said, Frank makes sure everyone gets paid. Definitely all in the family.

It's impossible to pull off being on the road for forty years without having a loyal and incredibly talented crew. Kenny Myers has driven us millions of miles for thirty-plus years. He gets us from city to city, safe and on time. The newest member of our road band and crew is Nathan Winkler, an unbelievable musician and sound engineer from South Africa. He plays bass in the show and mixes monitors, while tending to all the onstage sound needs. Dianna Luster, one of our most loyal and cherished team members, ran our office for over thirty years until she retired. Jenna Roher was with us for years as my assistant and resident rock star, with the very important role of arranging all of my basketball games.

I want to wrap up this section with a final thought about my mom. When I look back at where she started and what she was able to overcome, it is a testament to her faith in God. I remember a sermon where our pastor talked about how one person can change the entire trajectory of their family's future generations. After church, Madison and Gunnar acknowledged and pointed out to Lisa and me, "That's what Nanny did for us."

CHAPTER TWELVE

Travelin' Band

There were five of us thinking that we can
This is the life and times of a travelin' band

—**FROM THE SONG** "Travelin' Band"

OVER OUR FORTY YEARS as a band, we have journeyed millions and millions of miles on interstates, highways, and backroads all over this country and crisscrossed her skies thousands of times. Besides seeing the beauty of this nation firsthand, the greatest blessing has been the incredible people we have met along the way. But they say you can't truly appreciate America until you travel outside her borders to see how the rest of the world lives. I would have to agree with that.

One of the most bizarre trips we ever took was in the late-eighties when we were booked to play a series of shows in China. As odd as this sounds, a major US corporation gave us as a gift to some Chinese dignitaries. After searching through artists in multiple genres, they felt like our merging of styles was a good representation of American music. We took the compliment to heart and accepted.

We flew into Hong Kong, which at that time was still controlled by the British government. From the moment we arrived, they literally treated us like royalty. We had seen really nice places on the road, but this was an entirely different level we didn't know existed. I had never seen a hotel as elaborate as this. My suite was around three thousand square feet with a formal dining area. And each guy in the band had his own room.

After a brief stay there, we flew into China. Right away, we saw how vastly different life is in a communist country. One of the first signs was seeing multiple buildings with hundreds of bicycles parked outside. At first, we thought they must be schools, but then we were told they were factories. Most of them made cigarettes. Obviously, for all those assembly line workers, bicycles were their main source of transportation. No cars. We also noticed at any crossroads or intersections there were no signs or stoplights. You just had to figure it out with the other drivers. We also quickly realized the high level of government censorship, controlling what the people saw and heard. And, of course, the availability and variety of food was nothing like the US. Being raised in the South, after only a few meals, I figured out no one there used butter!

As we were driving through the city, another interesting thing I noticed, especially being a car buff, were these really cool trucks. They looked vintage, yet they also appeared to be brand new. After seeing quite a few, I asked our translator about them. He explained that someone had bought the molds from GM and Ford after they stopped production on those models in the 1940s and 1950s. Then they used the molds to make new trucks throughout China. As a truck lover, it was fun to see all these "new old" models out on the road.

I know a lot of foodies get excited about experiencing the cuisine in other countries, but not me. I'm a true Southern meat-and-three boy. Knowing that, someone had recommended that I pack a stash of peanut butter and crackers. I was glad I listened, because most days, that's what I survived on. When food was served, I had no idea what was on the plate in front of me. Of course, I was careful to never offend our hosts, but I was always conveniently "not very hungry, thank you."

Before we were allowed to play for the dignitaries, I had to meet with their staff to get our lyrics "approved." (Try explaining "Betty's Bein' Bad"! How does that even translate?) I was definitely nervous, well aware we were in a communist country where censorship is constant and "protection from Western ideals" is a very real thing. While the interpretation was difficult to wade through, it must have gone well, because they didn't take issue with any of our songs. (I would suspect that was a part of the vetting process before we were even invited, and this was just a formal double-check to be sure we weren't planning any propaganda.)

The shows we were scheduled to play for the dignitaries were at an auditorium at a university. Once we arrived on campus, they asked if some of the students could interview us. Of course, we agreed. As we were answering their questions through the interpreter, we realized they had never heard amplified music. They had never heard American rock and roll. All they knew was their own traditional music. So, since we were there and had the time, we volunteered to play for the students. Once the leadership agreed, we ended up doing six shows over the next two days for them. To accommodate their class schedule, the shows were at odd times like 3:20 p.m. and 5:10 p.m.

The campus theater seated about three thousand people. Five minutes before the show, there would be no one there. Then, suddenly, the back doors would open and they would walk in single file. Just like elementary school classes in the States. Right at start time, the room was full of students with no one saying a word. We came out like we always do with what must have been such strange music to them. When the intro to the first song blasted through the speakers, you could see them physically go back in their seats like being hit with G-force in a rocket launch. We literally scared them. But as the show went on, they began to settle in. Then they started to loosen up and laugh. They had just never seen anything like us before.

The coolest part of every show was, by the end, they were all standing up and dancing, having a great time. Funny how music creates such a natural response in humans. We had the privilege of witnessing this transformation, after they saw they had permission to have some fun. Fortunately, no one from the Party came in to stop the party. Those two days were honestly one of the highlights of our career, watching music overcome so many barriers and boundaries to touch people's hearts and souls, even if they couldn't understand a word.

Being in the Far East back in the pre-internet and pre–social media days, a lot of the people had never seen a westerner. They were especially fascinated with blond hair. And because they don't see many beards, they were mesmerized by a face full of hair. Between Jim's beard and my long blond hair, we felt like the Avengers arriving on the planet. People kept coming up, wanting to touch us. A crowd would literally gather around just to stare. It was a very bizarre experience. So much of that trip felt like we had been put in a time machine and sent back fifty years.

One of the most sobering moments was when we inquired about the bamboo scaffolding at our hotel, along with the places where drywall wasn't finished or areas weren't painted. After

I asked the translator when the hotel would be finished, he answered, "Oh, it's been done for about three years. What you see is because there's no motivation for the workers to come back and finish."

He told us that when a Chinese boy or girl graduates from high school, the government assigns each one a job for the rest of their lives for a very low wage. There was no motivation to care or have pride in your work. Of course, the super-intelligent kids were trained to be doctors, scientists, and so on, but everyone's destiny was determined by the government. We witnessed the futility and hopelessness of communism up close and personal.

The Show Must Go On

A major decision for any artist is when to make the call to postpone or cancel a show. While no one seems to know for sure, historians tend to think the showbiz phrase "The show must go on" originated with the circus in the nineteenth century. Whether the trapeze artist fell or a lion escaped, the rest of the entertainers had to go on and give the patrons their money's worth. The circus really is a great metaphor for what we have put on for four decades. And, in sickness or in health, the show has to go on. With over six thousand shows down, Sawyer Brown has *never* canceled a single one. But that does not mean we haven't had some major challenges.

One day before a show in Spartanburg, South Carolina, we were playing flag football in the parking lot. Suddenly, something felt like it popped in my leg and I went down. I had no idea what I had done, but I knew it was bad. Still several hours before the show, I went to the local ER. They took one look and said they didn't want to take any chances on my treatment. They recommended I wear a brace until we got home to Nashville and I could see a specialist. So, that night, I went onstage unable to dance and in a lot of pain.

The next night we were playing in Tifton, Georgia. When the promoter saw I was on crutches and in a brace, he said, "You know, Mark, we actually have one of the best knee surgeons in the country right here in Tifton. In fact, he's coming to the show tonight. His name is Dr. Jim Scott." At that time, he was also the team doctor for the Atlanta Falcons.

You're probably thinking what I was thinking: *Why is one of the best knee surgeons in the country in Tifton, Georgia?* That night, Dr. Scott came backstage and, after working on my knee for several minutes, reported, "Mark, you've torn your ACL, but I can fix it for you. If you want, I can do the surgery tonight after your show." We both agreed the sooner the better, so we made a plan. He would watch about half the show, then go back to his surgery room and prep his team. As soon as the show was over, I would be taken to the hospital, while the band and crew would go on to the next town as scheduled. When I told the doctor, "Now, I have a show to do tomorrow night in Columbia, South Carolina," he just laughed.

That night in Tifton, I sang and hopped around on one leg and had as much fun as possible. Then late that evening, I went to have the surgery and Dr. Scott operated on me most of the night.

Around 7:00 in the morning, I started to come out of the anesthesia. Hobie had stayed with me. Dr. Scott came in with his report. "Mark, you not only tore your ACL, but also the meniscus. You really hurt yourself. But I fixed it all. It's not going to be fun doing rehab, but you'll be back to normal soon." Trying to wake up, I responded, "Thanks so much, Doc, but I have to get to my show tonight."

Again, he started laughing—until I pressed, "No, I'm totally serious. A lot of people are counting on us and I can't cancel. That's just not an option." Dr. Scott paused to think for a minute, then he said, "Well, I have my own plane. I'm willing to take you. That way I can monitor you today and tonight. I'm game, if you are." I liked this guy!

With the IV still in my arm and the pain medication flowing, we loaded up for the airport. After the flight and the drive to the venue, I managed to change clothes. Just before they introduced us, Dr. Scott took my IV out. I went out to center stage and sat on a stool, explaining to the audience that I had gotten out of surgery about twelve hours prior. The good doctor stayed and watched some of the show, then packed up his medical equipment and went back to his plane to fly home.

I have to say that was the only Sawyer Brown concert that I was under the influence of any sort of substance. With the pain meds still in my system, I was feeling pretty great. But an added reason why that show was so important to me was because my grandparents and my mom had driven up to see us. My family's influence had taught me that when you get hurt, you just have to walk it off, shake it off, and keep going. And that is exactly what I did that night, thanks to Dr. Scott's incredible care. He referred me to a doctor in Nashville who took over my rehab and follow-up care. But, unfortunately, that was not the last time that I hurt that knee on the road.

A few years later, we were opening for Reba McEntire. I was dressed and ready for the show, hanging out back behind the stage in the arena when some crew guys started throwing a football around. Well, I had to get in on that.

Having too much fun, I lost track of time. All of a sudden, the lights went out, and I heard "Ladies and gentlemen, would you welcome ... Sawyer! ... Brown!" And then I heard the band launch into the intro of the first song. Panicked, I took off running for the stage. What I failed to see in the dark was a huge monitor speaker. I ran right into it—hard—in the soft part of my knee right where the ACL repair had been done. Because my adrenaline was on eleven, I knew it hurt really bad, but again, I had to just shake it off. I got to the mic just in time to start singing and dancing. We were rockin', getting the crowd ready for Reba.

The first time I looked over at Hobie, I saw he was staring at my leg with a horrified look on his face. But I was dialed in with the crowd and going strong, so I ignored whatever he was concerned about. Now, that night I had on bright yellow pants. Like *neon* yellow. When I finally glanced down, I realized the bottom half of one of my pant legs was now bright red. I had popped the ACL repair spot and was bleeding profusely. After our set, we got the bleeding stopped and bandaged my knee up. Back in Nashville, I got fixed up again. Lightning struck twice in the same place on me.

The first time we met Blake Shelton, he had an interesting story for us. He told us that we were his very first live concert to see at the Kerr Dome in Ada, Oklahoma. Also the first time he had ever seen someone from TV in person. Blake told me, "Mark, you had a broken leg, so you came out and had to sit on a stool the whole time to perform. It was probably the worst show of your life because you couldn't dance, but to me, it was just so cool that you weren't going to let that stop you." Blake was right. Nights like that were really hard for me. But it's great to know someone like him, even at a young age, could see the show-must-go-on mentality played out.

Over the years, I've found that the trying days like that are when God is able to reveal things to me. For example, I always felt like the fans came to see *that* guy—the little dancing man. But on those tough nights, sitting there on a stool, singing those songs with the kind of emotion I feel when we play, I realized I was getting the same response as if I were running around on the stage. I remember thinking, *Okay, well, that's pretty cool that we're still connecting. It's really about the music, about the songs that have touched these people.*

There was another time that I had a very different obstacle to overcome to make sure the show went on.

One of the promoters we had worked with for many years was struggling financially. We had agreed to do a show to help him pay off debt and get back on his feet. Usually, a couple of times a year, I get this funk on my vocal cords from the changing of seasons. It can be brutal for a singer. Now, it's one thing to go out when you aren't in good voice or you're hoarse, but it's quite another to have *no* voice. But we always say that our fans sing the songs louder than we do anyway. All we have to do is go out, get them started, and off we go. On this particular night, I could hardly make a sound. To help our friend, because the show was sold out, we not only couldn't cancel, but we had to hit a home run for him.

Earlier in the day, I found a throat specialist who gave me a cortisone shot. But things were not looking good and by sound-check I had nothing. That is, unless you wanted an impression of a grizzly. At dinner, the promoter came to me and nervously asked,

"Mark, what are we gonna do?" I managed to whisper, "Not sure. I'll figure it out." At showtime, I still had nothing. He asked me again, "Mark, *what* are we doing?" I answered, "Introduce us. I'll figure it out."

The guys launched into the first song and I walked out onstage. When it came time for me to sing, I motioned for the band to stop. Everyone froze and looked at me. It got really quiet, really fast. The guys had no idea what was about to happen, but I was just going with my gut on the spot.

Doing my very best to speak, I managed to get out, "Hey, everybody, we came all this way to spend the evening with you, but as you can tell, I won't be able to sing at all. Now, I got two guys up here who are fantastic singers. You've never gotten to hear *them* before, but they're gonna do every hit song we have. And there is nothing wrong with my legs, so I'm going to dance. To make tonight even more special, we've never done this before, but in the middle of the show, we'll do a Q-and-A session. Then afterwards, we'll be out in the lobby to take pictures and meet everybody here. We'll stay till the last person leaves." The crowd went crazy. Not one single person wanted their money back. That was a long but incredible night. We did an entire show in front of a sold-out crowd of happy fans. And I did not sing a lick all night.

One very cool story from that evening was that Shayne took the lead vocal on "The Walk." As he sang, I could see that he was emotional, trying not to choke up. After the show, he told me, "When I was singing those words, thinking about my two kids and also losing my dad not long ago, even though I have heard you sing it countless times, the song took on a whole new life for me tonight."

Ringmaster on the Road

If life in a band is like traveling with the circus, that must make me the ringmaster.

One thing we keep in the forefront of our minds is that our fans lay down their hard-earned money to spend an evening with us. They get their tickets, mark their calendars, and look forward to the show. That's why my attitude has always been, *It's your money, y'all. What do you want to do? We'll do whatever you want.* My job is to read the room and lead the band through pulling that off for them. That's why on any given night, we have all this energy locked and loaded.

Whether we are singing one of our high-energy songs, a mid-tempo, or one of our ballads, I have to figure out how to position them all and set them up right. I'm responsible for figuring out when to add songs, take them away, or pull something out of the hat. We're hitting everyone hard and I'm just taking them on a ride. But about five songs in, when we get to "The Walk," it's always a very impactful and moving moment. Winding everyone down, or back up, is an art form, as far as I'm concerned.

Our two most important moments onstage are when we walk out and then the last twenty to twenty-five minutes of the show. And everything in between has to have an impact. By the time we get to the finale, we're taking the horse to the barn. The closer we get, the faster they go. Shifting all the gears, up and down, is crucial to everyone having a great time. With any show, I know early on that I've got to make sure the crowd has enough energy to get through the whole night.

Because we don't have a set list, the band and I have

developed signs and signals as to what songs are next, where to go, etc., like a quarterback calling audibles at the line. Or a third-base coach giving signals to the batter. I'm very rhythmic in everything that I feel. So, some nights I'll want a song to be faster than usual. For the sake of that flexibility, we don't use a click track (a metronome the drummer or only the band hears). From night to night, the tempos may be a little different, depending on what I think the energy needs. Joe-Joe is great at adjusting with me, whether that's speeding up or pulling back.

An interviewer once asked Joe-Joe, "So, tell me about your relationship with Mark onstage." He answered, "Mark is really intense. Like *really* intense. But that's why we're here. Because he competes. So when he walks out, I've gotta connect with him. And if I make him happy, we're good to go. But some nights, that's not easy." When I heard his answer, I thought, *That is absolutely true. That's why I'm harder on him than anybody else in the band. But for forty years, thank God, he's put up with me.*

Once a show is over, good or bad, we never talk about it. When I walk off the stage, that's in the past and we're on to the next city, the next show. We're not going to rehash anything. I always tell our new crew guys, "You don't have to come up to me and say, 'Hey, good show.' I'm not that guy. I don't need that. You never have to tell me, because I know before anyone knows." A lot of artists have to constantly be affirmed by their crew, but I don't.

In my mind, we're never *not* going to have a good show, regardless of what may have happened. There's always something that can go wrong onstage, but I learned a long time ago that the crowd doesn't realize 99 percent of those things. You don't let them know and they don't care. They bought a ticket because they love you. The critics get in free. But everybody that paid, I just want to make sure they get what they came for. So we go out there and give them an amazing night. That's our job. I always say that we are in the service business. We didn't come to be served, but to serve. Just give the people an incredible and memorable evening.

To this day, it is such a great feeling to walk out onstage and see a drum set, a keyboard, and our amps there. No gimmicks. No tricks. We tell the crowd, "We're gonna hang with y'all tonight and play forty years' worth of music for you."

Every artist wants to be Elvis, and early on, I had to wrestle with that temptation too. But once you see fame for what it is and what it's not, you realize the illusion of it all. Every now and then you get recognized, or you get to go to the front of the line or get a better seat at the restaurant. But the truth for me is that I've had the blessing of living the dream by getting to be in a band with amazing guys, playing our own music, and doing what I love.

If people buy tickets to our show, have an incredible time, and make an emotional connection, then they'll listen to our music, wear our T-shirt, see us the next time we come to town, *and* bring their friends. I know that to be true because I'm a fan myself. There are artists I have listened to and followed for decades. I know what both sides of that coin feel like. True fans don't care what critics or the industry says. They know the artists they love, and that's all that matters. As the years passed, the fans became all that mattered to us too.

To put on the very best show we can every night, the sound-check is also a critical factor that I take very seriously. There are days in a tough room when we'll be in there for hours. I walk around the entire venue and listen from as many positions as possible while the band plays. I'll have the sound company move speakers or whatever it takes to get things sounding right. It's really important to me that no matter where you're sitting in the room, I want you to have the same experience that the people down front are having. Steve "Lightnin'" Lowrey, our front-of-house engineer on the road is also my studio engineer at home, so he knows me and knows us really well.

So many times while the band is playing as I'm walking around out front, I hear the guys and think how great they sound. I have a sense of pride that, to me, I'm in the best band in the world. We can go toe to toe with anybody. When we still have people tell us that we sound like our records or we sound just like we did in 1984, we're proud they feel that way. One of the ways we accomplish that is we are not a jam band. Everything is exactly like the arrangement on the album. Every guitar solo is the same every night, how it was on the record. Everyone plays what's on the record. It doesn't matter if we get bored with it, because the show is not for us, it's for the people who bought a ticket. I sing the same lyrics every night, so every note is going to be the same too.

They Just Keep Showing Up

Looking back, I am grateful that Lisa had the revelation from God about how He had cleared the deck in my life, all so I would have the time and energy to be a part of Casting Crowns. I am so grateful that He took the radio success away. But I'm doubly grateful He didn't take our touring away. The reason? Our incredible, loyal, faithful fans. So you can't turn on current country radio and hear us anymore. I'm good with that. As long as we can keep going out to see the people we have spent the past four decades with.

But not only did the Lord not take touring away, once we arrived at the right number of shows per year, that aspect of our career has *never* declined. In fact, some years have increased.

To this day, I'm always surprised when I walk out on that stage and there are actually people there. Especially when the room is packed and energized. Literally, every night in my mind, I prepare myself in case we walk out to empty seats. So, any night I see a packed house, I think, *How many concerts are you all going to come to?*

For years now, at every show, I ask, "How many of you have *never* seen Sawyer Brown before? Raise your hands." Pretty much any given night, three-fourths of the audience lifts their hand. At the least, it's half the crowd. We can't figure it out, but you know what? We don't have to. We just keep showing up and connecting.

But then here's my next question for those same folks who have never seen us before. I laugh and ask, "Why now? Why, after almost forty years, are you coming to see us now?" It's certainly no complaint or criticism, just curiosity!

What we know for sure is that we work very hard to give everyone the same show that they would have experienced in 1985. (Except for the hair; the hair is long gone.) And I believe we're better and more seasoned now.

Here's the reality about Sawyer Brown: even if we had continued beyond the twenty-one years with more hit records, we couldn't have done any more than we did in the music industry. We hit the ceiling and then kept bumping our heads on it. We had established such a strong catalog that there was no new level to achieve. No other place to arrive. We carved out our spot and have stayed there. That has been such a blessing.

In the early years, it always surprised me when people would come up and act like they knew me. But then I came to realize that was a sign they were comfortable. To a certain degree, they *did* know me. They had seen enough shows, watched enough videos, listened to or read enough interviews to get a good glimpse of who I am. So, for them, it's like seeing an old friend on the street. For many years, that has become a two-way street.

What you see onstage is a definite part of my personality that very few will see offstage. A perfect example is when the kids were growing up, they never saw me write a song. I remember Madison talking about going to school with Michael W. Smith's and Steven Curtis Chapman's kids and how they would talk about their dads playing music at home. Madison told them, "I don't think I've ever heard my dad sing at home." Because I'm an insomniac, my time to work was always at night when my family was in bed. I would tuck myself away and write, play, and sing. I just chose to never do that in the house with everybody gathered around. Some of that is likely because I am so introverted.

Our fans feel the strong connection, because we've been in the public eye since we were in our early twenties. That's our lifetime *and* theirs. Even back in the days when we were on TV, magazine covers, and billboards, I always engaged with people whenever being recognized in public. But truthfully, I'm more comfortable with *not* being recognized.

If you come to one of our shows today, you'll notice that about a quarter of the crowd is under thirty. Our only explanation for that dynamic is their parents played us when they were growing up and it's a good childhood memory. A lot of them come with their parents and/or grandparents. For us, that's the biggest compliment we can get—to see two or more generations coming to see us together. It's a family gathering in more ways than one.

That's why when we get to "The Walk," it can be a killer moment emotionally. Even for us. There are nights I can't even look up at the people, because it's so emotional with what I'm seeing in the crowd. There's such a connection with them, particularly with that song, especially if someone comes with their dad or granddad, or both.

One night in 2022 at a show in Montana, right as we came onstage, I saw in the front row a frail, elderly man with his grandson who looked to be in his late-twenties. Throughout the night, I watched them. There were times I was concerned about him holding up through the evening.

For the last several years, there is a point in the show when people come down front and crowd in at the stage. When I started to see people leave their seats and walk down, I was immediately concerned about the old man. The grandson caught the attention of a security guard, and they helped him walk the few feet from the front row to the front of the stage.

When we got to "The Walk," there was only one person I stepped out to shake hands with—that old man. When I did and he looked up at me to take my hand, the grandson, with one arm holding up his grandfather, started to cry.

Those are the times that I have no idea what the story is, but I can clearly see there is an incredible moment happening right in front of me. I have the privilege of singing someone's life back to them. To that old man and his grandson, they believe "The Walk" is not about anyone else; it's just about the two of them. It's for them and about them. And they finally, after all these years, got to be on the front row for me to sing those words to them.

In the Midwest, there are always a lot of young farmer kids that listened to us when they were out on their combines or tractors. Now they bring their wives or girlfriends. For a country boy who likes to rock, we're his band.

One of the unique things about Sawyer Brown is we don't really have a lot of *love* songs; we have *life* songs.

So, You Want to Close the Show, Huh?

Over the years, we have played shows with some great classic rock acts. One was with Starship (formerly Jefferson Starship). During a conversation with Mickey Thomas, the lead singer, he told me, "Man, I gotta tell you, when I saw we were opening for you, I was confused. I thought, *Why are we the openers?* Then I went on Wikipedia and saw all your hit songs and realized, *Oh my gosh, okay, I get it.*" But not all artists have …

Several years back, we were invited to play the famous Chili Cook-Off in Miami. Because KC of the Sunshine Band has been a longtime friend and he lives there, he came out to the show to hang with us for the day. We were supposed to be the show closer, but another artist on the bill demanded that he wouldn't play unless he closed. Our set had to be moved before his. The promoter came to us and explained his dilemma. We politely agreed to comply for his sake. But when another artist pulls a stunt like that with us, he or she has just thrown down the gauntlet, drawn a line in the sand, challenged us to a duel, or whatever metaphor you want to use.

I went to KC and said, "Hey, why don't you come out on our encore and we'll do one of your songs and then you sing with us on our last song?" He tried to talk me out of it, but I insisted. And I knew exactly what was about to happen.

In front of twenty thousand people, we finished "The Race Is On" and left the stage before coming back for our encores. With the entire place going crazy, I announced KC. When he ran out and launched into the classic keyboard intro to "Get Down Tonight," the energy of the crowd went through the roof. When he finished, we went straight into "Some Girls Do" with KC joining us. By now, the artist who had thrown the tantrum demanding to be the closer was standing in the wings, watching. Definitely, an "oh crap!" moment for him.

When we all jumped up in the air and came down on the last note, the crowd was in a frenzy, screaming and applauding. As I walked by the guy, I stopped, motioned toward the crowd, and announced, "It's all yours, buddy!" (Did I mention before that I'm competitive?)

The same kind of throw-down happened in Comstock, Nebraska, when a female country artist demanded to change spots with us and close. She couldn't understand why the promoter had intentionally placed us last, but she was about to find out the hard way.

Following her ultimatum, the promoter came to us. We just told him, "Hey, no problem. Do what you need to do." Remember the state I said the show was in? After our last encore, with the crowd waiting, I walked back out with an acoustic guitar to play "The Nebraska Song." Every single person in that crowd stood and sang every word with me. Doesn't matter how big of an artist you are, you don't want to have to follow an arena full of people singing their state's unofficial anthem about their beloved football team. The moral to that story is there are just some bears you don't need to poke.

The Next Chapter

Beginning in 2002, and especially after the *Mission Temple* record in 2005, we settled into a good groove of the band focusing only on doing around 125 shows a year. Cutting out the record label and radio meant a drastic reduction in interviews and media, all the time-consuming peripherals that come with maintaining your image as an artist. Life became much simpler for us all. For the next decade or so, outside of our tour schedule, I intentionally placed my time and energy on my family and working with Casting Crowns.

When we hit the decade of the 2010s, I began to sense it was time to release a new album. Fans were asking for new music and, as always, we heard them loud and clear. I had written some new songs that I was feeling really good about, so in the fall of 2011, we released *Travelin' Band* on my label, Beach Street Records. The theme of the album was to deliver a tribute to our longevity. From that project, there are two songs we play in the show, "Smokin' Hot Wife" and the title cut.

The first time my nephew heard "Travelin' Band," we were in the car together. When it ended, he asked me, "So, how long did it take you to write that song?" I laughed and said, "Twenty-seven years!" From start to finish, that song is our story in four minutes.

Today, as we celebrate hitting the forty-year mark, we know who we are and we also know what everyone's expectations are of us. We know when we get on the bus what our job is, where we're going, and what we're about to do. That's always a driving force for us. We pride ourselves in never allowing anyone the opportunity to say, "Man, they've lost a little bit. They're just not the same."

Reflecting back over the years, there are times that it seems like it was yesterday and there are times that it feels like forever.

I told you in the introduction that I believed there was definitely a divine plan for my life. Well, clearly there was. And, thank the Lord, the plan has worked.

Can we go another forty years?

Well, sure, we will if you will.

Travelin' Band

They were searchin' for stars
when we came along
It was rock 'n roll in a country song
There were five of us thinking that we can
This is the life and times of a traveling band
But Hollywood had a funny face
So we took our chances and we got away
We headed back to Nashville, Tennessee
Hobie, Bobby, Jim and Joe and me
No, the West Coast life didn't fit just right

You could see us on the television
It ain't easy bein' all that grand
So we put on our blue jeans and our t-shirts
And made off with our guitars in the van
And took our place on the stage
In a travelin' band

We heard our song on the radio
Along with "The Gambler" we hit the road
All across the USA
We were gypsies on parade
We were all about three chords and the truth
We wrote our songs on the bus, in the booth
Some go fast like "Some Girls Do"
Some go slow like "Used to Blue"

And when the lights went down
We could hear the crowd

We headlined our first show in Salt Lake City
We still make a stop there now and then
They've got all our faces on their t-shirts
You should have seen our hairdos
way back when
We took our place on the stage
In a travelin' band

Fame and fortune don't mean much
Without someone to hold and someone to touch
Some wives left, some stayed on
So who do you love when the beat goes on
Now we're 27 years and a million miles
Shiftin' gears and changin' styles
We said goodbye to old DC
Now it's Hobie, Shayne and Jim, the Joes and me
And when "The Race is On," they all sing along

Now I'd like to take this time to thank you
And though it's been a long and winding road
I count my blessings when I see your faces
And I look down at this guitar in my hand
And I take my place on the stage
In a travelin' band
I'm in a travelin' band

Sawyer Brown Discography

(1984–2017)

1. Sawyer Brown (1984 Capitol/Curb)
Producers: Mark Miller/Randy Scruggs
Chart Positions: #2 US Country, #140 Overall

1. Leona (Bill Shore, David Wills) 3:02
2. Feel Like Me (Mark A. Miller, Randy Scruggs) 3:05
3. Used to Blue (J. Fred Knobloch, Bill LaBounty) 3:20
4. It's Hard to Keep a Good Love Down (Miller, Scruggs) 3:04
5. Step That Step (Miller) 2:50
6. Smokin' in the Rockies (Frank Dycus, Dean Dillon, Buddy Cannon, Gary Stewart) 2:53
7. Staying Afloat (J.D. Martin, Don King) 2:44
8. Broken Candy (Miller) 3:27
9. The Sun Don't Shine on the Same Folks All the Time (Mark Gray, Danny Morrison, Johnny Slate) 2:49
10. Going Back to Indiana (Berry Gordy Jr., Alphonso Mizell, Frederick Perren, Deke Richard) 3:04

Singles:
1. Leona – October 1984 – #16 US Country
2. Step That Step – January 1985 – #1 US Country, #1 Canada Country
3. Used to Blue – May 1985 – #3 US Country, #1 Canada Country

2. Shakin' (1985 Capitol/Curb)
Producers: Mark Miller/Randy Scruggs
Chart Positions: #3 US Country

1.   When Your Heart Goes (Woo, Woo, Woo)
     (Mark Miller, Randy Scruggs) 2:28
2.   The Secretary's Song
     (Beckie Foster, Bill LaBounty, Quentin Powers) 2:45
3.   Heart, Don't Fall Now
     (Becky Foster, Bill LaBounty, Carolyn Swilley) 3:22
4. * Shakin' (Miller, Scruggs) 3:15
5.   Sharin' the Moonshine (Miller, Scruggs) 3:42
6.   Betty's Bein' Bad (Marshall Chapman) 3:15
7.   I Believe (Greg Guidry, David Martin) 3:50
8.   Lonely Girls (Miller, Scruggs) 3:15
9.   That's a No No (Miller, Scruggs) 3:07
10. Billy, Does Your Bulldog Bite (Ronny Scaife, Bobby Neal) 2:44

Singles:
1.   Betty's Bein' Bad – September 1985 – #5 US Country,
     #5 Canada Country
2.   Heart, Don't Fall Now – February 1986 – #14 US Country,
     #16 Canada Country
3.   Shakin' – May 1986 – #15 US Country, #7 Canada Country

3. Out Goin' Cattin' (1986 Capitol/Curb)
Producers: Mark Miller/Randy Scruggs
Chart Positions: #8 US Country

1.   Lady of the Evening (Mark Miller) 3:43

2. Better Be Some Tears
   (Kerry Chater, Bill LaBounty, Beckie Foster) 3:33
3. Not Ready to Let You Go (Steve Dorff, Mark Miller) 3:14
4. Out Goin' Cattin' featuring Joe Bonsall
   (Randy Scruggs, Miller) 2:53
5. The House Won't Rock (Frank J. Myers, Miller) 2:55
6. New Shoes (LaBounty, Foster, Susan Longacre) 3:02
7. Graveyard Shift (Gene Nelson, Paul Nelson) 3:51
8. Night Rockin' (Scruggs, Miller) 3:56
9. Savin' the Honey for the Honeymoon (J. Barry, Rick Vito) 3:07
10. Gypsies on Parade (Miller) 3:52

Singles:
1. Out Goin' Cattin' – September 1986 – #11 US Country,
   #4 Canada Country
2. Gypsies on Parade – December 1986 – #25 US Country,
   #23 Canada Country
3. Savin' the Honey for the Honeymoon – May 1987 –
   #58 US Country

4. Somewhere in the Night (1987 Capitol/Curb)
Producers: Mark Miller/Ron Chancey
Chart Positions: #16 US Country

1. Somewhere in the Night (Don Cook, Rafe Van Hoy) 3:20
2. Little Red Caboose (Steve Gibson, Dave Loggins) 4:07
3. This Missin' You Heart of Mine (Woody Mullis, Mike Geiger) 2:40
4. Dr. Rock N. Roll (Dennis Linde) 3:12
5. Still Hold On (Kim Carnes, Eric Kaz,
   Wendy Waldman, Dave Ellingson) 3:42

6. Lola's Love (Dennis Linde) 3:55

7. In This Town (Tom Shapiro, Michael Garvin) 3:04

8. A Mighty Big Broom (Mark Miller) 2:52

9. Still Life in Blue (Dennis Linde) 2:49

10. Old Photographs (Kenneth Beal, Kix Brooks, Bill McClelland) 2:54

Singles:

1. Somewhere in the Night – August 1987 –
   #29 US Country, #26 Canada Country

2. This Missin' You Heart of Mine – November 1987 –
   #2 US Country, #1 Canada Country

3. Old Photographs – April 1988 – #27 US Country,
   #35 Canada Country

5 . Wide Open (1988 Capitol/Curb)
Producers: Mark Miller/Ron Chancey
Chart Positions: #33 US Country

1. My Baby's Gone (Dennis Linde) 3:28

2. Old Pair of Shoes (Mark Miller) 2:45

3. What Am I Going to Tell My Heart
   (Gregg Hubbard, Bobby Randall) 3:44

4. Blue Denim Soul (Miller) 3:52

5. It Wasn't His Child (Skip Ewing) 3:38

6. Wide Open (Beckie Foster, Bill LaBounty, Alan LeBoeuf) 4:06

7. Falling Apart at the Heart (Hubbard, Miller) 4:00

8. Axe to Grind (Miller) 3:10

9. Running Out of Reasons to Run (Jim Rushing, J.D. Martin) 3:38

10. Field Hand (Miller) 4:37

Singles:
1. My Baby's Gone – October 1988 – #11 US Country,
    #5 Canada Country

2. It Wasn't His Child – December 1988 – #51 US Country

3. Old Pair of Shoes – September 1989 – #50 US Country

6. The Boys Are Back (1989 Capitol/Curb)
Producers: Mark Miller/Randy Scruggs
Chart Positions: #5 US Country / #85 Canada (Platinum)

1. Puttin' the Dark Back into the Night (Mark Miller) 3:08
2. Rosie Knows (Mark Miller, Gregg Hubbard) 3:47
3. I Did It for Love (Mark Miller) 4:35
4. The Race Is On (Don Rollins) 2:53
5. Hey, Hey (Jennifer Kimball, Ed Arkin) 2:47
6. Good While It Lasted (Don Cook, Bill LaBounty) 2:56
7. Locomotive (Mark Miller) 3:34
8. The Heartland (Mark Miller, Randy Scruggs) 4:05
9. I'm Gonna Miss You After All
    (Tony Haselden, Keith Worsham) 3:19
10. Gettin' Tough (Good Ol' Boy)
    (Steve Earle, Richard Bennett) 4:01
11. Passin' Train (Gregg Hubbard) 3:19

Singles:
1. The Race Is On – September 1989 – #5 US Country,
    #3 Canada Country
2. I Did It for Love – December 1988 – #33 US Country
3. Puttin' the Dark Back into the Night – September 1989 –
    #33 US Country

7. Sawyer Brown Greatest Hits (1990 Capitol/Curb)
Producers: Mark Miller/Randy Scruggs/Ron Chancey
Chart Positions: #26 US Country / Canada (Gold)

1. Step That Step (Miller) 2:47
2. Heart Don't Fall Now (Becky Foster, Bill LaBounty, Carolyn Swilley) 3:21
3. Betty's Bein' Bad (Marshall Chapman) 3:15
4. The Race Is On (Don Rollins) 2:53
5. When Love Comes Callin' (Mark Miller, Randy Scruggs) 2:44
6. Puttin' the Dark Back into the Night (Mark Miller) 3:06
7. Leona (Bill Shore, David Wills) 3:01
8. Used to Blue (J. Fred Knobloch, Bill LaBounty) 3:19
9. Out Goin' Cattin' feat. Joe Bonsall (Randy Scruggs, Miller) 2:52
10. Shakin' (Miller, Scruggs) 3:16

Singles:
1. When Love Comes Callin' – September 1989 – #40 US Country, #18 Canada Country

8. Buick (1991 Capitol/Curb)
Producers: Mark Miller/Randy Scruggs
Chart Positions: #23 US Country, #140 Overall

1. Mama's Little Baby Loves Me (Gregg Hubbard, Mark Miller) 3:08
2. My Baby Drives a Buick (Mark Miller, Randy Scruggs) 3:01
3. When You Run from Love (Mac McAnally, Mark Miller) 3:40
4. The Walk (Mark Miller) 3:44
5. Forty-Eight Hours till Monday (Gregg Hubbard, Mark Miller) 2:46

6. Superman's Daughter (Mark Miller) 2:18
7. One Less Pony (Mark Miller) 3:22
8. Still Water (Duet w/ Donna McElroy)
    (Mark Miller, Gregg Hubbard) 3:19
9. Stealin' Home (Mark Miller, Gregg Hubbard) 3:13
10. Thunder Bay (Mark Miller, Randy Scruggs) 4:45

Singles:
1. One Less Pony – February 1991 – #70 US Country
2. Mama's Little Baby Loves Me – April 1991 – #68 US Country

9. The Dirt Road (1992 Capitol/Curb)
Producers: Mark Miller/Randy Scruggs
Chart Positions: #12 US Country (Gold),
#68 Overall, #8 Canada Country

1. The Dirt Road (Gregg Hubbard, Mark Miller) 2:53
2. Some Girls Do (Mark Miller) 3:12
3. Another Trip to the Well (Gregg Hubbard, Mark Miller) 4:00
4. Time and Love (Mark Miller, Randy Scruggs) 3:18
5. Ruby Red Shoes (Mark Miller, Butch D. Myers) 3:03
6. Fire in the Rain (Mark Miller) 2:18
7. Burnin' Bridges (on a Rocky Road) (Mark Miller) 2:55
8. Sometimes a Hero (Mark Miller, Gregg Hubbard) 3:47
9. Ain't That Always the Way (Mark Miller, Gregg Hubbard) 2:40
10. When Twist Comes to Shout (Mark Miller, Terry McMillan) 3:19
11. The Walk (Mark Miller) 3:43

Singles:
1. The Walk – June 1991 – #2 US Country, #5 Canada Country

2. The Dirt Road – November 1991 – #3 US Country,
    #1 Canada Country

3. Some Girls Do – March 1992 – #1 US Country,
    #2 Canada Country

10. Café on the Corner (1992 Curb)
Producers: Mark Miller/Randy Scruggs
Chart Positions: #23 US Country (Gold),
#117 Overall, #10 Canada Country

1. Café on the Corner (Mac McAnally) 3:23
2. Trouble on the Line (Mark Miller, Bill Shore) 2:31
3. All These Years (Mac McAnally) 3:20
4. Travelin' Shoes (Mark Miller, Gregg Hubbard) 2:59
5. A Different Tune (Mark Miller, Gregg Hubbard) 3:01
6. Lesson in Love (Mark Miller, Gregg Hubbard, Duncan Cameron) 2:32
7. Chain of Love (Mark Miller, Gregg Hubbard) 2:25
8. Homestead in My Heart (Duncan Cameron, Michael Mikulka) 3:52
9. I Kept My Motor Runnin' feat. Donna McElroy (Mark Miller, Randy Scruggs) 2:55
10. Sister's Got a New Tattoo (Mark Miller, Gregg Hubbard) 3:57

Singles:
1. Café on the Corner – August 1992 – #5 US Country,
    #2 Canada Country
2. All These Years – November 1992 – #3 US Country,
    #42 US Adult Contemporary, #2 Canada Country
3. Trouble on the Line – March 1993 – #5 US Country,
    #7 Canada Country

11. **Outskirts of Town** (1993 Curb)
Producers: Mark Miller/Randy Scruggs
Chart Positions: #13 US Country (Gold), #81 Overall,
#2 Canada Country (Gold)

1. The Boys and Me (Mac McAnally, Mark Miller) 3:23
2. Farmer Tan (Gregg Hubbard, Mark Miller) 4:07
3. Outskirts of Town (Duncan Cameron, Mac McAnally) 3:20
4. Thank God for You (Mac McAnally, Mark Miller) 3:18
5. Listenin' for You (Gregg Hubbard, Mark Miller) 2:56
6. Eyes of Love (Duncan Cameron,
   Gregg Hubbard, Mark Miller) 3:06
7. Hard to Say (Mark Miller) 3:24
8. Drive Away feat. Dana McVicker (Mark Miller, Bill LaBounty) 3:47
9. Heartbreak Highway (John Flanagan, Mark Miller) 2:34
10. Love to Be Wanted (Mark Miller, Bill Shore) 2:31
11. Hold On (Gregg Hubbard) 3:30
12. The Boys and Me (Dance Remix) (Mac McAnally, Mark Miller) 5:05

Singles:
1. Thank God for You – June 1993 – #1 US Country,
   #17 US Hot 100, #1 Canada Country
2. The Boys and Me – October 1993 – #4 US Country,
   #2 Canada Country
3. Outskirts of Town – February 1994 – #40 US Country
4. Hard to Say – June 1994 – #5 US Country,
   #20 Canada Country

12. Sawyer Brown Greatest Hits 1990–1995 (1995 Curb)
Producers: Mark Miller/Randy Scruggs/Mac McAnally
Chart Positions: #5 US Country (Gold), #44 Overall / #7 Canada
Country (Gold), #35 Overall

1. Some Girls Do (Mark Miller) 3:12
2. Thank God for You (Mac McAnally, Mark Miller) 3:17
3. All These Years (Mac McAnally) 3:21
4. The Dirt Road (Gregg Hubbard, Mark Miller) 2:52
5. This Time (Mark Miller, Mac McAnally) 3:43
6. The Walk (Mark Miller) 3:43
7. Trouble on the Line (Mark Miller, Bill Shore) 2:31
8. Café on the Corner (Mac McAnally) 3:22
9. I Don't Believe in Goodbye
    (Mark Miller, Scotty Emerick, Bryan White) 3:51
10. The Boys and Me (Mac McAnally, Mark Miller) 3:23

Singles:
1. This Time – November 1994 – #2 US Country,
    #5 Canada Country
2. I Don't Believe in Goodbye – March 1995 –
    #4 US Country, #8 Canada Country

13. This Thing Called Wantin' and Havin' It All
(1995 Curb)
Producers: Mark Miller/Mac McAnally
Chart Positions: #10 US Country, #77 Overall,
#2 Canada Country (Gold)

1. Nothing Less Than Love (Mark Miller, Gregg Hubbard) 3:38

2. Big Picture 3:57
3. I Will Leave the Light On (Duncan Cameron) 3:10
4. (This Thing Called) Wantin' and Havin' It All
    (Dave Loggins, Ronnie Samoset) 3:28
5. Another Mile (Mark Miller, Gregg Hubbard) 3:43
6. Round Here (Mark Miller, Gregg Hubbard, Scotty Emerick) 4:02
7. She's Gettin' There (Mark Miller, Scotty Emerick, John Northrup,
    M.C. Potts) 4:04
8. Treat Her Right (Lenny LeBlanc, Ava Aldridge) 3:29
9. Like a John Deere (Mark Miller, Bill Shore) 2:34
10. Small Town Hero (Mark Miller, Gregg Hubbard) 3:56

Singles:
1. (This Thing Called) Wantin' and Havin' It All – July 1995 –
    #11 US Country, #5 Canada Country
2. Round Here – November 1995 – #19 US Country,
    #19 Canada Country
3. Treat Her Right – March 1996 – #3 US Country,
    #19 Canada Country

14. Six Days on the Road (1997 Curb)
Producers: Mark Miller/Mac McAnally
Chart Positions: #8 US Country, #73 Overall,
#2 Canada Country (Gold)

1. Another Side (Mark Miller) 4:41
2. Talkin' 'bout You (Mark Alan Springer) 3:39
3. This Night Won't Last Forever (Bill LaBounty, Roy Freeland) 3:56
4. Six Days on the Road (Earl Green, Carl Montgomery) 2:53
5. Small Talk (Mac McAnally, Mark Miller) 3:42

6. With This Ring (Mark Miller) 3:12

7. Transistor Rodeo (Mark Miller) 3:06

8. Night and Day (Mac McAnally) 3:35

9. Half a Heart (Gregg Hubbard, Mark Miller) 3:02

10. Between You and Paradise (Neal Coty, Mark Alan Springer) 4:15

11. A Love Like This (Mark Miller, Bill Shore) 2:50

12. Every Twist and Turn (Gregg Hubbard, Mark Miller) 3:11

13. Hidden Track :04

14. Hidden Track :04

15. Hidden Track :04

16. Hidden Track :04

17. Hidden Track :04

18. The Nebraska Song (Mark Miller) 2:53

Singles:
1. Six Days on the Road – March 1997 – #13 US Country,
    US Top 100 #17, #9 Canada Country

2. This Night Won't Last Forever – June 1997 – #19 US Country,
    #19 Canada Country

3. Another Side – February 1998 – #55 US Country

4. Small Talk – April 1998 – #60 US Country

15. Hallelujah, He Is Born (1997 Curb)
Producers: Mark Miller/Mac McAnally
Chart Positions: #42 US Country, #17 US Christian

1. Glory to the King (Gregg Hubbard, Mark Miller) 3:48

2. Sweet Mary Cried (Gregg Hubbard, Mark Miller) 4:13

3. Oh, What a Night in Bethlehem (Mark Miller) 4:30

4. Hallelujah, He Is Born (Gregg Hubbard, Mark Miller) 4:12

5. Where Christmas Goes (Gregg Hubbard, Mark Miller) 4:12

6. Christmas All Year Long (Mac McAnally) 3:12

7. He Sent a Carpenter (Mark Miller, Bill Shore) 3:11

8. Angels We Have Heard on High (Traditional) 5:02

9. The Little Drummer Boy
    (Katherine K. Davis, Henry Onorati, Harry Simeone) 4:02

10. Just One Night (Mac McAnally) 2:43

11. The Wiseman's Song (Scotty Emerick, Gregg Hubbard) 3:07

12. Little Town of Bethlehem
    (Gregg Hubbard, Bishop Phillips Brooks) 3:14

16. Drive Me Wild (1999 Curb)

Producers: Mark Miller/Mac McAnally
Chart Positions: #10 US Country, #99 Overall,
#9 Canada Country

1. Break My Heart Again (Marc Jordan, Stephan Moccio) 3:30

2. We're Everything to Me (Mark Miller, Gregg Hubbard,
    Mike Lawler) 3:14

3. I'm in Love with Her (Chuck Cannon, Allen Shamblin) 3:32

4. Drive Me Wild (Mark Miller, Gregg Hubbard, Mike Lawler) 3:35

5. Moon Over Miami (Scotty Emerick, Mark Miller) 3:57

6. All Wound Up (Mac McAnally) 2:47

7. 800 Pound Jesus (Billy Maddox, Paul Thorn) 2:54

8. It All Comes Down to Love (Chuck Cannon) 3:05

9. Every Little Thing (Scotty Emerick, John Scott Sherrill) 2:47

10. Playin' a Love Song (Gregg Hubbard, Mark Miller) 3:34

11. Soul Searchin' (Mark Miller, Mike Lawler, Anthony Crawford) 3:28

Singles:
1. Drive Me Wild – November 1998 – #6 US Country
2. I'm in Love with Her – May 1999 – #47 US Country
3. 800 Pound Jesus – January 2000 – #40 US Country

17. Sawyer Brown: The Hits Live (2000 Curb)
Producers: Mark Miller/Brian Tankersley
Chart Positions: #35 US Country

1. Six Days on the Road (Earl Green, Carl Montgomery) 2:58
   Recorded live December 17, 1999, in Joliet, IL
2. Hard to Say (Mark Miller) 3:19
   Recorded live February 25, 2000, in Ogden, UT
3. This Time (Mark Miller, Mac McAnally) 2:38
   Recorded live February 25, 2000, in Ogden, UT
4. Café on the Corner (Mac McAnally) 3:20
   Recorded live November 6, 1999, in Taylorville, IL
5. The Walk (Mark Miller) 3:47
   Recorded live December 19, 1999, in Spirit Lake, ID
6. Step That Step (Mark Miller) 3:01
   Recorded live January 26, 2000, in Mount Pleasant, MI
7. The Dirt Road (Gregg Hubbard, Mark Miller) 3:08
   Recorded live December 17, 1999, in Joliet, IL
8. This Night Won't Last Forever (Bill LaBounty, Roy Freeland) 3:43
   Recorded live November 6, 1999, in Taylorville, IL
9. All These Years (Mac McAnally) 3:49
   Recorded live December 28, 1999, at the Ryman Auditorium, Nashville, TN
10. The Boys and Me (Mac McAnally, Mark Miller) 4:27
    Recorded live February 25, 2000, in Ogden, UT
11. Thank God for You (Mac McAnally, Mark Miller) 2:57
    Recorded live February 25, 2000, in Ogden, UT

12. The Race Is On (Don Rollins) 3:04
    Recorded live February 25, 2000, in Ogden, UT
13. Drive Me Wild (Mark Miller, Gregg Hubbard, Mike Lawler) 3:29
    Recorded live November 19, 1999, in Warsaw, IN
14. Some Girls Do (Mark Miller) 3:47
    Recorded live February 25, 2000, in Ogden, UT
15. Perfect World (Mark Miller, Chuck Cannon, Billy Maddox, Paul Thorn) 3:18
16. Garage Band (Mark Miller) 3:34
17. 800 Pound Jesus (Billy Maddox, Paul Thorn) 3:04
18. Lookin' for Love (Wanda Mallette, Bob Morrison, Patti Ryan) 3:36

Singles:
1. Perfect World – June 2000 – #50 US Country
2. Lookin' for Love – November 2000 – #44 US Country

18. Can You Hear Me Now (2002 Curb)
Producers: Mark Miller/Brian Tankersley
Chart Positions: #39 US Country

1. Can You Hear Me Now (Mark Miller, Dave Loggins) 3:41
2. I Need a Girlfriend (Mark Miller, Dave Loggins) 3:45
3. Circles (Dave Loggins, Marv Green) 3:33
4. Where Was I (Billy Maddox, Paul Thorn, Anne Graham) 3:53
5. Hard, Hard World (Jamie Hartford) 2:54
6. She's an 'I've Got to Have You' Girl (Mark Miller, Dave Loggins) 3:53
7. When the Sun Don't Always Shine (Mark Miller, Gregg Hubbard) 2:54
8. Someone (Bill LaBounty, Rick Chudacoff) 4:01
9. Come Back, Baby (Mark Miller) 3:35
10. I Got a Plan (Mark Miller, Dave Loggins) 5:35

Singles:
1. Circles – February 2002 – #45 US Country
2. Can You Hear Me Now – May 2002 – #57 US Country

19. True Believer (Compilation, 2003 Curb)
Producers: Mark Miller/Brian Tankersley/Randy Scruggs/
Mac McAnally

1. Travelin' Shoes (Gregg Hubbard, Mark Miller) 3:00
2. I Got a Plan (Mark Miller, Dave Loggins) 5:36
3. Lord, Would You Do That for Me
    (Anthony Crawford, Mike Lawler, Mark Miller) 3:37
4. The Walk (Mark Miller) 3:44
5. Still Water (with Donna McElroy)
    (Gregg Hubbard, Mark Miller) 3:19
6. Circles (Dave Loggins, Marv Green) 3:34
7. It Wasn't His Child (Skip Ewing) 3:37
8. The Sun Don't Shine on the Same Folks All the Time
    (Mark Gray, Danny Morrison, Johnny Slate) 2:50
9. 800 Pound Jesus (Billy Maddox, Paul Thorn) 2:54
10. Building a True Believer (Mark Miller) 3:47

I'll Be Around (Craig Wiseman, Tim Nichols)
Single released by Lyric Street Records in August 2003
#48 US Country

20. Mission Temple Fireworks Stand (2005 Curb)

Producer: Mark Miller

Chart Positions: #47 US Country

1. Mission Temple Fireworks Stand feat. Robert Randolph (Billy Maddox, Paul Thorn) 3:08

2. Tarzan and Jane (Steven Curtis Chapman) 3:45

3. They Don't Understand (Dean Chance, Teresa Chance, Steve Miller, Jeff Wood) 4:17

4. With You Daddy (Danny Green, Doug Johnson) 4:07

5. Your Faith (Mark Miller) 3:40

6. Keep Your Hands to Yourself (Dan Baird) 2:41

7. Ole Kentuck' (Mark Miller, Dale Oliver) 3:10

8. All I Want Is You (Gregg Hubbard, Mark Miller) 3:55

9. One Little Heartbeat at a Time (Steven Curtis Chapman) 4:06

10. Ladies' Man (Steven Curtis Chapman, Mark Miller) 2:48

11. There Was a Time (Gregg Hubbard) 2:50

12. Tryin' to Find a Way to Make It Last (Steven Curtis Chapman, Mark Miller) 3:20

Singles:

1. Mission Temple Fireworks Stand – December 2004 – #55 US Country

2. They Don't Understand – August 2005 – #36 US Country, #15 US Christian

21. Best of Sawyer Brown (2008 Curb)
Producers: Mark Miller/Randy Scruggs/Mac McAnally
Chart Positions: #47 US Country

1. Step That Step (Mark Miller) 2:50
2. The Race Is On (Don Rollins) 2:56
3. The Walk (Mark Miller) 3:44
4. The Dirt Road (Gregg Hubbard, Mark Miller) 2:53
5. Some Girls Do (Mark Miller) 3:14
6. All These Years (Mac McAnally) 3:23
7. Thank God for You (Mac McAnally Mark Miller) 3:20
8. This Night Won't Last Forever
   (Bill LaBounty, Roy Freeland) 3:58
9. Six Days on the Road (Earl Green, Carl Montgomery) 2:54
10. They Don't Understand (Dean Chance, Teresa Chance, Steve Miller, Jeff Wood) 4:18

22. Rejoice (2008 O–Seven)
Producer: Mark Miller

1. Go, Tell It on the Mountain (Traditional) 4:13
2. Do You Hear What I Hear (Traditional) 3:59
3. God Rest Ye Merry Gentlemen (Traditional) 3:33
4. Rejoice (Mark Miller, Gregg Hubbard) 4:12
5. The First Noel (Traditional) 4:42
6. O Come, O Come Emmanuel (Traditional) 2:59
7. Gloria (Mark Miller, Gregg Hubbard) 3:00
8. O Come All Ye Faithful (Traditional) 3:39

23. Travelin' Band (2011 Beach Street)
Producer: Mark Miller

1. Ain't Goin' Out That Way (Robert Ellis Orrall, Stephen Barker Liles, Brad Douglas Warren, Brett Daniel Warren) 3:05
2. Smokin' Hot Wife (Mark Miller) 3:10
3. Walk Out of the Rain (Harley Allen) 2:48
4. Travelin' Band (Mark Miller) 4:22
5. Come Along feat. Ernie Haase & Signature Sound (Mark Miller) 3:44
6. New Set of Tires (Jeffrey Steel, Bob Dipiero) 3:55
7. Closer to Me (Mark Miller, John Waller, Jason Hoard, Scott Johnson) 3:55
8. Cool Night (Paul Davis) 3:25
9. Deliver Me (Mark Miller, Gregg Hubbard) 3:55
10. Y'all Ready (Mark Miller, Rob Jackson, Tom Douglas) 3:55
11. Runaway Heart (Mark Miller) 2:56

24. Sawyer Brown All-Time Greatest Hits (2017 Curb)
Producer: Mark Miller

1. Leona (Bill Shore, David Wills) 3:02
2. Step That Step (Miller) 2:49
3. Used to Blue (J. Fred Knobloch, Bill LaBounty) 3:19
4. Betty's Bein' Bad (Marshall Chapman) 3:21
5. Heart Don't Fall Now (Becky Foster, Bill LaBounty, Carolyn Swilley) 3:23
6. The Race Is On (Don Rollins) 2:53
7. The Walk (Mark Miller) 3:44
8. The Dirt Road (Gregg Hubbard, Mark Miller) 2:55

9. Some Girls Do (Mark Miller) 3:13

10. Café on the Corner (Mac McAnally) 3:24

11. All These Years (Mac McAnally) 3:21

12. Trouble on the Line (Mark Miller, Bill Shore) 2:32

13. Thank God for You (Mac McAnally Mark Miller) 3:18

14. The Boys and Me (Mac McAnally, Mark Miller) 3:24

15. Hard to Say (Mark Miller) 3:26

16. This Time (Mark Miller, Mac McAnally) 2:42

17. I Don't Believe in Goodbye
    (Mark Miller, Scotty Emerick, Bryan White) 3:51

18. (This Thing Called) Wantin' and Havin' It All
    (Dave Loggins, Ronnie Samoset) 3:28

19. Treat Her Right (Lenny LeBlanc, Ava Aldridge) 3:39

20. Six Days on the Road (Earl Green, Carl Montgomery) 2:52

21. This Night Won't Last Forever
    (Bill LaBounty, Roy Freeland) 3:56

22. Drive Me Wild (Mark Miller, Gregg Hubbard, Mike Lawler) 3:35

23. Mission Temple Fireworks Stand feat. Robert Randolph
    (Billy Maddox, Paul Thorn) 3:09

24. They Don't Understand (Dean Chance, Teresa Chance, Steve
    Miller, Jeff Wood) 4:15

Acknowledgments

A HUGE THANK YOU to Robert Noland who patiently led me through this process and helped me put to paper the big-fish stories of my life.

I'd like to especially acknowledge the incredible Sawyer Brown fans. Your unwavering support has carried me down this highway for the last forty years!

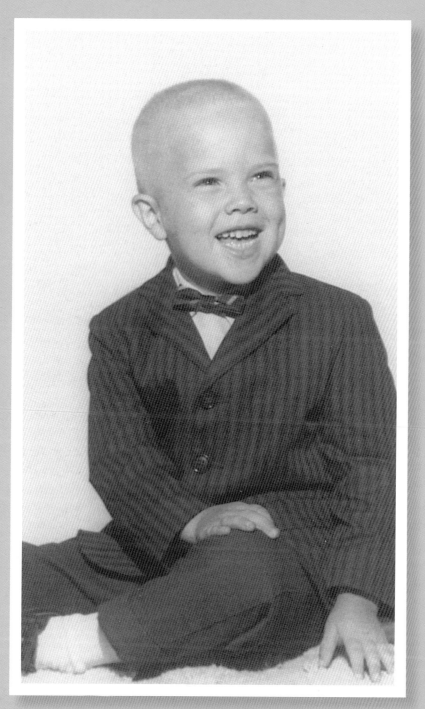

Dressed for my mom's college graduation.

One of the few pictures I have with my dad.

My mom always said she dressed
Frank and me just like the Kennedys.

ABOVE: This is why everyone thought Frank and I were twins.

LEFT: Winning the talent show in second grade.

TALENT SHOW WINNER — And he's Mark Miller, shown here with his cousin who accompanied him on the guitar.

**Mom, Frank, and me outside of
our first home in Apopka, FL.**

ABOVE: The Zoo Crew basketball team.

LEFT: My high school basketball picture. Go Blue Darters!

Chilling on break from the ski show.

ABOVE: Practicing new tricks for the ski show.

LEFT: Pinocchio getting some air in the ski show.

Writing my first song.

ABOVE: Me and Hobie (still Gregg at this point) at our first recording.

LEFT: My first concert at my mom's school, Ocoee Junior High.

ABOVE:
Much to my
children's
dismay,
I rocked
the 80s.

LEFT:
Ahh, gold lamé
in
the 80s.

ABOVE:
Switching
hats with my
good friend,
the legend
Charlie
Daniels.

RIGHT:
"Captain of
the 80s."

ABOVE:
Singing the
Nebraska Song in
Brook's jersey.

LEFT:
Gunnar
tuning up
to go on stage
with me.

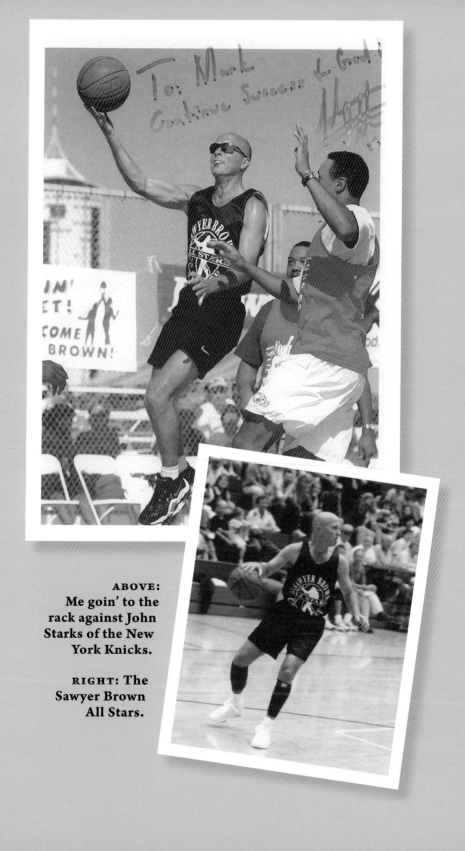

ABOVE:
Me goin' to the rack against John Starks of the New York Knicks.

RIGHT: The Sawyer Brown All Stars.

ABOVE: Me and Gunnar cheering on the Bucks.

LEFT: On location with Madison filming her TV show.

In Greece with Jequan.

Lisa and I with the two newest rock stars, Jack and Eli.